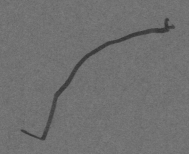

WOLVERINE

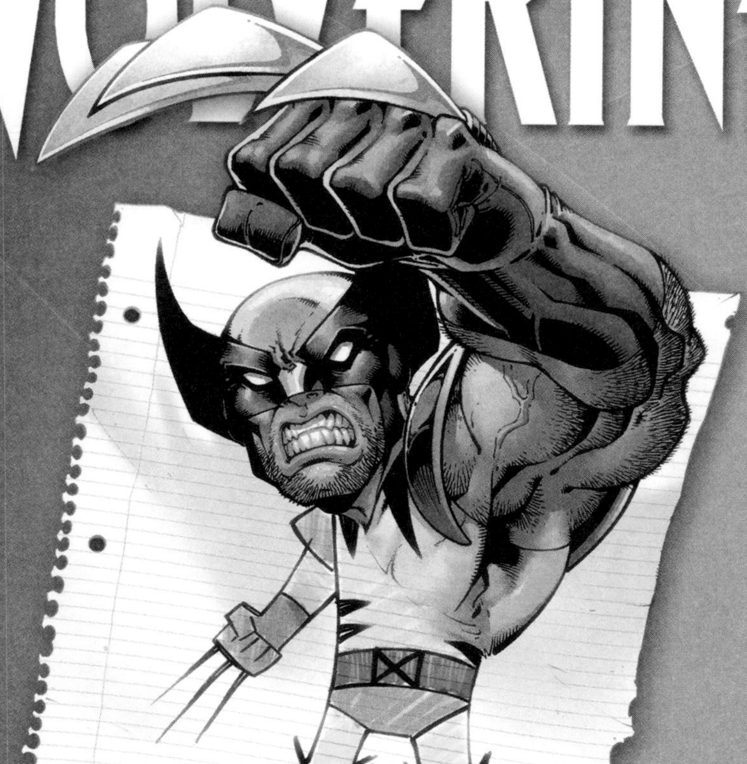
NAUCK
RAUCH

WORST DAY EVER

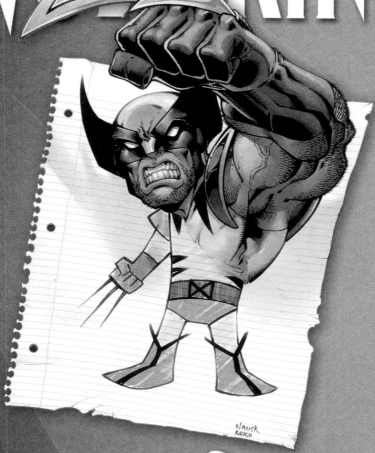

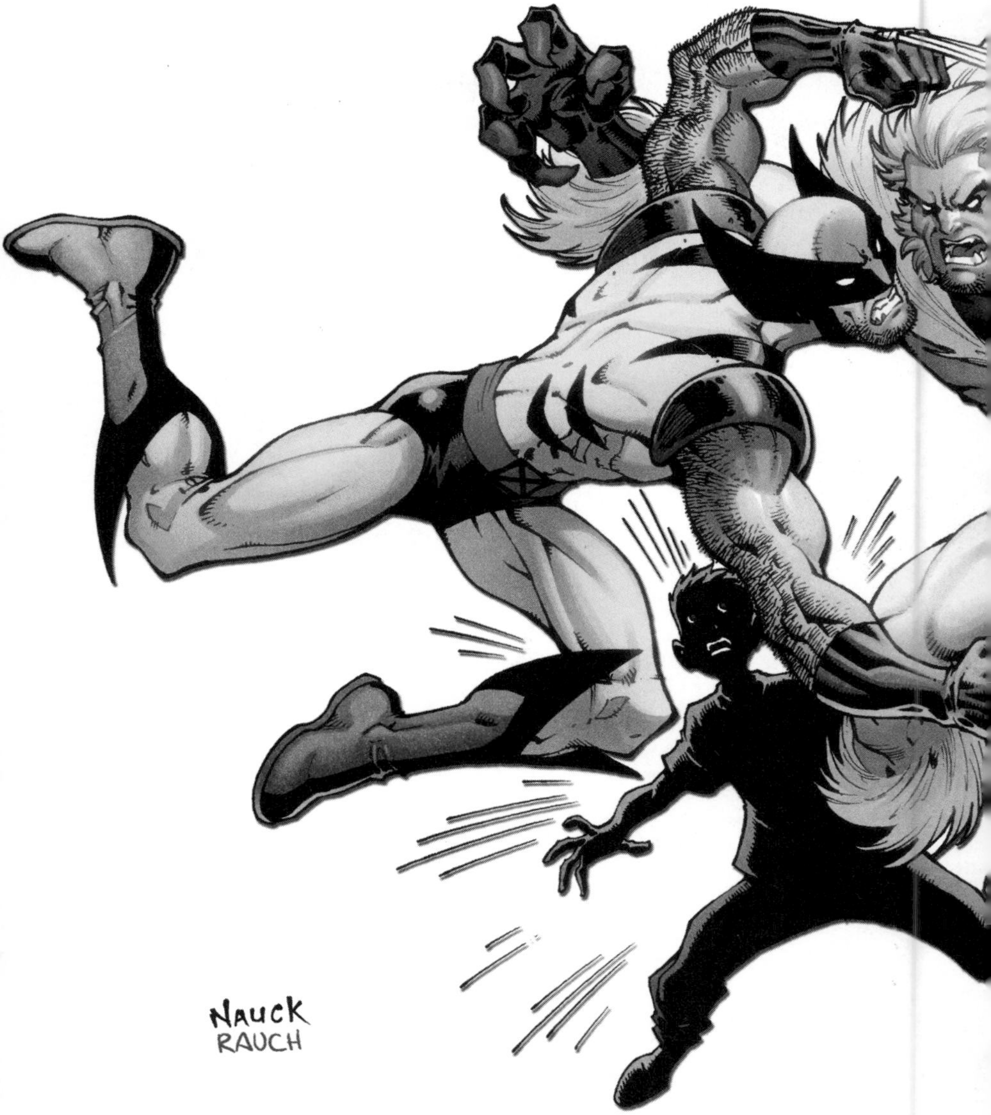
NAUCK
RAUCH

00111

7 59606 13757 2

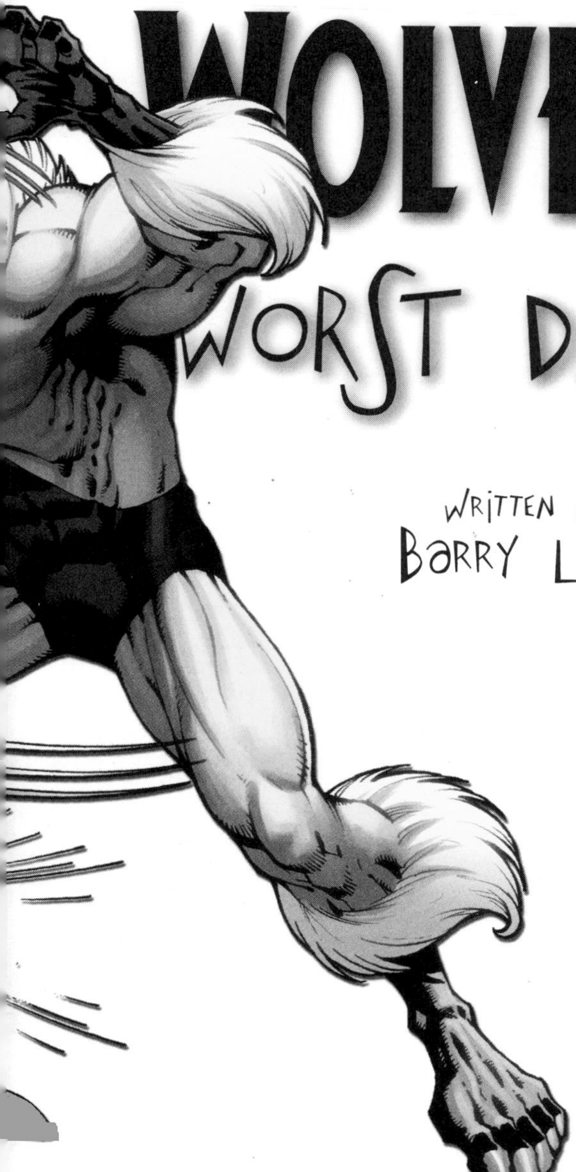

WOLVERINE

WORST DAY EVER

WRITTEN BY
BARRY LYGA

MARVEL ENTERTAINMENT, INC
New York • Manhattan Beach • London

Please visit us on the World Wide Web: **www.marvelkids.com**

WOLVERINE: WORST DAY EVER

$14.99 per copy in the U.S. (GST #R127032852);
Canadian Agreement #40668537.

First printing 2009. ISBN #: ISBN# 978-0-7851-3757-3.Published by MARVEL PUBLISHING, INC., a subsidiary of MARVEL ENTERTAINMENT INC. OFFICE OF PUBLICATION: 417 Fifth Avenue, New York, NY 10016.

ALAN FINE, CEO Marvel Toys & Publishing Divisions
DAN BUCKLEY, Publisher
JIM SOKOLOWSKI, COO Pubishing
DAVID GABRIEL, SVP of Publishing Sales & Circulation
DAVID BOGART, SVP of Business Affairs & Talent Management
MICHAEL PASCIULLO, VP Merchandising & Communications
JIM O'KEEFE, VP of Operations & Logistics
CHRIS ALLO, Editorial Talent Coordinator
JOHN PARETTI, Book Market Coordinator
ALEX STARBUCK, Editorial Assiistant, Special Projects
JEFF YOUNGQUIST, Senior Editor, Special Projects
STAN LEE, Chairman Emeritus.

Editor: RUWAN JAYATILLEKE
Book Designer: SPRING HOTELING
Production: NELSON RIBEIRO

Cover Art by TODD NAUCK and JOHN RAUCH

10 9 8 7 6 5 4 3 2 1

Printed in the U.S.A.

FEATURING ARTWORK BY

Roland Boschi • John Cassaday • Phil Jimenez • Julia Bax • Kris Justice
Hugo Petrus • Francis Portela • Roger Cruz • Andrea Di Vito • Salva Espin
Clayton Henry • Steven Cummings • Bob McLeod • Sal Buscema
Matteo Lolli • Jim Calafiore • Andy Park • Dave Cockrum
Mark Robinson • GURIHIRU • Joe Barney • Joe Madureira
Mike Norton • Juan Santacruz • Julia Bacellar

The author would like to thank everyone at Marvel -
especially Ruwan, David, and Spring - for such a fun time.

Also, special thanks to Robin Brande and Eric Lyga
(sounding boards par excellance),
to Janna Morishima, and to Kathy Anderson.

"If It's Tuesday, It Must be Magneto and the Brotherhood of Evil Mutants"

This entry posted on May 1 at 12:03:10 pm by Eric.

That's what Wolverine said right before he popped his claws — SNIKT! — and jumped into battle.

Wolverine leaps into action! I wish I could leap into action. It looks fun.

They're not *really* called "the Brotherhood of Evil Mutants," btw. Because they're bad guys and bad guys never think they're evil. They just *are* evil. They actually simply just call themselves the Brotherhood of Mutants.

I'm a mutant, but I'm no brother of theirs.

Anyway...

Sure enough, it was Tuesday. And sure enough, the Brotherhood attacked the Xavier School for Gifted Students. The main building ("the mansion," we call it). Right during lunch, can you believe it?

In case you need a cheat sheet, the Brotherhood of (Evil) Mutants is made up of:

Magneto
Master of Magnetism. He's the leader of the team and you won't find a nastier or more evil mutant around.

Quicksilver
Fastest mutant alive.

Scarlet Witch
Way too pretty to be evil... but she is anyway. Can "affect probability," which is a fancy way of saying that she makes people luckier or unluckier.

The Toad
I swear to God I'm not making this one up. He jumps around and he has a long tongue. I'm serious. I thought *my* mutant power sort of sucked and then I heard about this guy.

Then again, at least he gets to *use* his power...

But let me get back to the action.

Right after lunch. I was sitting alone — like always — eating whatever was left over when the other students were finished — like always — when the wall to the cafeteria buckled and collapsed — *not* like always.

The next thing I knew, silverware was flying everywhere! Magneto walked through the hole in the wall like it was a door someone had opened for him.

The silverware chased the other kids around until they ran screaming from the lunchroom. I ducked under a table. Don't ask me *why* I was hiding. With my mutant power, I never need to hide. I guess it was just reflex.

Wolverine and Colossus were hanging around the cafeteria because it was their day to be Lunch Monitors. By the time Magneto had come into the room, Wolverine had already popped his claws and jumped up onto one of the lunch tables, growling out, "If it's Tuesday, it must—"

Well, you read that part already.

Next thing I knew, the room was *full* of evil mutants! Scarlet Witch started twisting her hands in the air and tables flipped all over the place. The silverware chased Colossus around the room. A wind whipped up from nowhere and then I realized that the wind was a *person* — Quicksilver, moving so fast that you could barely see him.

And Toad. I could hardly believe what I was seeing — he used his tongue like a grappling hook, shooting it out of his mouth, latching onto a hanging light fixture, then swinging into the room to land on a table behind Wolverine.

It happened to be the table I was hiding under. THUD! I thought it was going to collapse on me! For a little guy, that Toad sure does pack some weight.

Next thing I know, Toad's leaping at Wolverine, the two of them snarling. The wind from Quicksilver started whistling and howling — the room felt like ground zero at a tornado strike. I grabbed a table leg and held on for dear life.

Colossus had metaled up and the silverware kept flying at him, sparking and clashing against his steel skin. It was like thousands of knives being sharpened all at once, the sound of screaming, clanging blades filling the air.

Wolverine dodged Toad, but lost his balance as his table shifted suddenly. Scarlet Witch. Her mutant luck powers!

"Time to put the witch's lights out!" Wolverine called out to Colossus.

"Right!" Colossus called back, sweeping one enormous arm to knock away about a million knives and forks. "Fastball special!"

Oh, a fastball special! This would be good. That's when Colossus grabs Wolverine and throws him at the bad guy. I *love* that!

I crawled out from under the table to get a better view. This would be something to see! With all that silverware flying around? And with the wind? It would look *awesome* when Wolverine went soaring through the air, straight at the Scarlet Witch, to knock her on her butt. Maybe he would even bounce off of her and smack into Magneto.

Could I actually be lucky enough to *see* that?

I slid on my butt across the floor, closer to Colossus. *Excellent* vantage point. I would see everything from here.

Wolverine hurtled through the air and right into Colossus' arms. Colossus spun around once to get some momentum and then took a step and...Yeow! —smashed into me! Almost stepped right on me with that ginormous steel foot of his!

Now, Colossus is a big, strong guy...even when he's *not* made out of ten billion pounds of stainless steel. But no matter how big and strong you are, if you're lunging in some direction and something trips you up, it's *not* gonna be pretty. Take it from me — like I said before, I had a great vantage point for all of this.

"What're you doin'?" Wolverine shouted as Colossus staggered and then fell flat on his face. It sounded like a big, huge frying pan slapping hard concrete.

And Wolverine went flying all right...but not in that "fastball special" kind of way, a cool arc that launches him up in the air, coming back down to unload two fistfuls of righteous anger on a bad guy.

No, he hurtled straight ahead, throwing out his arms like a clumsy guy tripping over a log, and then crashed headlong into a wall, never coming anywhere *near* Scarlet Witch.

"I...tripped...!" Colossus said.

"Ya think?" Wolverine shook his head and started to get up.

I didn't know what to do. Apologize? In the middle of a big fight? It's not like Colossus could know he tripped over me...

"Ending Danger Room simulation," said a very familiar voice.

Professor X.

Oops. Now I was in *big* trouble.

More later.

Instead of hitting his head on the wall, I bet Wolverine could have chopped through it. Like this!

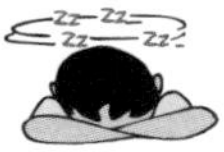

Backing Up for a Second

This entry posted on May 1 at 5:04:58 pm by Eric.

OK, first of all, let me back up and explain something: Like I said before, I'm a mutant. Yeah, like the ones you see on TV and read about online. But you'll never see or read about *me*...except for this blog.

I shouldn't even *have* this blog. It's way against the rules here, and if Professor X ever found out about it, I would be *so* totally busted it's not even funny.

In case you don't know what a blog is, I'll tell you. Because I'm helpful like that. A blog is like a diary, only it's on the Internet. (And if you don't know what a blog is, why the heck are you reading this?)

I'll be honest with you: even if you *do* know what a blog is, I *still* don't know why you're reading this. I don't even know how you *found* it – it's not like I linked it from anywhere. It's not like anyone knows me.

Anyway, just to make things easier on you, I've tagged a bunch of the entries with icons so that you know what's what:

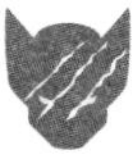

This is when Wolverine does something cool or rad or both.

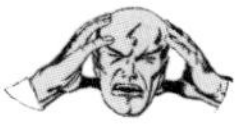

This is when I get yelled at by Professor X. You'll see this one a lot, I think.

This is when I talk about the X-Men.

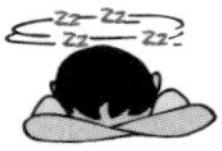

This is when I talk about me. I'm boring.

And be on the lookout: I posted some pictures here, too, but I also posted some of my drawings of things, for when I didn't have my camera. I draw in a lot of different styles because it keeps me from getting bored. If you don't like it, tough! It's my blog. :P

I bet none of the other kids have a blog or a journal or a diary or whatever. . . They obey the rules. But I need to be sure that someday, when I'm gone, there will be evidence that I was here at all. And no, I'm not trying to be "melodramatic." (That's the word my mom uses whenever I whine.) This might be the only way anyone will ever know I was here.

See, my mutant power is. . .

It's hard to describe. Basically, people don't notice me.

I don't mean like I'm shy or anything like that. I mean that people just don't notice me. I could walk into a room totally naked, playing an accordion while juggling chainsaws, and people *might* get the idea that something's a little *off* in the room.

If I concentrate *really* hard and make an effort, I can get people's attention. And as long as I keep talking and stay in their line of sight, they usually don't forget I'm there. But. . . man! It's a lot of effort, you know? It's tiring.

Everything was normal until about six months ago. I was just a normal kid, had just turned thirteen. I was looking forward to finishing middle school and going to high school. And then, suddenly, my friends stopped talking to me. Teachers stopped calling on me in class. I started getting detention for skipping school, even though I was right there!

(Turns out that's the age when mutant powers tend to pop up. So you're cruising along just fine, enjoying your life, looking forward to being a teenager and then — whap! Life smacks you upside the head with a super-power. A sucky super-power, to boot.)

The next thing I knew, this guy Charles Xavier rolled up to my house in his wheelchair. Later, I learned that he was actually Professor X, founder of the X-Men and the most powerful telepath in the world. But on that day, all I learned was that just being around me gave him a massive headache. Turns out he telepathically *knew* I was there, but his other senses didn't notice me, and the combination was a big pain in the you-know-what.

(If you *don't* know what, I feel sorry for you!)

So, Professor X talked to my parents like I wasn't even in the room. I was sitting right there on the sofa next to my mom, but, of course, no one noticed me. He told them that I was special, that I was a mutant, and that he had a school in upstate New York where I could learn how to control my power. And best of all, I would be hanging out with a bunch of other mutants, so I wouldn't be alone.

Sounds good, right? Sigh.

Time for dinner. I'll write more soon.

This is the Xavier School. Looks sweet, huh? Don't be fooled - it's still school.

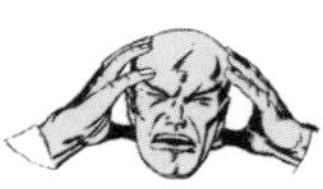

Why I'm in Big Trouble

This entry posted on May 1 at 7:00:20 pm by Eric.

Anyway, back to the cool stuff. You don't care about all that other junk, do you?

So, yeah, all that stuff I mentioned before? All that cool action? None of it was real. It was all holograms and stuff in the Danger Room, which is this special room deep under the school where Professor X trains the X-Men and the next generation of mutant super heroes.

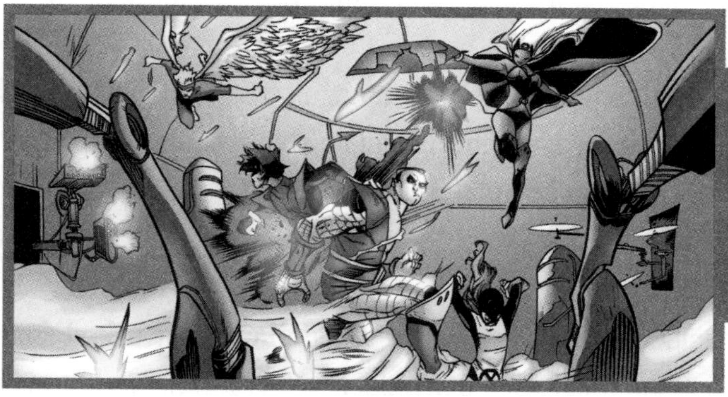

This is the Danger Room, with the X-Men. See how cool they are?

I am *not* one of the next generation of mutant super heroes. Again I'm just a guy with the world's most useless mutant super-power.

The funny thing is this: Even though Colossus tripped over me – even though he was lying on the floor *right in front of me* – he still didn't know what had happened! As the Danger Room holograms melted all around us, turning the "lunchroom" into four boring slate gray walls and an equally boring floor and ceiling, Colossus just looked around like someone had nailed him with a gigantic spitball.

"I don't understand," he said. "What did I trip over?"

"Me," I told him. "Sorry about that."

But he didn't hear me, of course. I sighed. I didn't feel like spending the energy to get his attention. Especially since it would just lead to me getting in trouble.

"I fear, Colossus, that you tripped over young Eric, our newest student."

Professor X's voice again. Only this time, it wasn't piped through a speaker from the Danger Room control center. This time it was right in the room with us — a door had slid open and the professor's wheelchair glided through, and stopped near us.

"I haven't misstated the case, have I, Eric?" the Professor asked, looking around the room. I could tell by the wrinkles in his forehead that he was concentrating. (Sometimes when he does that, I imagine I can see waves of thoughts shooting out of his head like the ripples a thrown stone makes in a pond. A *bald* pond.) "You *are* in here, correct?" he said.

"Yes, Professor." I stood up and waved my arms back and forth like I was trying to help a jet land during a thunderstorm.

Colossus was still looking around. "Who are you talking to, Professor?"

"Eric, please..." The Professor massaged his temples.

I jumped up and down and hooted and hollered. Colossus — who was standing no more than six inches away from me — suddenly jerked back. "What the — Where did *you* come from?"

Wolverine came up behind me. "Been here all along, haven't you, squirt?"

Professor X sighed and leveled his gaze at me and wouldn't look away. "Colossus, Wolverine, allow me to introduce Eric Mattias, the newest student here at Xavier's School for Gifted Students."

"Invisibility . . ." Colossus muttered.

"Not quite," Professor X said, and then went ahead and explained how my power worked, which was interesting because I had met Wolverine and Colossus once before already, but they must have forgotten. It's not like I'm all that memorable.

Colossus just shook his head and told me to stay out of his way from now on, then stomped off. He was made out of steel, so I don't think he was hurt (or even dented!), but I guess tripping over a kid like me and tossing Wolverine into a wall was sort of like stabbing his ego through the heart.

This is Professor X. Yes, he always looks this serious. Always. He was born without a smile. Poor guy.

"We have discussed this before, Eric," Professor X said. He was still staring at me so that he wouldn't forget I was in the room. And I kept fidgeting and bouncing from one foot to the other to help him out. "You simply cannot continue sneaking into places—"

"I wasn't sneaking!" I protested. "I just walked in. I was curious. I can't help it if no one saw me."

"Your powers can be very dangerous for you," he went on, as if I hadn't said anything. "And as you saw just now, they can be dangerous for your teammates as well."

Teammates? Ha! I actually did that "ha!" out loud without realizing it. "I'm never gonna be an X-Man. My power's useless. I don't have teammates."

He took a deep breath. "Perhaps. Perhaps not. In any event, you have to consider the consequences of your power on those around you, so that—"

"Back off." It was Wolverine. I'd forgotten he was standing right behind me. "Kid's figurin' out how to deal with his power, Chuck. Ain't that what this place is all about? You expect him to have it all nailed down after just six weeks?"

"Logan, we've had this conversation many times. And I'm quite certain I've asked you to call me Professor in the past."

"Right. Sorry, Professor Chuck. Give the kid a break. You know anyone here who's figured out their powers in six weeks? I'm the one who took a header into the wall and I forgive 'im."

They started arguing then and I realized that it had happened again — it was like I wasn't even in the room. As soon as they focused their attention on each other, they stopped noticing me.

Story of my life.

Speaking of which...

I'll get to that next time.

STORY OF MY LIFE

This entry posted on May 2 at 12:13:43 pm by Eric.

I used to have a pretty good life. I had a lot of friends. I wasn't the most popular kid in school, but everyone knew me and most of them liked me. There was a girl — Emily Hardy — that I liked and sometimes at lunch she would look over at my table and then look away quickly.

Not a bad life. Not bad at all.

And then the power developed and everything started to suck with the power of a thousand vacuum cleaners all running at once: VRROOOOOOOMMM!

My first week here at the school did *not* go well. First of all, I didn't realize how big a deal privacy was here. The school is *huge*, OK? Like, it's bigger than my middle school, and that's not even counting all the special X-Men rooms and junk like that hidden deep underground. So, I get dropped into this huge school with all these new people...Well, what would *you* do?

I explored.

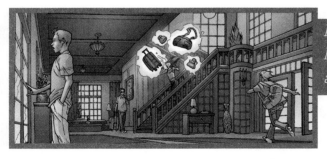

People levitating their luggage is normal around here.

I was still getting used to my power. It didn't occur to me that people couldn't or wouldn't see me when I went into their rooms or hung out around them. I wanted to be a part of the gang, wanted to be with the kids my age. So I would find a group and stick with them. I would chime in occasionally and no one would respond, so I just figured they were ignoring the new kid. I stuck with it, hanging around, listening.

I guess I didn't really think it through. I didn't make the connection: People didn't know that I even was around, so they thought they were having private conversations.

And just because I could walk into someone's room and look around without them telling me to get out didn't mean they were OK with it. It's just that they didn't realize I'd come in.

Eventually, Professor X figured out what was going on. And that's when I got my first big lecture on Power and Responsibility. (I swear he speaks in capital letters...)

Not the best start to my days at Xavier's School for Gifted Freaks— er, Students.

The only cool thing, of course, is that I'm living in the same building as the X-Men. That's *way* cool. They're like the superstars of the mutant world, the mutants other mutants aspire to be.

In case you've been living on the moon or in the Negative Zone for the last hundred years, here's the deal on the X-Men:

Cyclops

He's the team leader. Shoots energy beams out of his eyes. He's the one person I'm glad doesn't look my way!

Storm

She can control the weather. How cool is that?

Colossus

Big, strong dude who turns into big, strong steel dude.

Iceman

Come on! Do I really have to explain this one to you?

Angel

He can fly. He can *fly*!!!!!

Marvel Girl

Telekinesis. In case you were sick the day they taught basic science fiction in school, that means she can move stuff with her mind.

And then there's Wolverine. More about him later.

I drew this instead of doing my homework last night. I wish I could fly. Doesn't it look like fun?

A Little Bit Right Now

This entry posted on May 3 at 7:45:05 am by Eric.

Actually, a little bit about Wolverine right now, since I have a second before my first class.

Here's the thing about him. I pay the most attention to him, of all the X-Men. Because he's a loner.

And I need to learn how to be a loner.

I don't know why Wolverine likes to be alone. I don't know why he likes to go off by himself. I follow him sometimes. Just to see what he does. He usually just roams the grounds of the school. There's woods all over the place, so he goes out in the trees and moves real quiet and sniffs the air and walks like there's a path only he can see. Or sometimes, he goes racing off through the woods like it's the best, coolest thing in the world, the only thing that makes him happy.

Times like this are the only time I ever see Wolverine smile.

And at night, he...I don't think he sleeps a lot. I'm sort of an insomniac (a word my mom says comes from the Latin for "kid who is slowly trying to drive me crazy" — hey, I can't help it: if I'm awake, I want to talk to people and hang out, so I used to wake her up. Sheesh.), so I spend a lot of time wandering the halls at night, when everyone else is asleep. It's not like I can wake people up, right? If I'm practically invisible to people who are wide awake and staring right at me, I could probably walk right on top of their bodies and play the trombone in their ears while they're asleep and not bother them.

It's weird, nighttime. I'm used to being alone, but at night it's different because it's being alone like *other* people are alone. Does that make any sense?

At night, Wolverine prowls around the mansion. Every night, the same thing: After checking all the windows and doors, he heads to the kitchen, polishes off a huge sandwich and a tall glass of — get this — strawberry milk (You wouldn't think a tough guy like that would guzzle strawberry milk, but who am I to judge?) By now it's like three in the morning and he's finally ready to call it a night because he heads straight back to his room.

Funny thing, though — he always grabs the cookies from the top shelf and leaves them on the table...but never bothers to eat one. I want to know: What sort of man drinks strawberry milk and doesn't eat a cookie? Especially when the cookie is *right there!* (I figure those cookies exist for a reason — to be eaten — and I would hate for them not to fulfill their destiny, so I always eat a couple. And maybe a couple more.)

This is getting pretty long and I only really meant to tell you a little bit about him.

Anyway, look, here's the thing about Wolverine: I need to learn from him. Not because I want to. Because I *have* to. Face it: With my mutant power, I'm gonna be alone all the time. Even if other people are around.

Gonna be late for class — Alternate Futures and Paradoxes! Gotta go!

Just Thinking...

This entry posted on May 4 at 8:46:54 pm by Eric.

I've decided that if I ever *did* become an X-Man (which will *never* happen, but *if*) that my super hero code name would be Nowhere Kid. Or maybe Nowhere Boy. I haven't decided yet. And I think I would wear a cape. Why not? It's not like anyone will notice it.

About My Art

This entry posted on May 5 at 2:33:21 pm by Eric.

I draw. And take pictures. And sometimes I'll post that stuff in my blog Because even if people don't notice me, they at least notice something I've drawn. Sometimes I leave a piece of art lying around and just wait for people to find it. And I can stand there and listen to them talk about it and get honest feedback without worrying about people lying or trying to spare my feelings or whatever. Because I'm right there, but they don't know I'm right there.

That's, like, the only time in the world this power is any good at all.

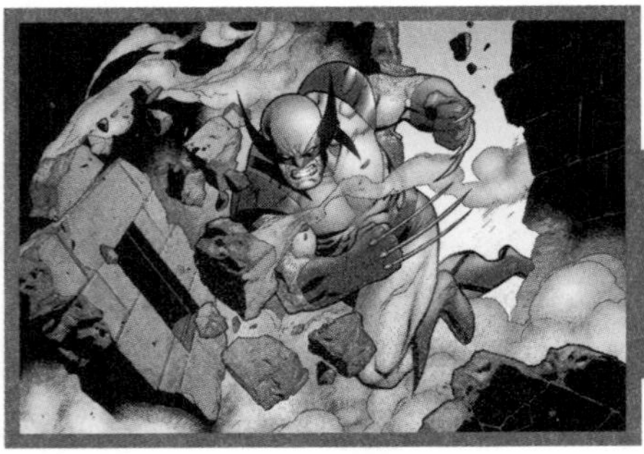

This is what it would look like if Wolverine busted through a wall. Awesome, right?

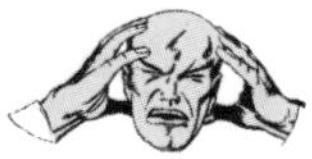

My First Mission-Six Weeks Ago

This entry posted on May 5 at 9:19:28 pm by Eric.

Remember a little while back how I said that my first week at the school wasn't all that great? Well, it wasn't. I was getting used to my powers, getting used to a new school, getting used to teachers and classes like "Mutant Development" and "Popular Super-heroics" and "Shape-Shifters: Threat or Menace?" And I got in trouble for wandering where I wasn't supposed to wander and eventually I ended up in Professor X's office, which is like going to the principal's office, only the principal can read your mind.

Plus, getting chewed out by a telepath like Professor X is no fun. Not only is he yelling at you, but you also keep getting this weird little "echo" in the back of your mind. It's like having someone shout in your ear while someone else is whispering the exact same thing in the *other* ear, only half a second later. It made it tough to concentrate on what he was saying, so he kept saying it over and over again. Plus, *he* was getting a headache just from focusing on me so much, so neither one of us was happy.

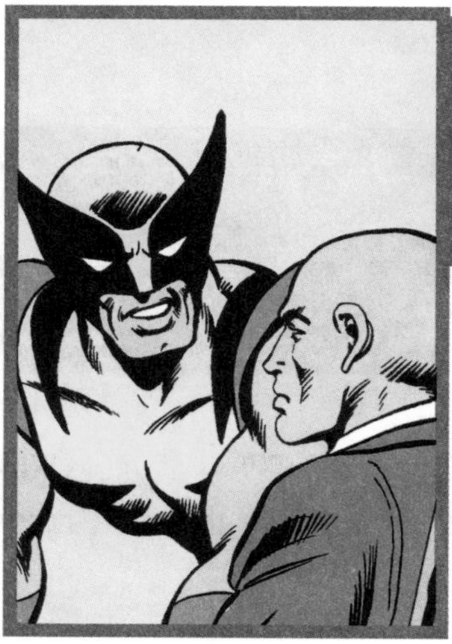

A quick drawing of Wolverine in one of his costumes, talking to Professor X. He has a couple different costumes. I guess so he doesn't get bored.

Fortunately, that first time, Wolverine interrupted by walking into the Professor's office without even knocking. (I always knock, but people never hear it, so I *have* to walk into rooms if I ever want to go in at all!)

"Ya wanted to see me, Chuck?"

Professor X gritted his teeth. I could almost see a little thought bubble over his head: *I've told you to call me Professor!!!!!*

Hey, the guy's a telepath — maybe I *did* see a thought bubble over his head. (It could happen.)

Anyway, then they got into an argument for a couple of minutes about how the Professor had summoned Wolverine ten whole minutes ago and Wolverine was late and blah blah blah. And by now neither one of them knew I was in the room, so I got to hear everything. Which isn't *technically* eavesdropping, is it? I don't know.

The Professor wanted Wolverine to take Angel and the X-Jet (he called it "the Blackbird" for some reason) and go bring a new mutant to the school. Turns out this new guy had just "manifested his powers," which means his mutant ability just turned itself on. He was living on the street, homeless, no family, and the bad guy mutants would be tracking him down to recruit him to be an evil mutant if we didn't get to him first.

They're still talking. They talk a lot. I drew it different to make it more interesting this time. Because I care about you, my nonexistent blog-reader.

"This is why," the Professor finished, "when summon you, it is imperative that you come to me immediately."

I wasn't too sure what "imperative" meant, but it sounded like "impressive" and it was a big, Professor X-type of word, the kind he tosses around so that you remember he's a professor and you're not. (As if you could ever forget. Duh. The guy's *name* is Professor X! That would be like forgetting Captain America is a captain. Or the Incredible Hulk is incredible. Or Doctor Doom is a doctor.)

I don't know about you, but flying on the X-Jet and meeting a new mutant sure sounded a lot better than hanging out in the Professor's office, getting yelled at for stuff that wasn't even really my fault.

When Wolverine left the office, I went with him. I even waved goodbye to Professor X, but he just turned back to his computer and started working on something. So it's not *my* fault. I tried.

I have to go to Basic Mutant Defense Techniques class. I'll tell you the story about my mission with Wolverine later.

I HAVEN'T FORGOTTEN
This entry posted on May 6 at 2:32:30 pm by Eric.

I haven't forgotten about that Wolverine story. I forgot that I have an extra hour of class. It's Wednesday. We have an extra class on Wednesday: "New Mutancy." That sucks. I don't know what's so special about Wednesdays.

I'll come back after class and write it up.

Oh, and we're learning about mutant popular culture during the last decade. Just FYI. In case you cared.

SOONER THAN I THOUGHT
This entry posted on May 6 at 4:47:13 pm by Eric.

OK, so this is still the story about what happened my first week at the Xavier School for Gifted Students (English translation: Place Where Mutants Live), so it happened about six weeks ago. If you remember from the last time I was telling this story, Nowhere Boy was about to help Wolverine track down a mutant. Yay! Adventure!

After being stuck at the Xavier School for a whole week without making any friends, the idea of going off on an adventure seemed pretty cool to me. It was actually beyond cool: It was *necessary*. Remember: It was still my first week. I was still new. I was breaking rules, not because I like breaking rules (mostly), but because I was still figuring out the rules.

I followed Wolverine to this part of the school that I'm not supposed to go to. (How do I know this? Well, I have a keen deductive mind and I found two important clues. The first one was the big sign on the door next to the fingerprint scanner, which read, "Upperclassmen and Grad Students Only!" The second one was the fact that my first day at school, Professor X took me to the door and said, "You're not supposed to go through there." So, that's how I knew.)

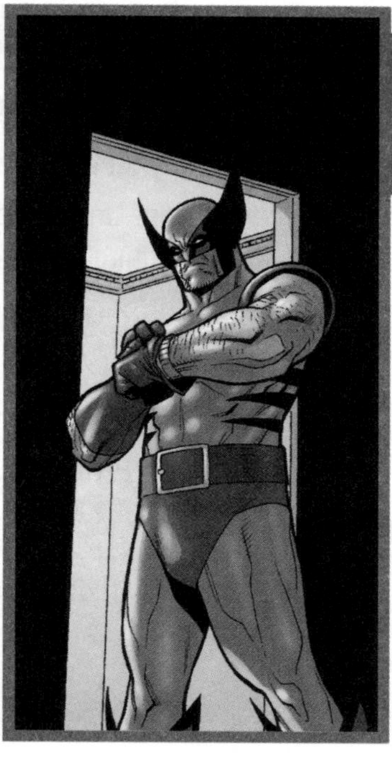

I had trouble keeping up with Wolverine at first, but then he stopped to check his watch and I caught up!

We walked down this short hallway, then took an elevator down like a billion stories. I was like, "Wow, the Professor has an elevator that goes to the center of the earth! Cool!"

Well, it didn't go to the center of the earth, but it did go into this way-cool sub-sub-sub-sub-sub-sub-sub-basement. Upstairs, everything was wooden and old and dusty. Downstairs, everything was polished metal and glass. Sort of like a high-tech laptop, only with hallways and doors.

Wolverine didn't run, but he walked fast down the hall. I kept getting distracted by stuff along the way: Doors labeled "DANGER ROOM!" and "CONTAINMENT!" and "UNIFORM DESIGN!" So I kept falling behind and then I would have to run to catch up to him. (I remembered the Danger Room because it sounded cool, and that's why I ended up in there just the other day, at the beginning of this blog. It took a little while to get in there when something cool was happening!)

By the time we made it to the hangar, I was winded.

 I didn't know it was a hangar at first. We just stopped at this ginormous door that looked like a big round hatch with a raised X crossing it. (Professor X is *obsessed* with the letter X. It's *every*where! On the doors and windows. On the school books. On the school uniforms. I think he needs help. Or maybe just a good interior designer.)

Wolverine typed on a keypad and a little hatch opened. Lights played all over his face and a computer voice (which sounded a lot like Professor X... the man's an egomaniac!) said, "Identify, please."

"Logan," said Wolverine, sounding bored.

"Passphrase, please," the computer said.

OK, now this next part is a little weird. But I thought about it a lot and I think I understand it. Here's the thing: After the computer asked for the passphrase, Wolverine grumbled and shook his head and then finally cleared his throat and...

And he sang.

No, seriously! I swear to God and Galactus. The man *sang*.

(Only slightly more disturbing than hearing Wolverine sing is realizing that he's got a pretty good voice.)

"Raindrops on roses and whiskers on kittens," he sang. *"These are a few of my favorite things."*

And the door opened.

Like I said before, I've spent some time thinking about it since then, and here's the deal: If you were a bad guy, like, say, Mystique, (who's a shape-shifter) and you were trying to break into the X-Jet hangar, you could duplicate Wolverine's eyes and maybe his fingerprints and all of that. And if he had a boring password, you could probably guess it, maybe.

But would you ever — in ten trillion years — think to yourself, "Hmm, I need to guess Wolverine's passphrase. I know! I bet he *sings*!"

Nah. You'd never think that.

I followed him into the hangar and *wow*!

It was *huge*. I couldn't believe that something this enormous was hidden underneath the school. It was almost like—

Well, no, it was *exactly* like someone put an airplane hangar under the mansion. I don't know how else to describe it.

You might think that putting a hangar underground isn't the smoothes move, and you'd normally be right. But when I looked up, I could see that the ceiling was designed to open. (Yes, in case you're wondering — the ceiling had a stylized X carved into it. Like I said: the man's an ego-hound.)

And I saw why Professor X called the X-Jet "the Blackbird" — it did sor of look like a black bird. A big, black bird made out of metal. With engines But otherwise exactly like a black bird.

Whatever. Everyone else just calls it the X-Jet.

Angel was already there, waiting. "What took you so long, Logan?"

"We ain't all hummingbirds, bub. Let's blow this popsicle stand."

The ramp to the X-Jet came down, whisper-quiet. The jet itself was al shiny black, like licorice.

Wolverine and Angel went up the ramp and I went with them. The firs adventure of Nowhere Boy!

This is getting long. I'm going to break it into two posts because my fingers are tired. Besides, no one will read anything this long on the Internet...

NOWHERE BOY RETURNS

This entry posted on May 6 at 8:24:57 pm by Eric.

When last we left our hero (me), he (I) was on the X-Jet with Wolverine and Angel. (This was all still six weeks ago, back when I first came to the school.)

You can guess what happened next, if you've been paying attention at all: The ceiling opened up and the jet shot right up into the sky, popping up from underground in a field behind the school. That's pretty smart of Professor X to have that field back there, I have to admit.

WHOOSH! That's what it looks like when the X-Jet takes off. Bet you wish your school had its own jet!

"You're more surly than usual," Angel said as he piloted the X-Jet. (Two things: First, if I had wings like Angel's I would never fly anywhere in a plane again. Second, I looked up "surly" and it means sort of nasty and grumpy. Stick with me, OK?)

"Surly's my nature," Wolverine said. I was sitting right behind them strapped into a seat with a harness that — yes — clicked together to form a buckle with an X stamped on it. (Seriously, the Professor has issues!)

"Well, yeah, but it's been worse lately. You've been snapping at people left and right. More than usual."

"Ever think you talk too much?"

"Impossible!" Angel said. "I'm very charming."

Wolverine popped the claws on one hand — SNIKT! "Ya ever wonder if that charm's more'n skin deep?"

Angel just raised his eyebrows. "All right, then. I'll shut up."

SNAKT! Back went the claws. Claws would be a cool mutant power, too.

We kept flying for a little while. I guess there's not much to say after Wolverine shows you his claws.

After a few silent minutes, Angel suddenly straightened up in his seat like he remembered something. "Oh. Wait. I get it. I get why you're...It's almost that time of year, isn't it?"

Wolverine didn't say anything for so long that I figured he'd either fallen asleep or just wasn't going to answer. But then he said, "Mind yer own business, Chicken Little."

"Sorry, Logan."

Well, that made me *really* curious, but I didn't have much time to think about it. Angel landed the X-Jet and what was supposed to be a simple mission to grab a scared mutant kid soon got more complicated because of this guy. This guy named... (I can hardly say it. It's so ridiculous.)

It's getting late and I'm actually tired, so I'm going to bed. I'll finish this tomorrow. A guy named "Unus the Untouchable" deserves an entry all his own.

Unus the Untouchable

This entry posted on May 7 at 7:02:03 am by Eric.

I actually slept last night. What an accomplishment! I wonder if Wolverine had his sandwich and strawberry milk, like always?

I have a little time before I have to run to my class in Identifying Apocalyptic Evil, so I'm going to finish up that story about my first mission—the mission I had six weeks ago when I first moved to the Xavier School. And Unus the Untouchable. No, I'm not making this up.

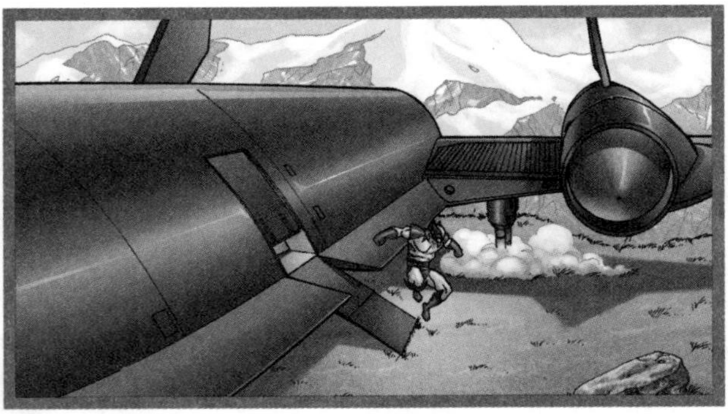

Angel landed the plane on the outskirts of this little town, near some buildings that looked sort of old, but still in use. I don't even know where we were – it's not like I have a GPS mutant power, all right? Anyway, Angel goes flying out of the plane the second the ramp goes down. Wolverine unbuckled his harness and followed him. I tagged along. No way was I gonna stay in the plane! I wanted to see this new mutant kid.

Turns out I wasn't the only one. This guy named Unus the Untouchable had beaten us to the punch. Don't ask me how he knew where to find the kid. I don't know things like that.

This is Unus the Untouchable. Be honest - would you ever touch this guy?

He's called Unus the Untouchable because he has some kind of force field that makes him, well, untouchable. But why would you want to touch him in the first place? If "untouchable" means you *can't* touch the guy, what would be the word for "who would want to touch him in the first place?" Because I don't get bragging about how you can't be touched when you're a mean, nasty, evil kind of person people would avoid touching anyway. That's like naming yourself "George the Handsome" when you're ugly, or "Lucy the Genius" when you keep tripping over your own shoelaces.

And get this: Angel and Wolverine were talking about Unus the Untouchable on the X-Jet before we landed, and I thought it was a *girl!* Because his name sounds like "Eunice," which is, like, the name of someone's old aunt or grandmother. I thought it was going to be a girl, but it was a guy and I found out later that he spells his name Unus, not Eunice. (Someone should tell him that it doesn't matter how you spell it. It's still a girl's name.)

Anyway, Angel came dive-bombing the guy out of the sky, which looked really cool until he totally bounced off the guy's force field and ended up sprawled on the ground. Ouch.

I was standing near Wolverine, so I heard him clearly when he grunted and said, "Stay back and stay safe."

I thought, *Wow. He's so focused he doesn't even realize that Angel is knocked out!*

SNIKT! SNIKT! Both sets of claws popped out and he ran towards Unus the Untouchable. (Does his mom call him that, too? "Unus the Untouchable! You go clean your room right now!")

Wolverine charging ahead! In way-cool Silouhette! I think this looks cool.

"Why are you bothering?" Unus the Untouchable taunted. "Even *your* claws can't cut my force field..."

"Who says I want to cut your force field, bub?"

And with that, Wolverine did something I totally didn't expect: He didn't jump at Unus the Untouchable — he jumped *over* him.

And grabbed a window ledge.

And pulled himself up higher.

And slashed out with his claws at a flagpole jutting from the wall.

And the flag came down, covering Unus the Untouchable, force field and all. Blinding him.

Wolverine did a back flip off the wall, landing next to the kid. Unus was struggling under the flag. Wolverine's claws slid back into his arms — SNAKT! — and he grabbed the scared mutant kid's wrist and hauled him up from the ground and ran back towards the X-Jet.

By now, Unus had shrugged off the flag. He roared and ran after Wolverine, who was a little slower than usual because he was carrying the mutant kid. Just before Unus could catch him, though, Wolverine suddenly *threw the mutant kid up in the air!*

I couldn't believe it.

He just tossed the kid up and spun around, the claws popping out again — SNIKT! — as he slashed at Unus.

Unus was right — Wolverine's claws couldn't get through the force field. There was a sound like metal on glass. Blinding sparks shot out where the claws hit the force field. Unus wasn't hurt, but I guess the sparks and the noise surprised him. He was stunned long enough to stop and take a few steps back.

And the kid? Angel swooped down low and plucked him right out of the air and headed toward the X-Jet, darting straight up into the plane, his wings barely missing the edges of the ramp opening.

Wolverine dashed back to the jet. "Get on the plane!" he shouted, even though Angel was already on board and firing up the engines. I scrambled up the ramp with him, and the door slid closed right before Unus could throw himself inside.

A minute later, we were airborne, the kid strapped into a seat next to me. He was breathing fast, looking around like he expected a monster to jump out at him at any moment. I guess I would be a little freaked out, too. Getting kidnapped by Unus the Untouchable. Then a guy with wings and a guy with claws show up and *re*-kidnap you.

I let him calm down a little bit before I tried.

"My name's Eric," I said, even though I knew it was useless. But maybe the kid's mutant power was the ability to see people like me.

Ha.

"Did you guys hear something?" he asked, looking around (and right through me), all nervous.

"Try to rest," Angel suggested. "We'll be at the mansion soon."

"Kick back, kid," said Wolverine. "We're the good guys."

Off to breakfast, then math. Yuck.

MEET...THE xPHONE!

This entry posted on May 7 at 3:52:19 pm by Eric.

All of that - Unus the Untouchable, Sam, the X-Jet - happened when I first came here, six weeks ago. We got back to the mansion without anyone getting hurt, and Professor X realized what I'd been up to and I got dragged into his office and got in trouble. Again. It's been like this the past six weeks. The other day in the Danger Room is just the latest.

Honestly, I'd sort of thought Professor X had forgotten about the whole deal in the Danger Room, with the Colossus-tripping and the Wolverine-into-the-walling. But no. Today, he tried to do something about it. He gave me a brand new xPhone.

This is my xPhone. You know you want one, too. But you can't have one.

I have to say, getting the xPhone *almost* made getting yelled at by Professor X worth it. It's pretty cool. It's an awesome little cell phone with all the latest Iron Man technology built into it. Holographic display with gestural user interface. Keyed to activate based on my mutant DNA signature. Stuff like that. You know.

(OK, maybe *you* know. I'm not sure what *any* of that means. I copied it off the box.)

The only downside to it is that it also has CPS built into. That stands for

"Cerebro Positioning System." Cerebro is this super-sophisticated computer that Professor X built. It can track mutants anywhere in the world. Which is kind of a scary thought, but I guess someone has to keep track of them and Professor X is a decent enough guy, so why not him?

So, CPS is some special gadget in the xPhone that lets the Professor track my movements. It's not perfect (because apparently my power even affects *satellites and computers*), but — in his words — "It will keep you from scampering off into harm's way again."

Professor X's favorite hobby is yelling at me.

Harm's way. Yeah. Like anyone even knew I was there! And how can a guy with an impenetrable force field hurt you? How can holograms in the Danger Room hurt you?

I think about that little trip on the X-Jet a lot. That mission. It happened weeks ago, but that's what sort of made me brave enough to do some other things, like eventually get into the Danger Room. Which got me in trouble.

The worst thing though, isn't getting in trouble. The worst thing is something else.

Right now, I'm sitting at the desk in my room. I can look out the window and I have a pretty good view of the volleyball court. A bunch of kids my age are playing volleyball. One of them is Sam, the kid Wolverine and Angel rescued from Unus the Untouchable six weeks ago.

As soon as he got of the X-Jet that day, he was hanging out with people and making friends.

Now he's down there, playing volleyball and laughing and having a good time.

He even has a cool mutant power: He can sort of hurl his body through the air. Not really like flying, but more like a bullet being fired from a gun. And when he does that, pretty much nothing can hurt him. So they called him "Cannonball," and I bet someday *he'll* get to be an X-Man.

It's not fair. Nowhere Boy will *never* get to be an X-Man.

The X-Men playing volleyball. I'm not drawing Sam joining them because I don't feel like drawing him. So there.

Still Feeling Sorry for Myself

This entry posted on May 7 at 7:29:38 pm by Eric.

So, a few hours have gone by and they're not playing volleyball down there any more, but I'm still feeling sorry for myself.

When I get like this, I feel like I should talk to someone about it, but that's tough for me to do. So instead, I write on this blog.

And when *that* doesn't help, I go exploring.

Which isn't tough, for me.

I think today I'm going to check out Wolverine's room. Just because I can.

Wolverine's Room

This entry posted on May 7 at 9:11:19 pm by Eric.

OK, so I'm back.

Wow, that was pretty cool!

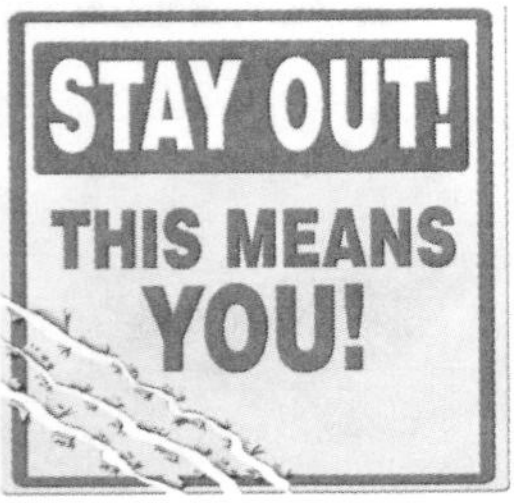
STAY OUT!
THIS MEANS
YOU!

First of all, I stood outside the door for a few minutes, too scared to go in. I don't know why. mean, I knew that Wolverine was hanging out with some of the other X-Men because I'd heard his voice from one of the meeting rooms on my way here.

Maybe it's because I knew that it was wrong to invade someone's privacy like that. But I figure I'm a special case. I mean, if I couldn't wander around a little bit, I'd have almost *nothing* to do here. (Except for school, but that doesn't count as "something to do" — it's school!) That would really suck.

So I finally got the courage to open the door and go inside.

And it wasn't anything like I expected.

I don't know — I guess I figured with Wolverine, his room would be sort of barren. Just a bed and maybe a little dresser and that's it, right? Or maybe it would be some kind of outdoorsman's place, with furniture made out of logs.

But it was Japanese.

I just stood there for a minute, shocked. And then I realized that people don't notice *me*, but they *would* notice if Wolverine's bedroom door stood open for no reason. I went inside and closed the door behind me.

It was like walking into a new world. It was like that book I read once, the one where the girl goes into a closet and pushes her way through these hanging fur coats and then suddenly discovers that she's outside in the snow, in another universe. That's what it felt like.

Standing screens blocked off one corner of the room. When I peeked around them, I saw comfortable cushions on the floor. I wondered what they were for, but then an image formed in my head: Wolverine, sitting cross-legged on the cushions, his eyes closed...

Meditating! Wolverine *meditated!*

There was a stand with two samurai swords on it. (I touched one and almost cut my finger off — they were real...and sharp!) Hanging from the wall was a full suit of samurai armor, just like in the movies. I couldn't believe it.

Can you picture Wolverine fighting a ninja or something? I can, and it would totally look like this!

Along one wall, there was a low shelf. It had a framed picture of a Japanese woman and some other stuff: An old, battered helmet that looked like the ones in pictures from World War II I'd seen in history class. A bayonet, rusty and chipped. Stuff like that. Old stuff.

Where did it all come from? Did it belong to Wolverine? Did someone give it to him? Or was it his all along? And if *that* was the case, then... how old *was* he?

I started to get nervous that Wolverine might come back any minute. And besides, I still had the xPhone in my pocket, so the Professor could suddenly decide to push some buttons and find out where I was.

But before I left, I noticed something hanging on the wall: A calendar. With red marker, Wolverine was crossing off the days. He'd circled the twelfth. I peeled back the calendar to look at the other pages. He'd been counting down to the twelfth for a while now. I don't know what that's all about.

I got out of there pretty fast, my heart pounding real hard and real loud until I got back here.

CHANGE OF PLANS
This entry posted on May 7 at 11:15:56 pm by Eric.

I'm not following Wolverine around tonight. I feel sort of guilty abou
going into his room without permission.

WHOA!
This entry posted on May 8 at 12:36:38 am by Eric.

Just woke up and I had to write this down because I think I understan
what the calendar in Wolverine's room was about. Sort of.

I remember that first mission. When I was on the plane with Wolverin
and Angel, Angel said to Wolverine something like, "Getting to be th
time of the year." Something like that.

That's around the time Wolverine started counting down to the twelft
of this month!

So every year on the twelfth of May, Wolverine does something.

Or maybe…

Maybe something *happens* to him…

Ooh, spooky, right?

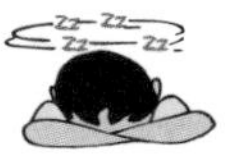

"The Most Important Meal of the Day," My Mutant Butt!

This entry posted on May 8 at 8:00:46 am by Eric.

Now, I know what you're thinking. You're thinking, "Hey, this is a blog, right? Why is he telling all these long stories? Why isn't he telling us all the usual blog stuff, like what he ate for breakfast today?"

Well, first of all, smarty-pants, I tell long stories here because I have no one to talk to, OK?

And second of all... I'll be happy to tell you what I eat for breakfast.

I had oatmeal for breakfast today. Oatmeal! What is the Xavier School kitchen staff thinking? How am I supposed to grow up to be a big, strong mutant without my daily dose of Sugary Spider-Bombs?! Or Mighty Avenger Flakes (I love the Hulk marshmallows)?!

You can add a ton of sugar and cinnamon to oatmeal. You can pile on sliced bananas and almond slivers and blueberries. But nothing you do to it will ever in a billion years make oatmeal worth eating. Trust me. I know these things.

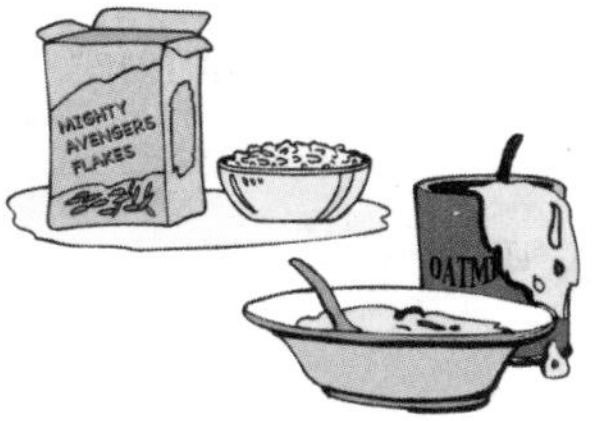
MIGHTY AVENGERS FLAKES

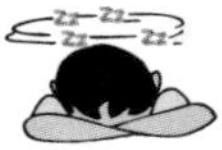

Back to the Oatmeal

This entry posted on May 8 at 8:10:37 am by Eric.

OK, look, about the oatmeal... Here's the problem. If you get some cold cereal and you toss it in milk, it's going to be good, right? No matter what.

But with oatmeal, if you end up with the stuff scraped off the bottom of the pot, it's always gonna be clumpy and chunky and gross.

And the people who serve the food here never notice me (imagine that!) so I always get served last and I always get the junk stuck at the bottom of the pot.

That's why I don't like oatmeal.

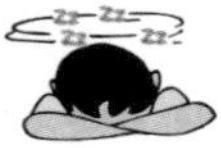

My Worst Day Ever

This entry posted on May 8 at 4:51:24 pm by Eric.

Wow, I thought things couldn't get any worse than oatmeal for breakfast. I was wrong. Today will go down in history as The Day That Was Worse Than Oatmeal.

I guess I have to back up a little bit here. And tell you some private stuff that I've never told anyone. I'm a little nervous about doing that. But no one will ever read this blog until—

Oh, never mind. I'll just tell you.

After class today, I went back to my room — like always — and read some books and played some computer games. And then I made the mistake of looking out my window.

There were the usual kids playing games out there, which always hurts a little bit, but I'm sort of used to watching that now. Watching and not participating at all.

But Dani was there, too.

Dani Moonstar. Most of the kids call her "Mirage" because she can make illusions in the air. Which is a *very* cool mutant power. If you think about it, it's sort of the opposite of my power — she makes things appear where there's nothing, and I make something (me) disappear even though it's still there. (Did that make any sense? It made sense to me!)

Dani Moonstar. She's perfect. Don't argue with me - she is.

Anyway, Dani is just really cool. I used to hang around her and her friends a lot, but no one ever talked to me and I started to feel creepy, so I stopped.

But today I looked out my window and there she was, so I thought it was going to be a good day.

But then Sam walked up to her.

Right outside my window!

He walked up to her and they started talking and then they sat down together under the big sycamore tree.

That sort of sucks.

I pulled my blinds, even though I like the sunlight. Nowhere Boy has to get used to the dark.

I sat down to write this entry. And now, for some reason, I'm thinking about Wolverine. About the Japanese woman in the picture in his room. I never see Wolverine with any of the girl X-Men. Is that Japanese woman his girlfriend or something?

I guess it doesn't matter. But I wonder.

IN HISTORY CLASS
This entry posted on May 9 at 11:22:56 am by Eric's xPhone.

I just discovered that I can blog from my xPhone! Is that the coolest thing or what?

Storm is teaching us about the D-Day invasion during World War II. I have a question, but she hasn't noticed me raising my hand.

Or jumping up and down. Or hollering at her.

So I'm going to walk up to the front of the room and if she *still* "ignores" me, I'll probably have to take one of the erasers, go back to my seat, and throw the eraser at her head.

WELL, THAT WORKED...
This entry posted on May 9 at 11:26:01 am by Eric's xPhone.

Finally got my question answered. And now I've been sent to Professor X's office. I should have my own chair there.

This is Storm, mutant goddess of the weather. She can get thrown through walls, beat up by bad mutants, zapped with lasers, and knocked down by flying garbage cans, but she can't take an eraser to the head.

PUNISHED

This entry posted on May 9 at 12:05:12 pm by Eric.

Professor X thought that sending me to my room after the school day was "adequate reprimand for acting out, Eric." He also said a bunch of other very big, very impressive words that didn't make much sense to me, but I got the gist. He wants me to behave, to be helpful and courteous, blah blah blah.

I don't get it. This is a school, right? I'm here to *learn*, right? I had a question and I made sure it got answered. How am I supposed to learn anything if I can't ask questions?

So, I basically don't know why I'm in trouble. Storm's an *X-Man* (X-Woman?). She gets punched and kicked and thrown through walls by bad guys all the time. Why is it a federal case when she gets hit in the head with an eraser? I mean, maybe I helped her — maybe she's going to face an evil mutant whose power is to throw erasers some day, and thanks to me, she'll be ready! It could happen.

And it's not like sending me to my room is a big deal. I'm here most of the time anyway because there's no point going anywhere else. (I used to watch TV on the mondo huge flatscreen in the student lounge, but people kept changing the channel.)

Unlike all of the other kids here, I have my own room, which is nice. The Professor figured that if I had a roommate, it wouldn't be fair to him because he could never be sure if I was in the room or not. And it probably wouldn't be fair to me, either, because if I was trying to study or sleep my roommate might make a bunch of noise without realizing I was around to be bothered.

Sigh. There's a kid here whose mutant power is – no lie – snot that can freeze things solid. I would give a lot for that mutant power. I would actually, seriously give *anything*.

Oh, Gross!

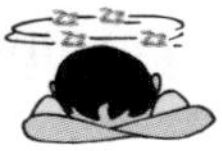
zz
zz
zz
zz

This entry posted on May 9 at 3:49:52 pm by Eric.

I don't even think I want to tell you about this, but no one is reading my blog anyway, so I might as well.

Right after class, I had to go to the bathroom. Don't laugh or anything – mutants have to go to the bathroom, too, you know. *Everyone* has to go to the bathroom at *some* point. Even teachers and parents. It happens.

Normally I use the little private bathroom in my room, but I was sort of in a hurry because I had, like, ten chimichangas for lunch, so I ducked into one of the public bathrooms on the main floor.

I was sitting there minding my own business and I guess I forgot to lock the door because suddenly I looked up and there's big, huge rear end headed my way! It was Colossus! He was about to sit on me!

I started yelling and screaming and kicking and slapping at him and he finally got the point that something was not right here and he shuffled away, mumbling something that I couldn't understand. Come to think of it, I probably didn't *want* to understand it, either.

I guess I'm lucky he wasn't in his steel form, right? Because then he never would have felt me kicking him and he would have sat on me and that ton of metal would have made me go splat. (I wonder how you go to the bathroom when you're made of solid steel? Actually, on second thought, I don't want to know.)

Lesson learned: From now on, Nowhere Boy only goes to the bathroom in the Nowhere Bathroom.

(Poor Colossus. I don't think he's *ever* going to like me.)

Colossus walks around shirtless all the time!
Yeah, we're all impressed, big guy.

IN WOLVERINE'S ROOM. AGAIN.

This entry posted on May 9 at 6:27:46 pm by Eric's xPhone.

I must have a death wish or something. Either that, or I'm really, really bored hanging out in my own room.

So I'm in Wolverine's room, checking out the picture of the Japanese woman. I can't tell how old the picture is. Is it someone he knows now? Someone he knew a long time ago?

I try to picture Wolverine on a date with his Japanese girlfriend. It would probably look like this. (I don't picture him wearing a tie. Ever.)

The calendar is still counting down to May 12. Three days from now. I get a shiver when I think about it. Somehow, I don't think it's counting down to a birthday party.

LATE NIGHT STUFF

This entry posted on May 9 at 11:39:56 pm by Eric.

I still follow Wolverine around at night. Not *every* night, but my insomnia is still pretty bad, so if I'm up, I wander the mansion. And he's usually the only other one up.

Tonight he seemed especially jumpy. He didn't even finish his sandwich. He sort of picked at it for a while, then got disgusted and threw the whole thing away. He sat at the kitchen table for a little while, staring off into space, drumming his fingers. Then he got up and went back to his room.

This is sort of how worried he looked.

As usual, he left the cookies on the table. I took pity on their loneliness and ate three of them. Then I ate one more, just to keep things even.

IN DANGER

This entry posted on May 10 at 3:17:22 pm by Eric.

I decided to sneak into the Danger Room again.

Yeah, I know Professor X got all angry at me for doing it last time. But I don't think it's *my* fault Colossus tripped over me. That could have happened even if I wasn't there. He could have tripped over some rubble. Or his own giant, steel feet.

In fact, I think I probably *helped* him by being there. Now, when he grabs Wolverine for a fastball special, he'll be more careful where he puts his feet and how he steps. See? I'm like a special added bonus to the Danger Room. Professor X ought to pay me.

(Well, he lets me live here for free, so I guess I won't charge him for my valuable services. I'm cool like that.)

The Danger Room seemed boring at first. No one was in there. When it's not activated, it's just this huge chamber with metal walls, floor, and ceiling. Nothing really worth blogging about.

But as I hung around, waiting for something to happen, I suddenly heard Professor X's voice over the loudspeaker. "This will just be a basic targeting run, Sam. No reason to worry."

Sam?

I turned and the door opened and Sam came cruising in. He was wearing an X-Man uniform!

Oh, man, I *hated* him right then. He had a little swagger in his walk and he seemed way too confident for someone who's just a kid. I remembered how he'd been so scared when Wolverine rescued him from Unus the Untouchable. Not swaggering around then, were you?

"I'm ready, Professor X," he said.

The bright Danger Room went dim for a second and then — like magic — Sentinels appeared.

This is what it looks like when the X-Men fight a Sentinel. Much cooler than when Sam fights one.

Sentinels are these enormou robots that hate mutants. Some gu built them a while ago and eve though the X-Men stopped him from destroying all the mutants in th world, his robots were still out there. Someone is always reactivating on or building a new one from blueprints they bought on the Internet. An even though everyone thinks they can control the Sentinels, it always turn out that the Sentinels revert to their original programming and start huntin down mutants no matter what.

Sentinels are BAD NEWS.

My first day at the school, Professor X gave me a rundown on all th enemies the X-Men face, all the bad guys who hate mutants. Most of th time, his advice was "Run" or "Get help." But when he showed me a pictur of the Sentinels, he added, "Pray."

Tired of typing. More soon.

OUT OF DANGER AND IN TROUBLE
This entry posted on May 10 at 5:26:54 pm by Eric.

I just can't catch a break. I couldn't catch a break if I had the world's biggest baseball glove and the break was thrown underhand by the weakest softball pitcher in the world. I *still* wouldn't catch the break.

It's not my fault! I swear!

Well, maybe it *is* my fault. But I didn't mean to do it, so that means people shouldn't blame me, right?

Here's what happened in the Danger Room:

The Sentinels started coming after Sam. I sort of pressed myself into a corner and tried to disappear. I don't mean the way I usually disappear — I mean actually vanish and reappear somewhere else. Sentinels were serious trouble — they were what the older mutants used to scare the younger ones (like me). They were the boogeyman and a kidnapper and a crazy man rolled into one. I wanted no part of them.

I have to admit, though — Sam did pretty well. He was obviously scared, but he launched himself through the air at the first one, ricocheting off it at superspeed. I winced in pain. Throwing myself at the speed of sound headfirst into a mechanical giant made out of nearly indestructible metal is *not* my idea of a good time.

(In case you're wondering: My idea of a good time is playing *Iron Man Adventures* on my StarkTech 400 game console, with a big bowl of nachos and a tub of cherry soda on the table next to me.)

But Sam's power makes him just as nearly-indestructible as long as he's "cannonballing" at something, so when he bounced off that huge Sentinel, it was with a huge grin plastered across his way-too-good-looking face.

The Sentinel staggered backwards and collided with the Sentinel standing behind it. Sam landed just a couple of feet away from me, still grinning. "That all you got?" he drawled. (I forgot to mention before: He has this annoying accent that the girls all think is cute.)

The first Sentinel stepped aside, allowing the second one to come up next to it. "Secondary element detected," it said in its menacing metallic voice. "Initiate elimination protocols."

That didn't sound good. And I was right.

Next thing I knew, the Sentinels were firing laser beams out of their eyes. Sam screamed and cannonballed into the air, crashing into the ceiling. He dropped down, unhurt, but he was an easy target for the next blast of lasers.

Which never came.

Instead, the lasers started firing at *me*! Fortunately, they all missed. I was like the Sentinels had a general idea of where I was, but didn't know for sure. So they just started blasting away at the corner where I was standing. Lasers sizzled the air around me and the walls started smoking and burning.

"I've lost control of the room!" Professor X shouted over the loudspeaker. "Logan, get in there!"

The next thing I knew, the heavy plate glass that separated the control center from the Danger Room shattered as Wolverine barreled through, his arms outstretched, his claws already fully extended. One Sentinel turned to deal with him while the other kept firing in my general direction. I curled into a ball in the corner. I told myself that I was Nowhere Boy and that there was a chance that my power might protect me...but probably not.

Over the sound of alarms going off and lasers blasting all over the place, I heard the unmistakable sound of metal tearing metal. Like screws digging into sheets of steel. Squealing.

The Sentinel stopped firing lasers at me. I dared open my eyes and looked around. My Sentinel was busy defending itself as Wolverine danced on it, dodging and dipping low to slash with his claws.

"Danced" sounds sort of weak and wimpy, but that was the only word for it.

Wolverine, taking care of Sentinel business! Awesome!

The other Sentinel — the first one — was a pile of junk on the Danger Room floor. Its head had rolled into a corner, gears and wires and cables spilling out of it like the gory stuff in movies. Except, you know, robotic. Not bloody at all.

Wolverine hacked at the remaining Sentinel's head, cutting it open, exposing the wiring of its robot brain. It tried to turn and zap him with its laser eyes, but he moved out of the way and stabbed it in the back of the head with both sets of claws. The Sentinel made a weird noise — it sounded exactly like a burp, no lie — and pitched forward, sizzling, sparking, shaking. Then it stopped moving entirely.

The Danger Room was totally quiet for a minute. Sam just stared. Professor X watched in silence through the broken window.

Wolverine yawned and stretched, then cracked his knuckles. "I love doin' the recycling," he said.

My Fault, Of Course

This entry posted on May 10 at 6:21:09 pm by Eric.

Apparently, it was all my fault (as usual). The Sentinels weren't holograms from the Danger Room – they were old, scrapped Sentinels that the X-Men recovered and Professor X reprogrammed for training.

Then they detected me, but couldn't get a fix on my location. They had been programmed to test one mutant – Sam – but when they picked me up, their default programming kicked in and they went berserk.

I don't really think that's *all* my fault. I mean, Professor X didn't have to use real Sentinels, did he? And he didn't have to do *such* a good job restoring their programming, did he?

I don't think so. But no one seems to listen to my opinion about these things. (They probably should; things would run a lot more smoothly if I was in charge. Like, no more oatmeal for breakfast.)

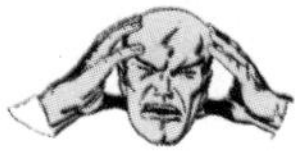

I Get Yelled at Again

This entry posted on May 10 at 8:12:05 pm by Eric.

Professor X told me that he has "no desire to invade your privacy, Eric," but that if I don't stop sneaking around and going where I'm not supposed to be, then he's going to permanently activate the CPS in my xPhone. Then Cerebro will always know where I am and will sound alarms every time I go somewhere I'm not supposed to be.

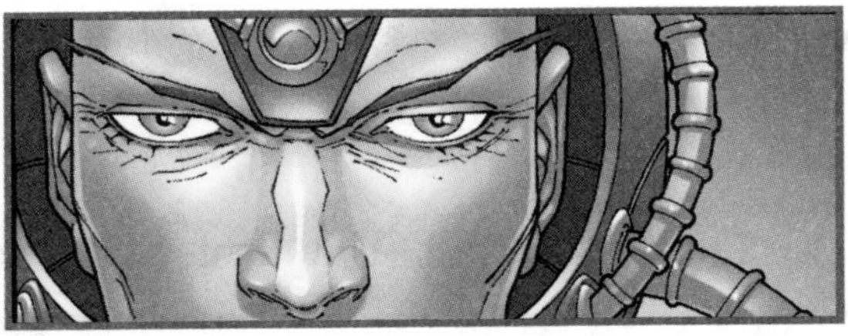

Can I just point something ou here? I don't "sneak around" a all! I just walk around normally I'm not even trying to be quiet Heck, when I went into the Danger Room today, I'm pretty sure I was humming.

I mean, I get that people don't notice, so it might *seem* like I'm sneaking around but it's not *my* fault no one pays attention to me, so I'm getting sort of offended a all of this "sneaking around" stuff.

I was going to tell the Professor all of that, but by the time he took a breathe from yelling at me, we both had killer headaches and I just wanted to get out o his office and back here, where I could write this up.

So I said, "I understand, Chuck," sort of the way Wolverine would say it, an *that* was a big mistake because then I got a whole new lecture on respect and th headache just got worse. I don't see what the big deal is: Chuck is his name.

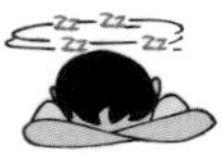

No One Understands

This entry posted on May 10 at 10:11:12 pm by Eric.

No one gets it. If I didn't go "where I'm not supposed to be," I would neve go anywhere at all. Because if I go to the "safe" and "approved" places, all see are shiny happy mutants, palling around and having fun together. Lik I need to see more of that. Barf.

Nowhere Boy, signing off.

POOR ME
This entry posted on May 10 at 10:15:54 pm by Eric.

I miss my mom. I miss my friends. I miss my life!

READ ME BEFORE THE EARLIER ENTRY!
This entry posted on May 10 at 10:16:39 pm by Eric.

I can't figure out how to delete the previous entry! Aargh! Ignore it! Don't read it!

 ## THE SCOOP ON WOLVERINE
This entry posted on May 10 at 11:52:01 pm by Eric.

Wow, so it just occurred to me, like, five minutes ago, that a while ago, I was talking about the X-Men and I listed stuff about all of them and then for Wolverine, I said I would talk more about him later. This is exactly what I said:

"And then there's Wolverine.

"More about him later."

But I haven't explained much about him at all!

OK, so since no one ever notices me, I get to hear all *kinds* of stuff.

I linger around the X-Men a lot and this is what I've managed to piece together about Wolverine:

1) He hates being called "Wolvie."

2) He loves strawberry milk.

3) And sandwiches.

4) He calls people "bub." A lot.

5) He's the only person in the history of the known universe to call Professor X "Chuck" or "Charlie" as opposed to "Professor Xavier" or "sir."

6) He's Canadian. (So, like, he can't vote. Oooh, bummer, right?)

7) His name is Logan. Not, like, "Bill Logan" or "Logan Smith." Just... Logan. (Not even "Logan Logan," which would at least be two names!)

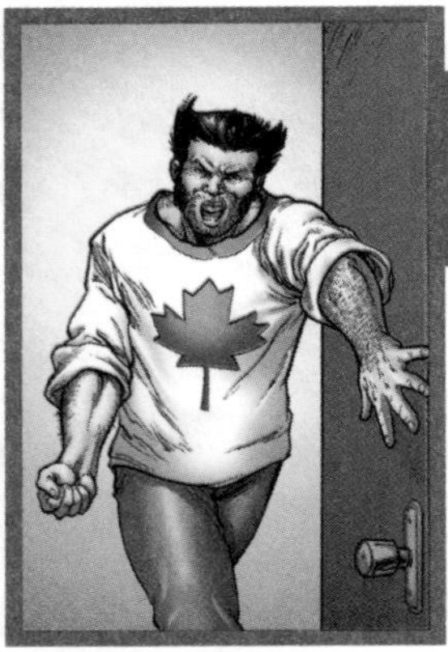

See? Canadian! Why else would he wear that shirt?

BTW, I thought a wolverine was some kind of tough wolf or wild dog because that's what it sounds like. But I looked it up on the Internet and a wolverine is actually — get this — some kind of smelly weasel

I don't know why Wolverine calls himself that. He doesn't really smell and he's not weaselly at all. Maybe he doesn't know what it means – but I'm not going to be the one to tell him!

Anyway, "Wolverine" *sounds* really cool, so maybe that's all that matters.

So, that's the basics. But here's the cool stuff:

First of all, no one knows how old he is. Even *he* isn't sure. It turns out his memories are all scrambled up and wiped out and some of them are even just plain deleted. He looks pretty young, but his healing factor could be keeping him youthful.

Right. His healing factor. That's the cool thing about Wolverine. Those claws? They're not even his main mutant power! It's totally not fair! He gets a cool power *and* claws.

His actual mutant power is healing. Like, if you punch him in the face and make his nose bleed, it'll stop almost right away. (I am *not* suggesting that you actually punch Wolverine in the nose. In fact, I'm specifically suggesting that you *not* punch Wolverine in the nose. Unless you like pain. Or unless you're Sam the Cannonball Who Hangs Around With Dani, in which case punch away. I'll watch.)

He can get shot, cut, dropped off the roof and all that stuff. He'll just bounce back. The worse he's hurt, the longer it takes to get better, but he *always* gets better. Eventually.

At least... So far.

Even when he's hurt, Wolverine can still kick your butt!

Anyway, so that's his power. And I am *way* jealous of it because I banged my knee running up to my room to type this, and it *still* hurts, and I bet I'm going to have a bruise for, like, a week. So I could use a little healing factor right now, OK?

I'm not *too* sure about this next part, but from what I heard Cyclops and Marvel Girl saying the other day, it seems like a bunch of Canadian military guys grabbed Wolverine when he was younger and tied him down and injected this metal into his bones.

(That sounds way-cool and gross at the same time. There should be a word for things like that so that you don't have to say "Way-cool *and* gross." What if we call it "way-gross?" I'm going to try that from now on.)

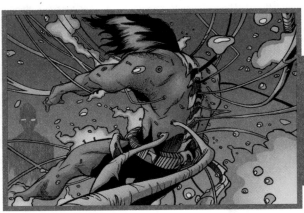

I guess it probably looked like this when the military was messing with him. Not fun.

They injected this way-gross metal into him. It's called Adamantium. (It took me *forever* to find it on the Internet. I kept spelling it with two d's and I thought there was a q in there somewhere.)

Adamantium is supposed to be totally unbreakable, which is way-cool, not way-gross at all. And they bonded it to his bones (I don't know how – with Super-Glue, maybe?) so now his *bones* are totally unbreakable.

I'm not clear on the claws – like, maybe he always had them, or maybe the military added them in. But either way – just to make things *perfect* – the claws are *also* made out of Adamantium.

Whew!

This explains why Wolverine is just so *tough*. I mean, you can't break his bones. You can't crack his head open. And when you *do* hurt him, he just gets better. Cyclops said that the only way to get rid of Wolverine for good would be to do so much huge, massive damage to him at once that his healing factor would be overwhelmed and he wouldn't be able to recover. But that's got to be impossible.

Right? Yeah, I think so. Impossible. Got to be.

I'm a little fuzzy on what happened to him after that. The Canadian army gave him the bones and the claws, and then he escaped from them. Or something. I don't know. And his memory was all goofed up like you wouldn't believe. But Marvel Girl says that it looks like his memory was messed up even *before* the military started messing around with him, so that might not be their fault.

Eventually, he ended up here, at the school. And even though he's not what you call a "joiner" or a "team player," he ended up being an X-Man. To fight the good fight and also get on Professor X's good side so that Professor X will help him recover his lost memories.

Well, maybe *mostly* to get Professor X's help and to fight the good fight a little bit.

I'm tired from typing all of that. I'm actually going to go to bed. Early.

CAN'T SLEEP

This entry posted on May 11 at 12:56:39 am by Eric.

I gave it a try. I really did. And even though I'm tired, I just can't fall asleep. Every time I close my eyes, I see this big tank of gooey stuff and Wolverine is floating in it and army guys are standing around while Adamantium gets pumped straight into his bones.

I never really thought about it before, but I bet it probably hurt a lot when they did that to him. That's probably why he ran away from Canada — they put him through a lot of pain, you know?

Like I said, pain. I really have trouble thinking about this too much.

STILL CAN'T SLEEP

This entry posted on May 11 at 1:25:37 am by Eric.

So I got out of bed and went to the kitchen. Wolverine was already there. His drink was almost empty and the sandwich was nothing but a crust and a bunch of crumbs. He was sitting at the table, real still and real straight. Alert.

He tapped his fingers on the table, like he was nervous. I started to wonder: What in the world could make *Wolverine* nervous?

And wondering that made *me* nervous!

I sat down across from him. I felt sad. I thought about the picture of the Japanese woman in his room. With his memories all screwed up, maybe he didn't even know who she was! Maybe he just had this picture that he carried around and he knew it was important, but he didn't know how or why.

That made me even sadder.

He had these cool powers and he was so tough and so awesome, but he was sort of lonely.

I wished that I didn't have my power. I wished that he could see me and hear me. Because I would have said to him, "Hey, Wolverine, I don't know what's bothering you, but maybe if you talk to someone about it, it'll get better. I don't know, but that always worked for me. And I would listen, if you wanted to talk."

And then I would say, "When I was a little kid, I used to have nightmares all the time. This was before my power kicked in. I would have nightmares and I would wake up screaming, and my mom or my dad would come running into my room and turn on the light and hold me and rock me until I calmed down and stopped freaking out."

And then I would say, "When he was holding me and rocking me, my dad would always ask what my nightmare was about. He wanted me to tell him about it. But I was always too scared. It was too real, you know? So I wouldn't tell him. I would tell him that it was too scary. Too scary even just to *talk* about. That's how scary it was."

And then I would say, "But my dad would always say to me, 'Eric, if you talk about it, it won't be as scary any more. If you talk about it, that helps make it go away.' And you know what, Wolverine? You know what? He was right. Because one time I finally had the courage to do it. I finally told him all about my nightmare, in all of its weird, creepy, gory, gross details. And it didn't seem so bad after that. I was able to fall asleep. And I still had nightmares, but I talked about them right away and then they didn't seem so bad and pretty soon I stopped having them. Except for *sometimes* because everyone has nightmares *some*times, right?"

And then I would say, "So maybe if you talked to someone about what's bothering you, it wouldn't seem like such a big deal, Wolverine. I know I'm just a kid, so I don't have real good adult advice to give you, but that's the best kid advice I have."

That's what I would say. All of it. It would take a long time.

But he can't see me or hear me, so I didn't say any of it. I just thought it. I didn't say anything at all.

After a little while, he got up and sighed, really heavy, like he felt old all of a sudden. And he took the cookies down from the top shelf and put them on the table and didn't even look back. He just left them there.

It's weird. I didn't feel like eating any. So I came back here to think.

YUM

This entry posted on May 11 at 1:42:54 am by Eric.

OK, enough thinking. I went back to the kitchen and grabbed a cookie. Bed time now.

OH, MAN

This entry posted on May 11 at 3:18:09 am by Eric.

Shouldn't have eaten that cookie. Weird dream. Not really a nightmare. Just weird.

Following my own advice to talk about it, so here I am. In the dream, I had the exact *opposite* mutant power. Instead of no one noticing me, people *had* to notice me. They couldn't help it. Everywhere I went, people turned to look at me. I couldn't do anything at all because I was always being watched. Even in the bathroom with the door closed, people were constantly *aware* of me, so I couldn't do anything at all. Taking a shower was embarrassing. I couldn't even pick my nose — everyone would notice.

What a freaky dream. What a lousy power. I finally found the mutant power that sucks more than mine does, and it's in my own dream.

Feel better now. Back to bed.

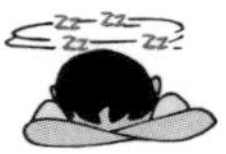

?????

This entry posted on May 11 at 7:22:10 am by Eric.

I feel like I'm forgetting something important today.

Off to class.

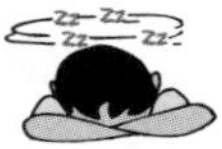

?????? x 2

This entry posted on May 11 at 10:54:06 am by Eric's xPhone.

In math class, blogging on the xPhone. Still feel like I forgot something important. Don't know what, though. Pancakes for breakfast. Not bad. I hate maple syrup, but raspberry jelly is *good*.

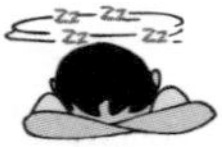

??????? x 3

This entry voice-posted on May 11 at 12:16:23 pm by Eric's xPhone.

Lunch. No, seriously. Something has slipped my mind. Don't know what.

Hamburgers today. *Mmmm*. Like mine rare. So rare you can almost hear the cow mooing.

Learned something new about the xPhone today: I can talk to it! I talk and it turns what I say into a blog entry. It's not perfect and it's sort of slow, but it's good for short entries like this one.

Good Day/Bad Day

This entry posted on May 11 at 5:45:29 pm by Eric.

Back in my room now and I think I might never leave.

Today was a good day and a really, really bad day. Why does life have to be like that? "Give with one hand, take with the other," my dad used to say.

(I haven't called my parents in at least a week. I feel bad about that. But I don't want them to know how miserable I am here, and if they hear my voice, they'll know. When I e-mail them, they can't tell unless I put in a bunch of :(and stuff like that. And I'm not an idiot, so I don't do that.)

Today right after lunch, a bunch of kids were hanging out in the student lounge. There was some kind of X-Men emergency, so all the teachers were gone. This happens every now and then. It's one of the perks of having super heroes for your teachers — when the world is about to end (which is like at least twice a month), school gets canceled. It's better than having snow days. Heck, three weeks ago there was this big chemistry final for the upperclassmen. Beast was the teacher — he's this big, burly guy who can do acrobatic stuff like a monkey, but he also happens to be a crazy super-genius. He's, like, legendary for his tough finals, so there were kids walking through the halls, going, "Oh, God, please let Galactus try to eat the earth. Please please *please* let there be an alien invasion by the Skrulls!"

That's Beast, going through the jungle all monkey-style with Angel. You wouldn't think a guy like that is also a genius, but he is.

I don't know what's weirder: That stuff like that happens here or that I'm pretty much used to it.

Oops. I forgot to explain why this was such a good/bad day.

Right. X-Men gone, school's out. Kids hanging around in the lounge. They had this cool movie on the big TV, so I was just hanging out, watching. I stood behind the sofa because usually when I sit down, someone ends up sitting on top of me — like Colossus that one time in the bathroom. (Then they notice me and usually get all ticked off, like it's my fault or something. Like I saw them about to sit down and *magically* teleported myself under their butt. Right.)

I was just really getting into the movie and there was this one part that was really funny and everyone laughed, including me.

And then something really weird and really cool happened:

One of the kids on the sofa turned around and looked at me and said — *to me!* — "Yeah, this is hilarious, isn't it?"

I just... I just *stood* there. Like a dope. Like a statue. Like a dopey statue. *He noticed me!* He heard me laugh and he turned around and saw me and *noticed me.*

I was so shocked that I didn't say anything back, and after a second, his eyes sort of flicked in that strange way people's eyes flick when I "disappear." I'm really used to that look now: It's this sudden burst of confusion, like, "Wasn't there something here a second ago?" and then they settle down as my power kicks in and messes with their brainwaves (or however it works — no one knows) and then it's like I'm not there and I was never there and I'm Nowhere Boy again.

But for that moment... For that moment, he *noticed* me.

I thought that maybe he had some kind of power that might counteract *my* power, but I checked him out and that's not it. His name is Roberto and he's from Brazil and his power is to, like, absorb sunlight and turn it into superstrength. (No, I don't know how he does it. But it's rad, and even though I always say I wish I had other people's powers, I *really* wish I had his power.)

The rest of the afternoon, while we watched the movie, sometimes I would just "click in" like that. Usually with Roberto (maybe because I was standing right behind him?), but sometimes with other people who were nearby, too.

When the movie ended, I came back here to think about all of this. And to write it down. Because eventually I'm going to talk to Professor X about it and I want to make sure I remember it all. But it was a pretty good day because maybe there's a way around my power. Maybe.

But when I got back to my room, the day turned bad.

My room is next to Sam's. He's roommates with the kid who can freeze his own snot, so I'm sure they have a lot to talk about, since Sam's a snot.

Anyway, I heard someone laughing in there, so I peeked in the room. (This was *not* spying! There's an open door policy at Xavier's School — between first bell and lights out, you're supposed to leave your door open unless you're getting dressed or you're sick or asleep or something like that.)

Sam was sitting on his bed and Dani was sitting at his desk and they were laughing hysterically about something.

And Dani said, "You're really cute when you laugh, Sam."

I wanted to throw up. But I didn't. Instead, I came back here, to my room to write.

Why did something really good and something really bad both have to happen on the same day?

 ???????²
This entry posted on May 11 at 10:17:19 pm by Eric.

Dinner was pizza. The X-Men were back from saving the world by the time everyone started hitting dessert. When they walked into the cafeteria everyone stood up and started applauding, which was cool. They tried to be all tough and nonchalant about it, but I saw Cyclops crack a little smile and Angel did a sort of fist-pump.

Wolverine was nowhere to be seen. I think he got hurt and was resting in his room.

I still feel like I'm forgetting something, but I'm tired, so I'm actually going to bed *on time* tonight. I know, I know — it's a world of miracles and sunshine, isn't it?

Yuck
This entry posted on May 11 at 11:05:05 pm by Eric.

Every time I start to drift off, I think of Dani telling Sam how cute he is when he laughs.

Whoa!
This entry posted on May 12 at 12:32:22 am by Eric.

Oh, man! I have to write this fast — I just remembered what I forgot!

Today is The Day!

May 12. The day Wolverine's been counting down to on his calendar. All day I've been thinking about it *without* thinking about it. It's been nagging at me. It's past midnight now, so it's May 12.

I'm going to see if I can find him and see what's up about this day.

I Can't Believe I'm Doing This...

This entry voice-posted on May 12 at 1:29:17 am by Eric's xPhone.

I'm about to get on a motorcycle in the middle of the night.

OK, let me back up real quick. I'm voice-blogging from the xPhone. I hope it can keep up with me. I'm in the garage. I'm *totally* not supposed to be here – not alone, not at night, not during the day, not *ever*.

But here I am. And I'm about to do something that is probably the stupidest thing in my life or the bravest thing in my life. Or maybe both. I don't know. But I do know that I want to get this down in my blog before I go. Just in case...you know...Just in case I don't come back.

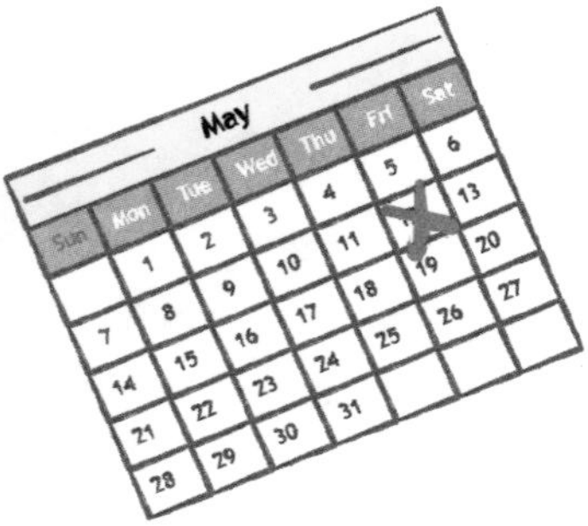
May
Sun
Mon
Tue
Wed
Thu
Fri
Sat

I went to Wolverine's room, but he wasn't there. The calendar had been torn off the wall and thrown on the floor. It lay there, crumpled and stepped on. I looked at it – May 12 was crossed through so hard that the calendar had ripped.

I ran down the hallway to the kitchen. Wolverine almost collided with me coming out, but I guess he was dizzy or something because he sort of stepped to one side at just the right moment and missed me. He looked *angry*.

He also looked a little less tough than usual. He wasn't moving as fast. Wolverine always has this way of moving, of standing. It's like he's ready or anything, but he's worried about nothing.

Watching him stomp down the hall, all I could think was that he didn't look ready for anything. And he seemed worried about *something*.

I just stood there, frozen. The idea of something worrying Wolverine... I figure anything that worries Wolverine should probably have me hiding under my bed. Even if I don't know what it is.

But I followed him anyway. I had to run hard because he had already gone around a corner by the time I managed to unfreeze myself from my spot outside the kitchen. I ran and rounded the corner and saw him just as he went through a door.

Why was I following him? I don't know. I just did it. Maybe because he was a loner, like me, and loners should stick together. Which would make them not loners any more, but maybe that's the point. What do I know? I don't have a big, gigantic Professor X-sized brain to think about these things. I just do stuff.

He went into the garage and opened the door and before I could do anything at all, he hopped on a motorcycle and took off.

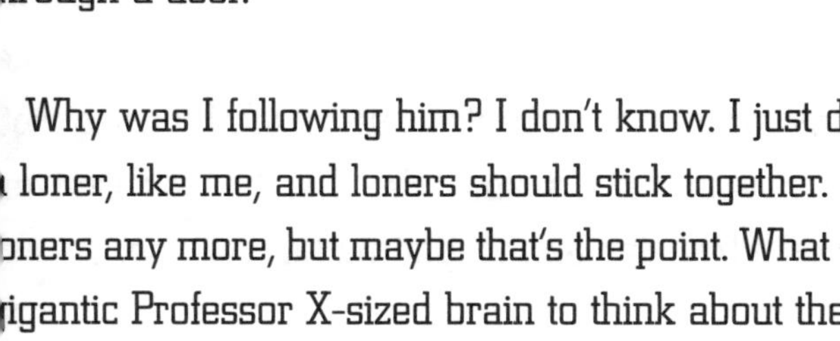

Wolverine tears out of the school garage. In a hurry. Duh!

And I'm going to follow him some more.

STALLED OUT

This entry voice-posted on May 12 at 1:49:52 am
by Eric's xPhone.

I guess I should explain something here: I really d[...]
know how to ride a motorcycle. Why? Because I a[...]
just super-cool like that. 'Nuff said.

I'm just not used to *this* motorcycle, so I stalled [...]
out. I'm waiting a minute to restart it because that'[...]
what my dad taught me.

My dad's the one who taught me how to ride. I was *way* too young — even [...]
know that — but we lived on a big farm and there was lots of flat, open space[...]
And Dad says that *his* dad (my granddad, who died during the Galactus riot[...]
when I was a baby) taught him how to ride a motorcycle when he was, like, ter[...]
so Dad took me out on my twelfth birthday and taught me how to ride.

Wolverine getting further
away from me because I
stalled out!

Motor's kicking back i[...]
I can hear Wolverine's bik[...]
over the rise. I'm gone.

WOLVERINE'S WORST DAY EVER?

This entry voice-posted on May 12 at 2:09:46 am by Eric's xPhone.

I can't believe what I just saw.

It came out of nowhere. It was like…It was like a bolt of lightning, but with fur and fangs and it *roared* and I think I smelled something like blood and…

Let me back up.

I have to talk about this. For just a minute. Because otherwise I'm going to lose my mind. It's like the bad dreams when I was a kid — if I talk about it, it'll be better.

I hope.

God, I hope.

This isn't a nightmare. Or maybe it *is* a nightmare, but it's a solid nightmare, one made out of real stuff, not brain stuff.

OK, so I was cruising along after getting the bike started again. I thought I was losing Wolverine, so I sped up into a curve, which is a *really* dumb thing to do, especially at night, especially on an unfamiliar road, but I wasn't thinking too clearly. All of a sudden, I knew that I had to keep up with him. If I had a rad mutant power like seeing the future or reading minds, I would figure that feeling came from the power. But since I have a sucky power, I knew that the feeling came from my gut, like normal people's feelings.

I almost lost control of the bike coming around the corner, but I managed to keep it on the road. Just ahead of me, Wolverine was bearing down hard tearing down the blacktop. The school is way out in the middle of nowhere — there were nothing but trees rising up on both sides of the road. In the darkness, some of them sort of looked like Sentinels, and that distracted me so much that I almost missed it.

It.

It came out of nowhere. One second, Wolverine was cruising along ahead of me, hunched low over the body of the bike. The next second, this...this *thing* launched itself out of the trees and tackled Wolverine right off the bike, like it was nothing. Like he wasn't going almost a hundred miles an hour. Like it was the easiest thing in the world.

I'll be honest — this scared the snot out of me!

The bike went skidding off one way, and Wolverine and the thing went the other, tumbling over each other, rolling across the road to the shoulder. The thing on Wolverine was huge, an orange-and-yellow blur that snarled and growled like a mad dog.

They slowed down just for a second and I caught a glimpse of it: A man. Well guess it was a man. It was man-shaped, with arms and legs and hair and a head and all of that stuff, but it looked more like an animal that someone had dressed up and taught to walk on two feet.

Seven feet tall. *Huge* muscles. A mane of dirty blond hair that came down to his shoulders.

He snarled and smacked Wolverine, knocking Wolverine off the road and into some scrub brush. Then he followed Wolverine.

I had stopped my bike when Wolverine got knocked off his. I stood there, watching, as the bad guy leaned over, picked up Wolverine, and threw him into the woods.

I couldn't believe what I was seeing. Someone was beating up Wolverine. Wolverine! The toughest mutant in the whole wide world, and he was getting his head handed to him!

The big guy stomped into the woods. I heard him growl and howl, then I heard branches snapping. He must have picked Wolverine up and thrown him again.

I don't know what to do.

DECIDED

This entry voice-posted on May 12 at 2:13:08 am by Eric's xPhone.

It's been a couple of minutes. I can't wait around any more. I have to do something.

Here's what I've decided: I'm going to go into the woods and find them.

I know it's sort of nuts. Like, what am *I* going to do against a mountain of crazy muscle and claws? But by the time I get back to the mansion, Wolverine could be really hurt. And by the time I manage to get someone's attention and explain what's going on, it could be too late. Everyone's asleep — it's tough enough getting people to notice me when they're awake. When they're asleep it's almost impossible.

So that leaves me with two choices — I can go into the woods or I can stand here like a lump and cross my fingers and hope that Wolverine gets the upper hand, even though the bad guy totally caught him off guard and looks twice as mean as Wolverine.

No choice. I'm going in.

[UNTITLED ENTRY]

This entry voice-posted on May 12 at 2:20:19 am by Eric's xPhone.

I think I'm lost.

JNTITLED ENTRY]

his entry voice-posted on May 12 at 2:25:26 am by Eric's xPhone.

I'm definitely lost. Oh, God.

It's really dark here. The trees are blocking out the moon. I followed a
ath of broken branches for a while. The leaves and grass on the ground
e all messed up and I followed that, too. But then it got too dark.

NTITLED ENTRY]

his entry voice-posted on May 12 at 2:32:02 am by Eric's xPhone.

I don't know why I'm even recording this blog now.

UNTITLED ENTRY]

his entry voice-posted on May 12 at 2:41:11 am by Eric's xPhone.

No one will ever find me. They don't notice me when I'm right in front of
em, so how will they ever find me?

I wonder if my super lame power will work when I'm dead? Will my
ody never be found?

[Untitled Entry]

This entry voice-posted on May 12 at 2:42:15 am by Eric's xPhone.

I just heard something. Maybe it was a rabbit?

[Untitled Entry]

This entry voice-posted on May 12 at 2:43:01 am by Eric's xPhone.

Not a rabbit. I heard growling. And yelling. I recognized Wolverine's voic but I couldn't tell what he was saying.

And I heard that *other* voice. Over and over. It's like a lion and a chargin elephant and a crazy person all at once. Just the *voice* scares me. An Wolverine is actually *fighting* him. I can't imagine what that feels like.

So do I go towards the voice? Or do I run in the opposite direction and hop to get back to the road?

[Untitled Entry]

This entry voice-posted on May 12 at 2:44:10 am by Eric's xPhone.

OK, I've made up my mind. I'm going to go towards the voice. I have t I'm not a super hero, but I'm a person and people are supposed to help othe people, whether they have super-powers or not. Right?

Right. Here I go.

In the Clearing

This entry voice-posted on May 12 at 2:47:25 am by Eric's xPhone.

There's a little clearing up ahead. I can see it because some moonlight is coming down there. That's where the noises are coming from.

That's where they're fighting.

Still Alive

This entry posted on May 12 at 4:06:52 am by Eric's xPhone.

OK. It's over. It's all over now, and I'm still alive.

So is Wolverine.

Wow. Wow, I can't believe what I saw. I can't believe what *happened.*

Wolverine is still recovering, so we have to wait here for a little while before we can go. Let me explain what happened.

I came to the clearing, as quiet as I could. It's the first time since my power started up that I've actually *tried* to sneak around. I guess because the fighting was so loud and so scary that my instincts just sort of kicked in.

I crept up around this big tree. I think it was a poplar. (Who *cares*, Eric? Sheesh.)

I looked into the clearing, and there they were.

Have you ever watched boxing on TV? The way the two boxers circle each other? It's like half the fight isn't even any fighting — it's walking in a circle, frowning at the other guy.

That's sort of what I saw in the clearing.

The big guy's name is Sabretooth. I know that now. He and Wolverine were circling each other, crouched down low. Snarling. I had never heard Wolverine make a sound like that before — it was like a dog protecting its master.

I stood there, frozen. I hadn't really gotten a good look at Sabretooth before because he was moving so fast. He had been plenty scary when I could barely see him, but now that I could actually study him, he was twice as scary.

Easily seven feet tall. Tallest person I'd ever seen in my life. His shoulders were as big across as I am tall. He was wearing this orange and brown outfit that had fur at the wrists and collar, and his hair was a dirty, gnarly mess.

His eyes were blank and dead. He had fangs — I could see them because he growled deep in his throat and flared his lips and it was like looking directly at a rabid wolf.

His hands... I looked at his hands and *that* was a mistake. Instead of fingernails, he had long, wicked claws that had bits of cloth and other gross stuff on them.

Wolverine vs. Sabretooth. I cleaned it up a little bit so that it won't freak people out, but trust me — it was really gross.

The cloth and other gross stuff came from Wolverine. He didn't look good.

For the first time since I'd met him, I was afraid for Wolverine and I felt sorry for him.

He looked like someone had been using him to practice surgery — he was a mass of torn clothes and torn skin, his body covered in his own blood. The claws on both hands were popped and I cheered a little when I realized that some of the cloth from Sabretooth's outfit hung off them.

Still, I could tell that he was in massive pain just by the way he moved — slow and a little unsure.

Sabretooth could tell, too. "Slowin' down, ain'tcha, pup?"

Wolverine's voice was low and a little shaky, but his words weren't shaky at all. "Fast enough for you, old man. I'm the best there is at what I do."

Sabretooth laughed. It was the least happy laugh I've ever heard in my entire life. I don't even know if it *was* a laugh, but he was smiling when he did it, so I guess it was. Sabretooth's sense of humor, I've decided, is not normal.

"Last year, you barely walked away from this," Sabretooth said. "This time, I'm gonna make sure you know who's the best. And it ain't you."

"You beat me, it don't mean nothin'," Wolverine said. "Just means even a low-down, miserable, lying, stealing, snarling dog like you can get lucky if he keeps tryin' long enough."

Wolverine and Sabretooth got THIS CLOSE!

Sabretooth howled so loud that I had to cover my ears. He jumped at Wolverine, his fangs open like he was going to bite Wolverine's head off and swallow it whole. Wolverine dodged to one side, but he was too hurt, too slow, and Sabretooth collided with him. They collapsed to the ground and rolled there, howling and screaming and stabbing each other with their claws.

I can't even tell you what that looked like. I'll never forget it. I'll have nightmares about it. But I won't tell you. Not now. It's too soon. Someday.

I saw Wolverine get in some good shots and I thought that even someone as big and as tough as Sabretooth would have to give up. It just had to hurt so much. Wolverine's claws were long and strong and made out of Adamantium. I can't imagine what it would feel like to have one go into you. You would have to give up, right?

But then I figured something out all on my own, just standing there. I'm not sure how I figured it out. Maybe it was the way they both snarled the same. The way they both seemed like animals there on the ground.

I realized all of a sudden: They *were* the same. Sabretooth was bigger and stronger and his claws were at the ends of his fingers, but he was just like Wolverine: He had a healing factor, too. He could take every shot Wolverine gave him and come back for more.

He was on top of Wolverine now, beating him. It was horrible. It was the worst thing I've ever seen in my life. Wolverine could barely move – he was pinned down by Sabretooth's huge body. He had one arm free and he could block some of Sabretooth's punches, but not all of them. It was too much.

I remembered Cyclops saying that the only way to stop Wolverine for good would be to hurt him so much and so bad that his healing factor wouldn't have time to catch up. I was no expert, but it looked like that's what Sabretooth was doing.

I had to do something. Me. It was the only way Wolverine would survive.

I looked around. If I jumped on Sabretooth's back, it wouldn't do anything. I'm too small. Even if I didn't have the world's suckiest mutant power, he still wouldn't notice me. I'd be a flea on a elephant.

But I could throw something at him, right? Just like I'd thrown that eraser to get Storm's attention in class. I could throw something and my power wouldn' affect the thing I throw.

I tried to find something big and heavy. I had this great idea that I woul do my own "fastball special" and whip a gigantic rock right at Sabretooth's fat head.

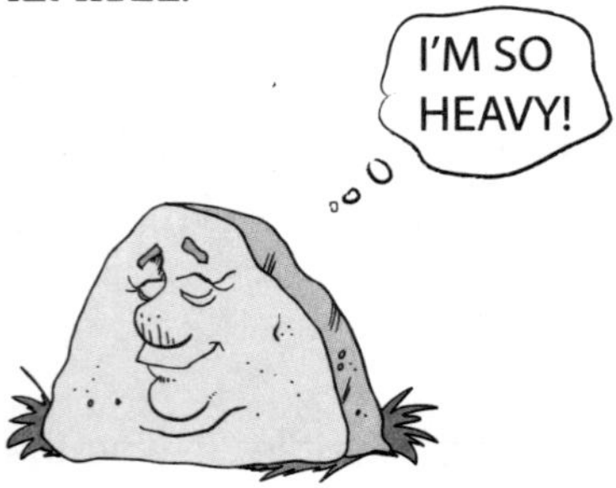
I'M SO
HEAVY!

I found a huge rock, partly buried in the ground The ground was soft, but I couldn't lift that rock much less throw it.

Big sticks. They wouldn't do anything to a gu

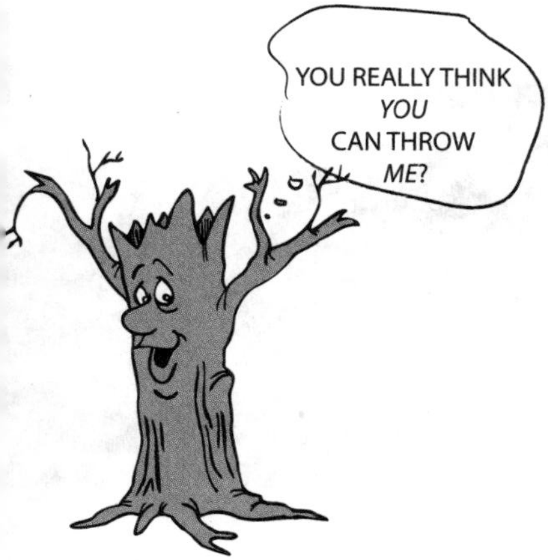
YOU REALLY THINK *YOU* CAN THROW *ME?*

Sabretooth's size. I'd have to throw a tree at him. (Ooh, that would be cool...)

Small rocks. Yeah, right. Like that would do anything.

That was my only choice, though. I gathered up an armful of rocks and started throwing them at Sabretooth, aiming for his face.

I missed with the first one and hit Wolverine instead. Oops.

"What are you doing?" Wolverine shouted, like he was angry. Wow, after Sabretooth beats him up all this time, *now* he asks what he's doing? The man needs to work on his priorities.

I kept throwing and eventually I hit Sabretooth in the face with a pretty good-sized rock. He paused for a second and looked around.

Then he did something weird — he *sniffed* the air.

I stood real still. When I stand still and don't make any noise, no one can notice me. Never.

But Sabretooth... He kept sniffing the air...

And then...

And then he *looked right at me!*

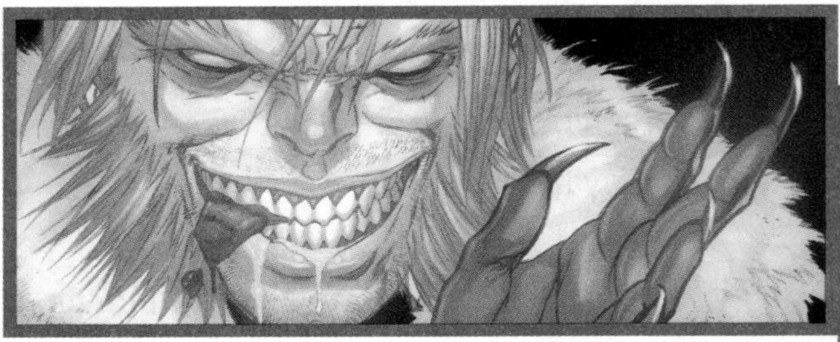

This is what it was like when Sabretooth looked at me. I will never, ever forget it. Brr.

His lip curled over a fang. I realized that was Sabretooth's version of a grin

Terrific. Just my luck. Someone finally noticed me and he was a psychopath!

"Whatta we got here, pup? A *real* pup! We—"

The next thing out of his mouth was a scream. It was a real good one, too. I think it shook the trees. I've never heard anything like it in my life and I hope I never do again.

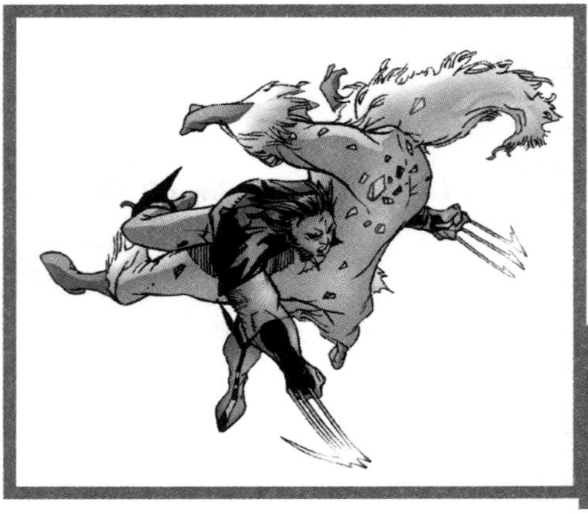

Why the scream? Well, because my little rock-throwing distracted Sabretooth for just a second. And then Wolverine jabbed up with his claws and—

Wolverine finally nails Sabretooth real good! (I cleaned this one up, too. No need to gross you out.)

It's actually pretty disgusting. But since it happened to Sabretooth, it was way-gross.

Next thing I knew, Sabretooth was up and running away. I think his head was sort of half hanging off his neck because when he shouted while he ran, it was tough to understand him.

"See you again next year, pup!" That's what he said.

And then he was gone.

I was still alive. Wolverine was still alive.

Wow.

Home

This entry posted on May 12 at 8:19:36 am by Eric.

Back at the mansion now. It's morning. Wolverine and I were out in the woods all night. I should probably be asleep by now and believe me – I am *exhausted*. But so much happened *after* Sabretooth left and I want to get it all down so that I can always remember it. Because even though it was the scariest night of my life, I think it was probably also the best night, too.

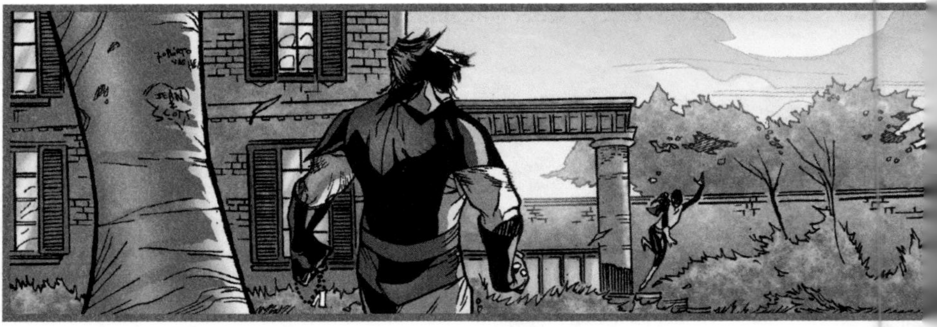

Here's the thing: Wolverine *noticed* me. He *noticed* me.

Let me explain. It's cool. And complicated. But mostly cool.

He was lying there on the ground, looking like a dog that's been run over by a tractor trailer. And then the tractor trailer backed up and ran over him a couple more times, just to be sure. I don't want to go into too much detail because I don't want people to throw up. I felt like I was going to throw up, just by being there.

I was still in shock that we were both alive. In shock that I'd actually thrown rocks at Sabretooth. In shock that he had noticed me, had looked at me. And then in shock again that I was still alive because — man — when Sabretooth looks at you, you sort of figure your number's up, your farm is bought, and your bucket has been kicked clear into the next county. Brr.

I finally managed to move my feet and I sort of shuffled over closer to Wolverine, even though he was gross. (*Not* way-gross. There was nothing remotely cool about it.) I didn't know what to do, or even *if* I should do anything. He was hurt pretty bad, but maybe his healing factor could keep up with—

"You just gonna stand there and not say nothin', squirt?"

I checked over both shoulders, figuring someone had come into the clearing. Maybe one of the X-Men. Maybe another student. But no — it was still just Wolverine and me.

He groaned and shifted his weight a little bit. "I gotta lay here all night healin', the least you can do is provide some sterling conversation."

I glanced both ways again. Still no one. Who was he—?

Oh my gosh.

"Are you..." I stuttered as it came out. "Are you talking to me?"

He snorted. "You see anyone else around here, kid?"

"You can see me? You notice me, even when I'm just standing here?" I almost reached down and shook him by the shoulders, but...

1)   He still looked weak and out of it,

2)   It's really not polite to shake people,

3)   His claws were still popped and I wasn't going anywhere near them.

"Kid, I *always* notice you."

Now, sometimes when people get surprising news, they say something like, "It blew my mind!"

I have to tell you: This news from Wolverine didn't just blow my mind. Oh no. Basically, it was like having a professional demolition team — those guys who blow up buildings on TV — crawl into my head through my ears, plant dynamite in all the right places, lay down their wires, crawl back out, give the "Go!" signal, and then detonate the explosives, totally destroying my brain.

What I'm saying is, this news blew my mind *professionally*.

"You notice me. Always."

He grinned. Well, I *think* he grinned. His mouth wasn't really the shape of normal mouths right about then.

"I got these heightened senses. Smell. Taste. Hearing. Sight. All of 'em. It ain't easy, but I know when you're around. Why do you think I leave the cookies out for you every night?"

And just like that, it's like all of a sudden I could rewind and re-watch the last six weeks at the school. Every time I was around Wolverine...

Yeah, he left the cookies for me, but he also...

When we fought Unus the Untouchable (well, *he* fought and I watched): Wolverine said, "Stay back and stay safe." I thought he was talking to *Angel*, but he was talking to *me*!

And other times, too. Like just a little while ago, before we both left the school. He came out of the kitchen and *almost* bumped into me, but swerved at the last second.

Around about this time, Wolverine made a coughing, groaning sound and I realized I was standing there in the middle of a flashback while he was hurt really bad. No joke!

"Should I go get help?" I asked. "I'm not sure how to get back to the school, but—"

"Nah, don't worry about it. Healing factor is kicking in just fine. It'll take a couple hours, but I'll be up soon. Just don't go wandering off. I don't know what's lurking in these woods tonight."

I shivered. "That guy..."

"Sabretooth. Don't worry — he's halfway to Canada by now. I hurt him pretty bad. Good job, distracting him like that."

"I didn't think he would notice me."

"He's got the same senses I got. Once you hit him with a rock, he stopped focusing on me and he sniffed you out."

That should have been scary to me, but instead it was the best news I've ever heard — there *were* people who could notice me! It wasn't easy, but was possible.

It made me think of yesterday (or is it two days ago now? Staying up all night has me confused). In the lounge with the other kids, and Robert noticed me. Maybe there's more to my power than I thought.

Then my imagination stopped wandering and my curiosity piped up. had to know...

"Speaking of that Sabretooth guy..."

Wolverine shrugged. "This is just something he does. Every year. On my birthday."

"Happy birthday," I said. It was lame, but what else could I say? You're supposed to wish people a happy birthday.

Wolverine just laughed. He explained that this fight was like Sabretooth big birthday tradition. Every year, he tracks Wolverine down — with those heightened animal senses — and they fight. Because Sabretooth wants to prove that he's stronger than Wolverine. Tougher. Better.

Yeah, Sabretooth even looks scary eating a steak.

He wants to try to prove who's top dog. Uh, cat. Or, uh, wolverine. Whatever. To try to prove whoever's the best.

Yeah, it's a pretty simple tradition, but Sabretooth's a pretty simple guy.

"You shouldn't have come out here," Wolverine said. "You coulda gotten hurt real bad. Sabretooth doesn't take it easy on kids just because they're kids."

"But I helped! I distracted him! You said so yourself."

"He's been hunting me down once a year for a long, long time, kid. He ain't gotten rid of me yet, and it wasn't gonna happen tonight. You gotta look out for yourself. Power like yours, not a lot of other people will be able to do it for you."

"Yeah, no one cares..." And even though I didn't mean to be whiny and lame, I couldn't help it. After all this time, I finally had someone to listen to me. Someone who not only *could* listen to me, but who pretty much *had* to listen because his legs still weren't working, so he couldn't get up and walk away.

So I sat down next to him while his body slowly healed itself and told him everything. About missing my life. About feeling rejected, even a Xavier's school, where I'm supposed to be welcomed and accepted. The loneliness. Dani and Sam. The boredom. All of it.

"We're mutants," Wolverine told me. "That means we got dealt some lous cards. So you gotta decide — you gonna play those cards or you gonn walk away from the table? Look, I got a beast in me, kid. A berzerker rag that I sometimes can't control. But you know what? I work through it. Th X-Men are my family. You need to work through what you got in you."

"But you have a cool power," I said. "You have useful powers. You ca sense things and you can heal and you have claws. I have a useless powe I'll never be a superhero. I'll never be an X-Man. Everyone else at th school is training to be a superhero someday. I'm just...here."

Wolverine shook his head. "You're lookin' at this all the wrong way. Ki I'm the best there is at what I do..."

"But what you do isn't very nice, is it?" (Yeah, it was rude of me t interrupt. People with healing factors and claws should be allowed t finish their sentences.)

"No. It ain't. But look, that's not my point. There's two paths, kid. M 'n' Sabretooth, we're the same. Got the same powers, got the same craz beast livin' inside us. But he went one way, and I went the other. You got decide which way you're gonna go. That's what makes you who you ar Yeah, I'm the best there is at what I do. You need to be the best there at what *you* do."

"I don't *do* anything, though."

"Everyone's got something, kid. You just gotta keep trying."

We sat in silence for a little while. His mouth started to look normal, and his one eye slipped back into place. (Did I forget to mention before that he had an eye popped out?)

"Does it hurt?" I asked.

"Like you wouldn't believe, kid. Just because I heal doesn't mean I don't feel pain. I feel a lot of pain."

I thought about that for a little while. Deep gouges on his throat started fusing back together. He was starting to look a lot better and that made me a little bit sad. Sort of that selfish sad you get sometimes. Once he was better, we would have to go back to the mansion. Right now, I felt almost normal, having a conversation with someone.

So I figured I should talk while I had the chance.

"You know what I really want? I want to go on a mission with the X-Men. That time you and Angel rescued Sam from Unus the Untouchable was really cool. I want to do more stuff like that. And I figure it's totally safe. No one notices me. Not even the bad guys. That Sentinel was right on top of me and it couldn't hit me with its lasers. I think the *lasers* didn't know I was there."

"Not the craziest thing I've ever heard in this business, bub. But I think you ain't ready for it yet."

"But it's the best way to use my power. I could sneak up on the bad guys. You said that I should—"

"I said you gotta figure out what you're best at. I never said that was using your power." He sat up a little bit, moaning in pain, then gritting his teeth against it. "Listen to me: We're not our powers, kid. We're not even our natures. We're what we decide to do with those things."

"I don't understand." Because I didn't. I'm not a dummy, but I'm no genius either. And I felt like this was important stuff Wolverine was telling me, so I wanted to get it right.

"I was like you, kid. When I was younger. No one saw me. No one noticed, 'til one day it was too late and then *everyone* noticed."

"I don't know what you mean by that."

He sighed very dramatically. A little *too* dramatically, if you ask me. It's not like I was asking stupid questions. I think he was cranky because one ear was still hanging off his head, but maybe that's just me. *I* would be cranky if one ear was hanging off my head, but maybe Wolverine doesn't mind having one ear hanging off his head.

He held out his hand and I stared at it — the powerful fingers, the claws jutting out, gleaming and dangerous.

"Oh, sorry," he said. SNAKT! The claws vanished, sucked back into his forearms in less than the blink of an eye. He kept his hand out.

"Hey, kid — help me up." Oh. Right.

I grabbed his hand. His grip was so strong and powerful that I couldn't imagine him needing help, but who am I to judge? He almost pulled me down, but we managed to get him standing. It was a wobbly sort of standing, but his feet were on the ground and his head was pointing at the sky, so it counts.

I helped Wolverine get up. Because I'm cool and helpful.

He sniffed the air and jerked his head off to the left. "Mansion's that way, kid. I'm gonna need to lean on you."

"Shouldn't we go back to the motorcycles?"

He shook his head. "We're actually closer to the mansion after all that runnin' through the woods. Besides, after gettin' tackled by Sabretooth, my machine? She's a dud." Then he grinned at me. "I like you and all, kid, but Wolverine don't ride piggy-back with no one."

"Got it."

We walked through the woods like that, him leaning on me, his hand heavy on my shoulder, making slow progress as the sky began to lighten.

I couldn't believe I'd been up all night.

I got bored walking, so I figured we should talk some more.

"Hey, Wolverine, I gotta ask: What's the deal with the strawberry milk?"

He looked at me sort of mean and squinty. "You got your strawberry. You got your milk. What's not to like, kid? You got a problem with strawberry?"

"Uh, no."

"Well, then."

We walked a little more.

"I guess I just don't get it," I said. "Why strawberry? Why not chocolate?"

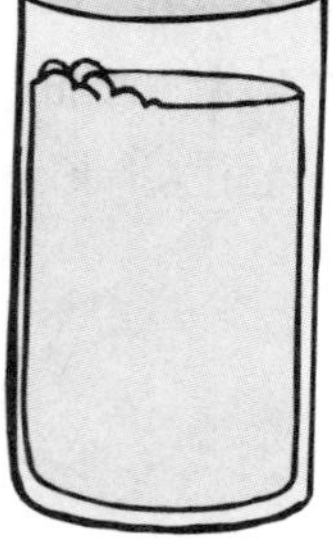

"Everyone drinks chocolate milk. Takes a tough guy to drink something that's pink."

"Huh."

So, yeah, we didn't talk about that any more.

Finally, we pushed through some brush and found ourselves on the soccer field behind the school. The mansion looked tiny in the distance.

Wolverine took a deep breath and tried standing on his own. He didn't end up on his butt, so the experiment was a success.

He didn't look at me as he spoke. He looked up at the sky, now grayish with morning light.

"I've lived a long time, kid. Seen a whole lotta bad in the world. Know what? Seen a lot of good, too. And most things — *most* things — only get better. They're never perfect. They sometimes ain't even great or good. But they usually end up better'n they started.

"We don't *defeat* our mutant powers. We don't *conquer* them. We learn how to live with them."

And that was the last thing he said to me before we went inside.

I came right here and started writing. Now I am beyond exhausted and I have an instant message from Professor X saying that I'm supposed to report to his office this afternoon, but I'm too tired to be scared or annoyed.

I'm going to sleep.

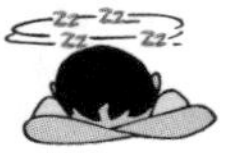

Awake!

This entry posted on May 12 at 12:31:49 pm by Eric.

I didn't sleep much, but I feel pretty good. I was just tossing and turning in bed for the last hour and I decided to get up.

I don't have to see Professor X for a while, so I'm going to go get something to eat. I am *starving*.

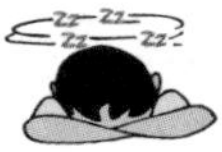

Food

This entry posted on May 12 at 1:04:23 pm by Eric's xPhone.

Lunch: Pizza. *Bacon* pizza. I love bacon. It's nature's most perfect food.

Professor X's Office

This entry posted on May 12 at 3:17:05 pm by Eric.

That wasn't nearly as bad as I thought it was going to be. You'll notice haven't put my usual "Professor X yelling at me" icon on this post. That's because he didn't really yell at me.

I knocked really loud at his door and yelled really loud *through* his door and I also *thought* as loud as I could in his general direction until he said "Come in, Eric."

I didn't sit down because it's easier to keep his attention if I'm up. I sort of paced back and forth, waving my arms a lot while we talked. I got the double-X effect: His voice and his mental voice. My head started to hurt.

"Wolverine has informed me of your little excursion, Eric. I am tempted to reprimand you, but he speaks quite highly of your involvement."

"Really?" I shouted it so that he would be sure to hear.

"Yes. The idea of a child of your age confronting an insane monster like Sabretooth fills me with a dread you cannot imagine, Eric."

Oh, boy! Why can't he just say he doesn't approve? Does everything have to be a lecture? I think because he's telepathic he likes hearing his own voice out loud.

(I didn't think that *then!* He's a telepath! He would have read my mind. I thought it later. Like now. While I'm writing this.)

"Still," he went on, "I cannot deny that you were helpful to Logan in this instance. And I must confess that children not much older than you at this school are facing, have faced, and will face similar dangers."

At this point, I still wasn't sure if I was in trouble and, if I was, exactly how much.

But it's funny. I realized that even if I was in trouble, it didn't bother me. I wasn't scared of Professor X. Hey, I faced *Sabretooth* and lived to talk about it. What's a bald guy who can read my mind going to do to me?

"I try to spend a significant amount of time with each student," Professor X went on, "especially in their early days at the school. Developing mutancy is complex issue, especially given the age at which it occurs, and there should b a certain amount of handholding. I fear I've been remiss in doing so with you Eric. Granted, there was an Onslaught Protocol and other issues demanding my attention, but while there may be reasons, there are no excuses."

OK. Whatever.

He sighed. "In short, Eric, I am apologizing to you."

Apologizing? To me? I was so surprised that I stopped pacing an Professor X said, "Did you leave the room?"

"No. Sorry." I started moving again.

"As I was saying, I owe you an apology. I'm sorry that I haven't spent a much time with you as with some of the other students. It's too easy not t pay attention to you. But I promise you — that's going to change."

"Thanks, Chuck." It just slipped out.

"Did you say something, Eric?"

"Me? Nope."

"I plan to spend more time studying your power. Given that you *can* b noticed and given that Wolverine can notice you with a little effort, I believe ther must be some sort of psychochemical control mechanism that will allow..."

And blah.

And blah.

And blah.

He went on for a while and I sort of tuned out and then tuned back in. But the upshot was that he thought my power might not be "absolute." That there might be ways around it.

So that was the best time I've ever had in Professor X's office.

STUDENT LOUNGE

This entry posted on May 12 at 6:27:41 pm by Eric.

I went by the student lounge a little bit ago. Something happened there and I feel pretty good about it. I don't want to overdo it or anything, but feel pretty good.

A bunch of kids were sitting around watching TV. Dani was one of them she was sitting next to Sam on the sofa.

I walked up behind them. I started to think really hard. About Roberto About Wolverine.

Then I got sort of distracted b the TV. It was this reality show *Big Shots*, about these peopl who were accidentally expose to these things called Pym Particles when Captain America and Thor and Iron Man wer fighting a bad guy in New York Pym Particles are what Ant-Mai uses to shrink real small, an this accident made it so thes people all shrunk to, like, si inches tall. So it's all about thei lives now that they're tiny.

I got all caught up in it an

before I realized what I was doing, I said, "I like this show. It's cool," even though no one would hear me.

But Dani sort of sat up a little straighter and turned to Sam and said, "Did you hear that?"

He shrugged. But maybe that was enough.

Because I've been thinking ever since then.

Roberto was watching a movie. The same movie I was watching. Dani was watching the same TV show.

Now, I'm no Professor X. I'm no genius. I don't think I'm going to figure out how my power works all by myself. But like Wolverine said, maybe it's not about that. Not really. Maybe it's about figuring out what I'm best at.

So I scrounged around in my desk drawers and found some of my favorite artwork. Some of the stuff that I think is my best.

And now I'm going to pretend to be a scientist and try a little experiment.

IT WORKED

This entry posted on May 12 at 9:58:16 pm by Eric.

I sort of can't believe what I'm about to type:

I was just hanging out with my friends.

Yes. My friends.

I brought my artwork to the rec room and left it on one of the tables. Pretty soon, a bunch of kids were checking it out, commenting on it.

I waited until they were all talking really loud. And then I said, " drew that."

Some of them ignored me. But a couple of them turned to look at me.

"I drew all of it," I said. "My name's Eric."

"Where have you been?" one kid asked. "I thought you left the school."

I get that a lot. "No," I said. "I've been here all along."

They stopped noticing me. I almost gave up right there. My mutant abilit was too powerful. I couldn't overcome it.

But then I remembered what Wolverine said about not conquering ou powers, but learning how to live with them.

So I went right into the thick of the crowd. Dani was looking at my artwork, really studying it hard. And I stared at my own artwork and I remembered when I'd drawn each piece and why and how, and what each piece meant to me.

And I said, "Do you like any of it?"

She turned to me. "Oh, you're back. Sweet. You drew this?"

She held a drawing of Wolverine out to me. I stared at it, focusing as hard as I could. "Yeah, I drew it."

Check out my drawing on the next page, the Wolverine drawing Dani liked. It took me a loooooong time to draw it, so I wanted to show it really big!

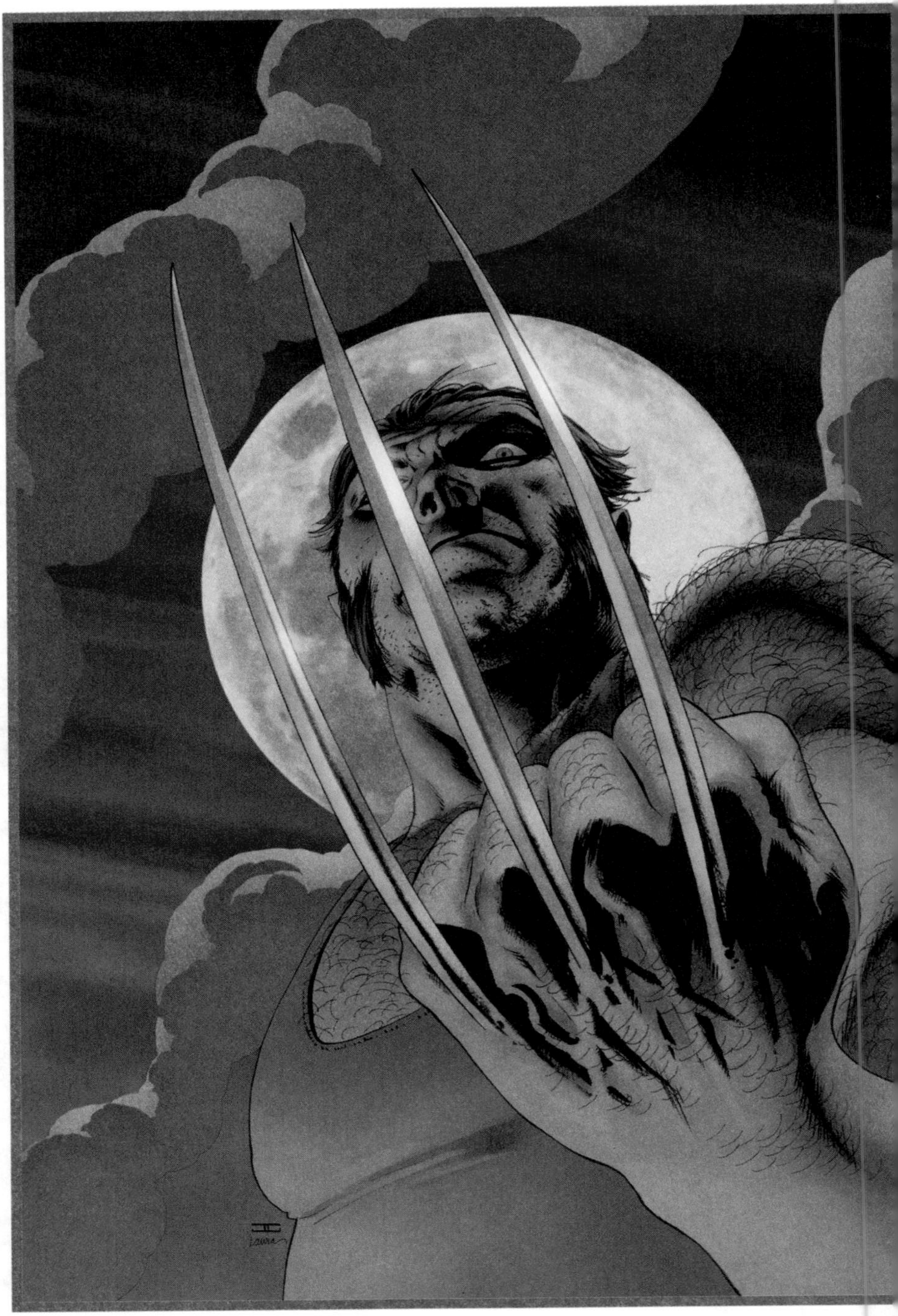

See, I had a theory. Maybe — just maybe — when I was thinking about the same thing as other people... Well, it just seemed like then they sort of noticed me. A little bit.

And Dani grinned and said, "It's cool. You're really good."

And I'll tell you, that was awesome. Not just because she liked my art. Not even because it was Dani, who's really nice and really cute. But because — other than Wolverine or Professor X — it was like the first real back-and-forth conversation I'd had in a while.

"My name's Dani," she said.

"Yeah, I know. I'm Eric."

"You're sort of blurry," she said. "Is that your mutant power?"

I didn't want to get into a whole conversation about my power, so I just told her it was.

And then I kept concentrating on *me* because that was the focus now. And some other kids focused on me, too.

And I made some friends.

I did look up and break my concentration for a second, though. That's when I caught someone coming into the lounge out of the corner of my eye.

It was Wolverine.

If you hadn't known that he'd been beaten almost to death just twelve hours earlier, you'd never know by looking at him. He looked fine. No scrapes, bruises or scars, and he was walking like nothing had happened.

When he saw me, he flashed me a quick grin and gave me a thumbs-up.

I fired it back at him. Thanks, bub.

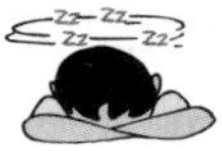

Best Day Ever

This entry posted on September 21 at 7:24:01 pm by Eric.

It's been a while since I've written in this blog. I've been making some friends. It's not easy for me, but it's not impossible either. So when something falls between those two things, that means you can do it if you really want to badly enough.

I haven't totally figured out how my power works, but between the whole "focus" trick and some help from Professor X, I'm making a little bit of progress. It takes time. But at least I'm not alone all the time. *Most* of the time, but not all the time. And for me, the difference between "most" and "all" is *huge*.

I even figured out how to use the xPhone to help me. A lot of the other kids have cell phones, too (none of them as cool as the xPhone, though), so I realized that I could walk up to someone and send a text message from the xPhone. That would get them thinking about me, and if I send enough texts fast enough, they start to see me. And then I can talk and make jokes and keep them focused on me long enough that we can talk.

So by giving me the xPhone, Professor X really helped me out. He liked it when I told him that. "You have gratified me enormously, Eric," is what he said. Which, translated, means, "Gee, thanks."

Anyway, I'm not blogging as much as I used to, but I wanted to blog about something really quick.

It was so cool. It was the best day ever...

Things are better here, but not perfect. So I still wander around. I still pop into the Danger Room every now and then, just for the heck of it.

Yesterday, I followed Wolverine into that special elevator again, down to the hangar. He was talking out loud to himself, which means that he was *really* talking to Professor X, who was talking in his head. He was saying stuff like, "I'm gettin' tired of chasin' down new mutants" and "I work best alone" and "Why do I have to take someone with me?" and all that.

He sang his passphrase to the hangar lock and went in through the big ego door.

(I like Professor X a lot more now, but the man is still an ego-maniac!)

Kitty Pryde was waiting for him there. She's a student, too, but older than me, and she's already been on a bunch of missions. She has the power to walk through walls. Very cool.

"Let's make this one quick," Wolverine growled. "I got ten bucks on the opening game of the hockey season, and I want to get back in time to watch it."

"Haven't you ever heard of TiVo, old man?" she teased him.

"Button your lip." He walked up the ramp before her, then suddenly stopped. Turned around.

"You comin', squirt?"

"Hold your horses!" Kitty snapped. "And don't call me squirt!"

"Wasn't talkin' to you," he told her.

I stood there for a second. I wasn't sure...

But then Wolverine waved me on board. Kitty looked around like he'd lost his mind, but she just shrugged her shoulders and joined him.

Us, I mean. Joined us.

Sweet! Going on a mission! An X-Man-in-training at last!

And what happened on that mission? You wouldn't believe it even if I told you. But maybe I will. Someday.

Barry Lyga is a recovering comic book geek. When he was a kid, everyone told him that comic books were garbage and would rot his brain, but he had the last laugh. He used to work for a living, but now writes full-time because, well, wouldn't you?

He is the author of *The Astonishing Adventures of Fanboy & Goth Girl*, *Hero-Type*, and the upcoming *Goth Girl Rising*. Also, this book in your hands (duh!). Visit him online at www.fanboyandgothgirl. com or myspace.com/fanboyandgothgirl.

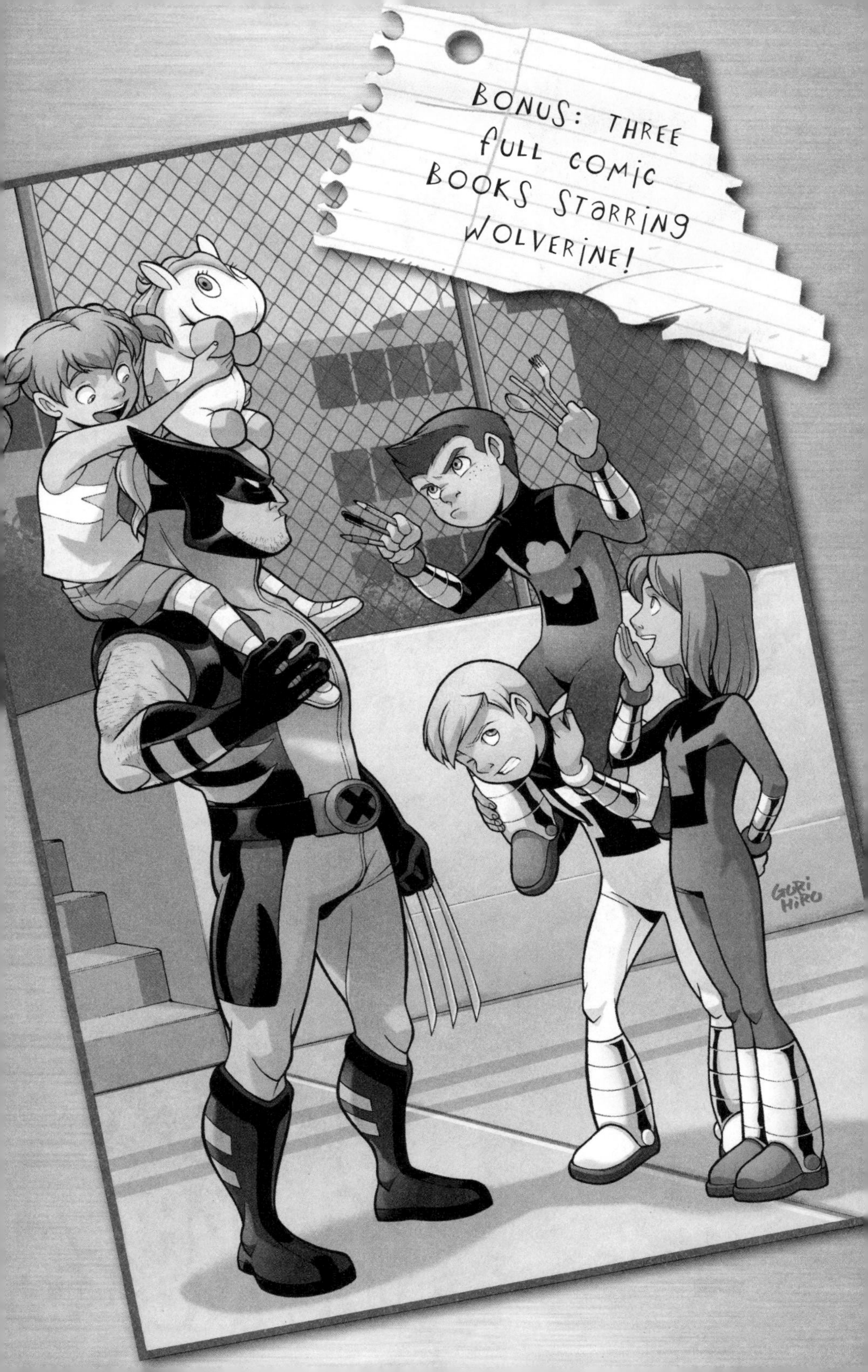
BONUS: THREE FULL COMIC BOOKS STARRING WOLVERINE!
GURIHIRU

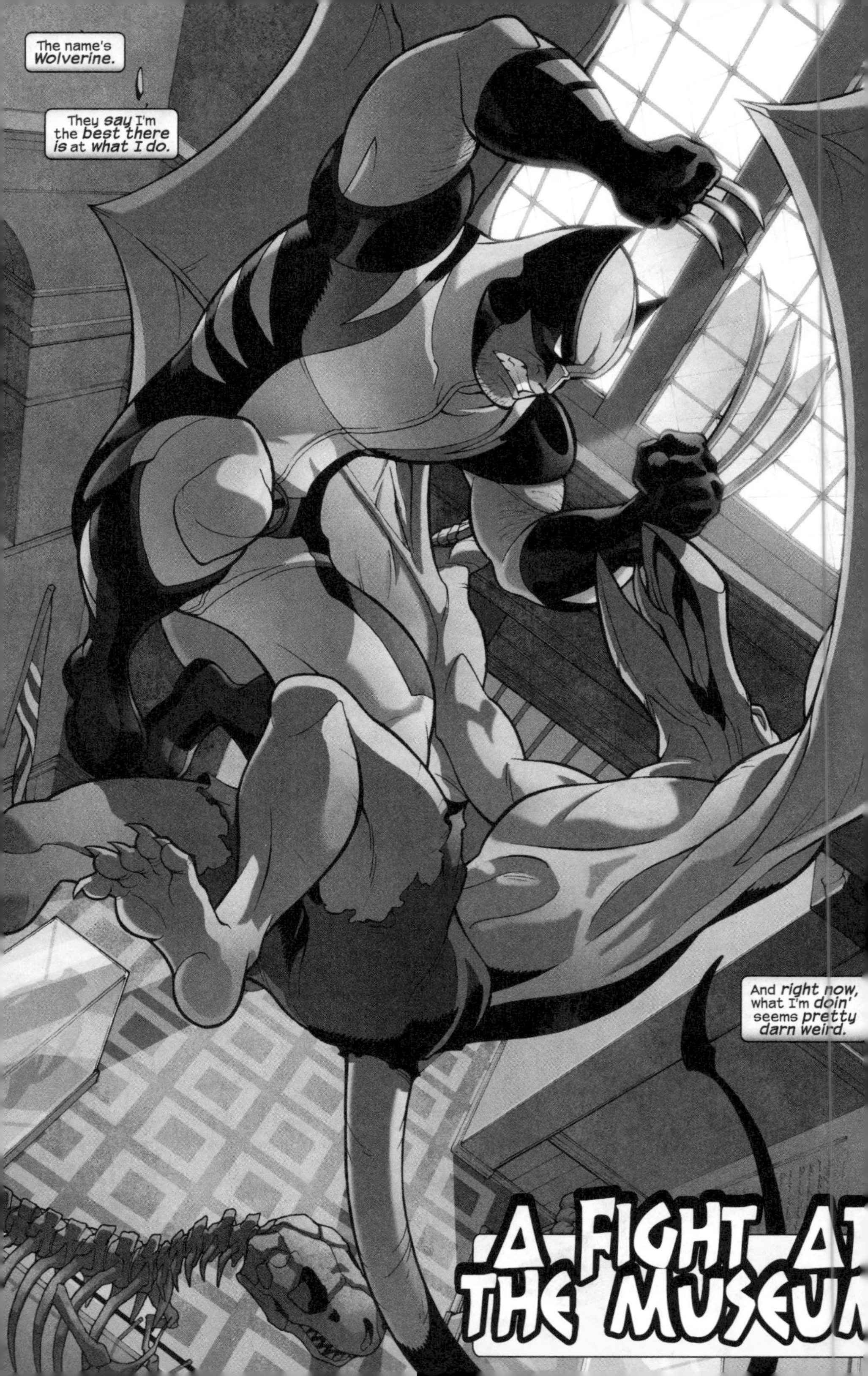

The name's Wolverine.
They say I'm the best there is at what I do.
And right now, what I'm doin' seems pretty darn weird.
A FIGHT AT THE MUSEUM

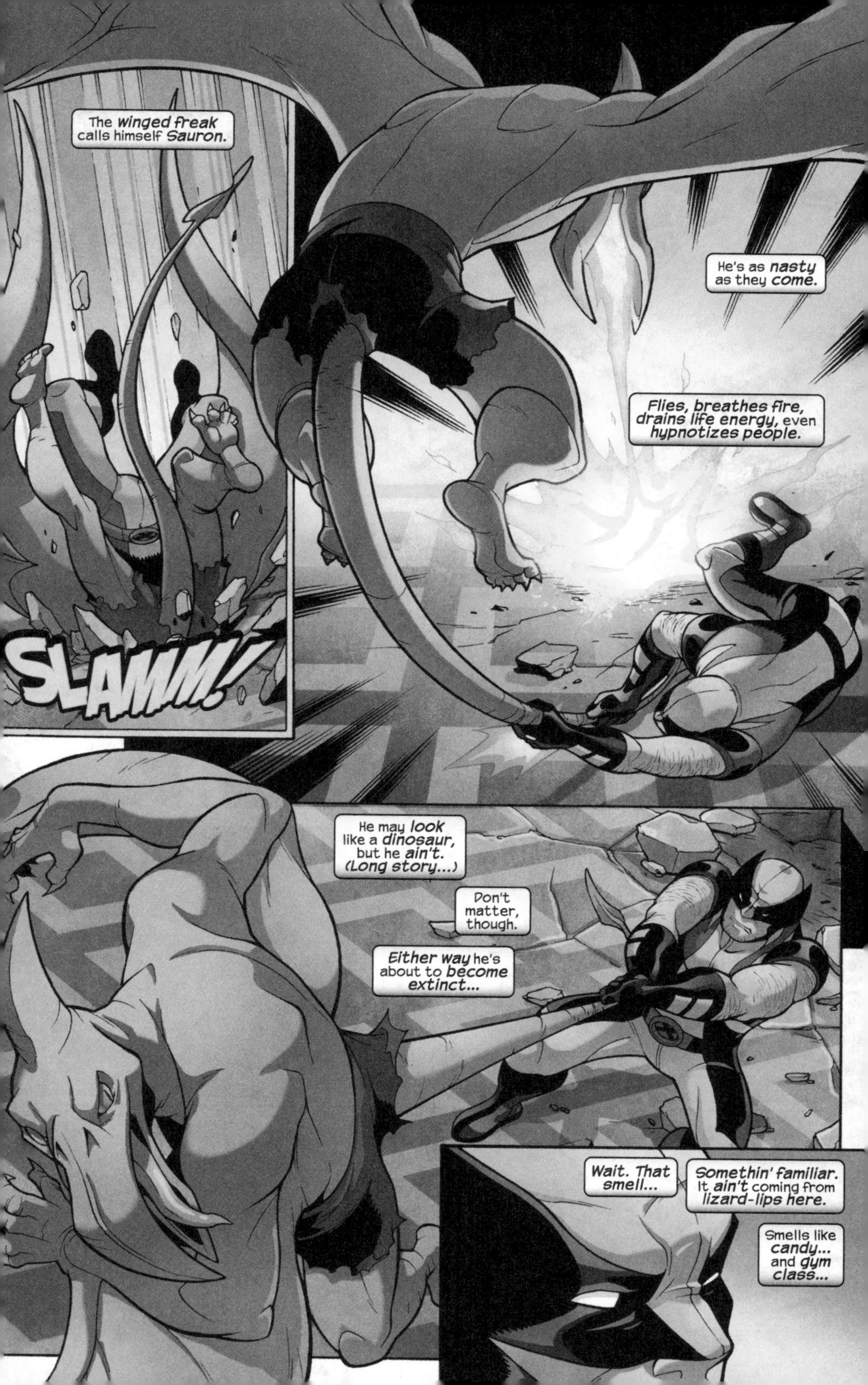

The winged freak calls himself Sauron.
SLAMM!
He's as nasty as they come.
Flies, breathes fire, drains life energy, even hypnotizes people.
He may look like a dinosaur, but he ain't. (Long story...)
Don't matter, though.
Either way he's about to become extinct...
Wait. That smell...
Somethin' familiar. It ain't coming from lizard-lips here.
Smells like candy... and gym class...

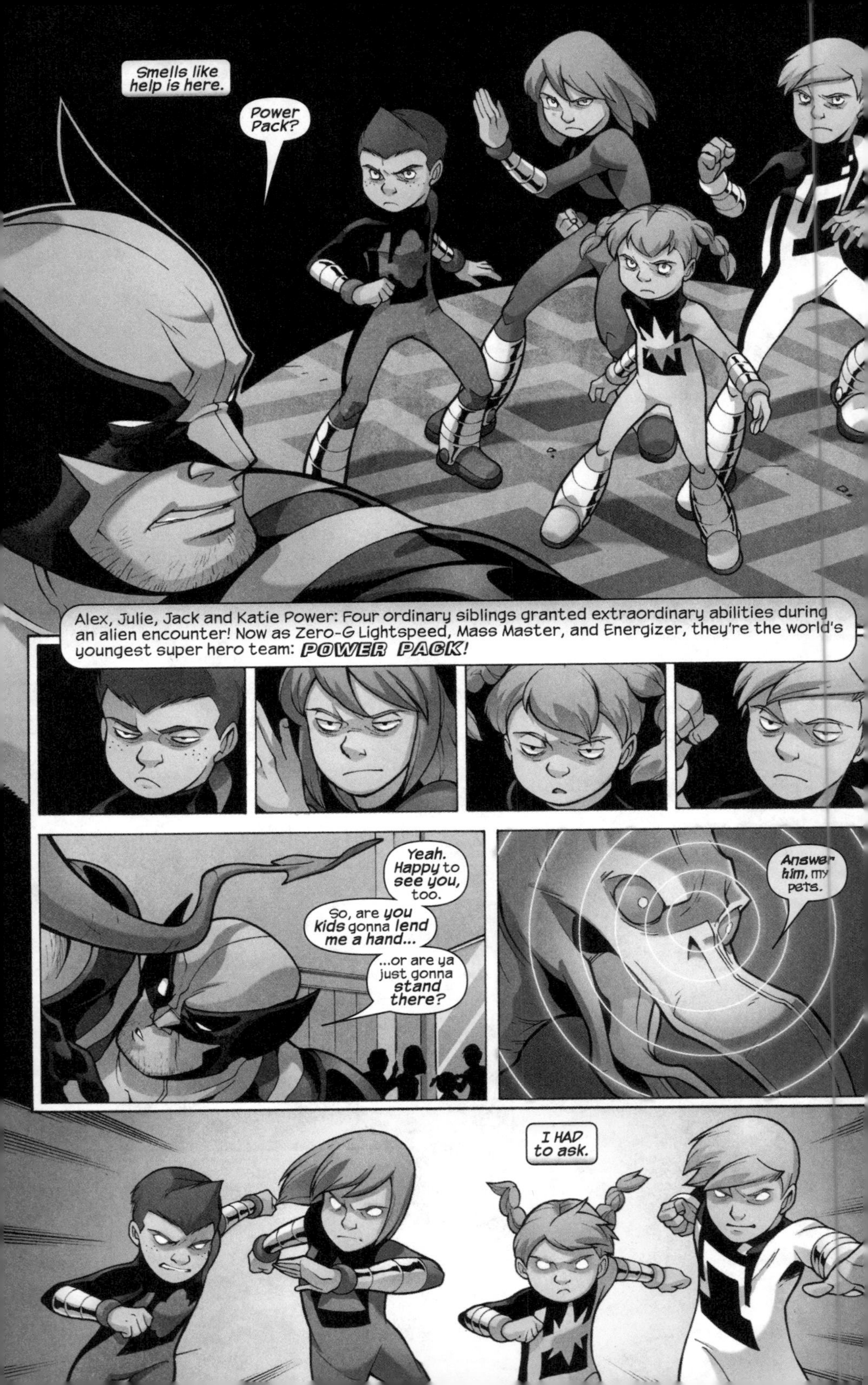
Smells like help is here.
Power Pack?
Alex, Julie, Jack and Katie Power: Four ordinary siblings granted extraordinary abilities during an alien encounter! Now as Zero-G Lightspeed, Mass Master, and Energizer, they're the world's youngest super hero team: POWER PACK!
Yeah. Happy to see you, too.
So, are you kids gonna lend me a hand...
...or are ya just gonna stand there?
Answer him, my pets.
I HAD to ask.

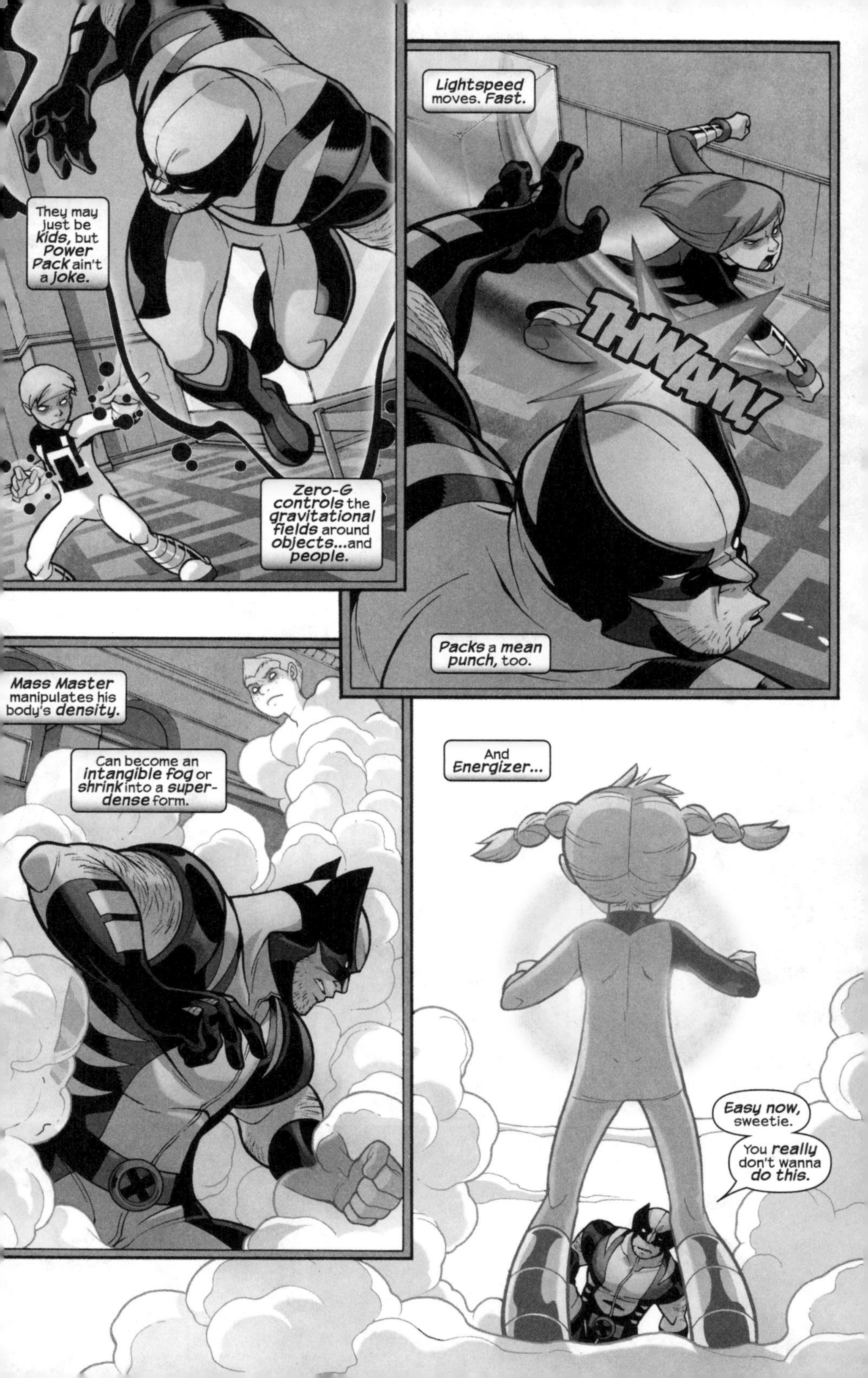
They may just be kids, but Power Pack ain't a joke.
Zero-G controls the gravitational fields around objects...and people.
Lightspeed moves. Fast.
THWAM!
Packs a mean punch, too.
Mass Master manipulates his body's density.
Can become an intangible fog or shrink into a super-dense form.
And Energizer...
Easy now, sweetie.
You really don't wanna do this.

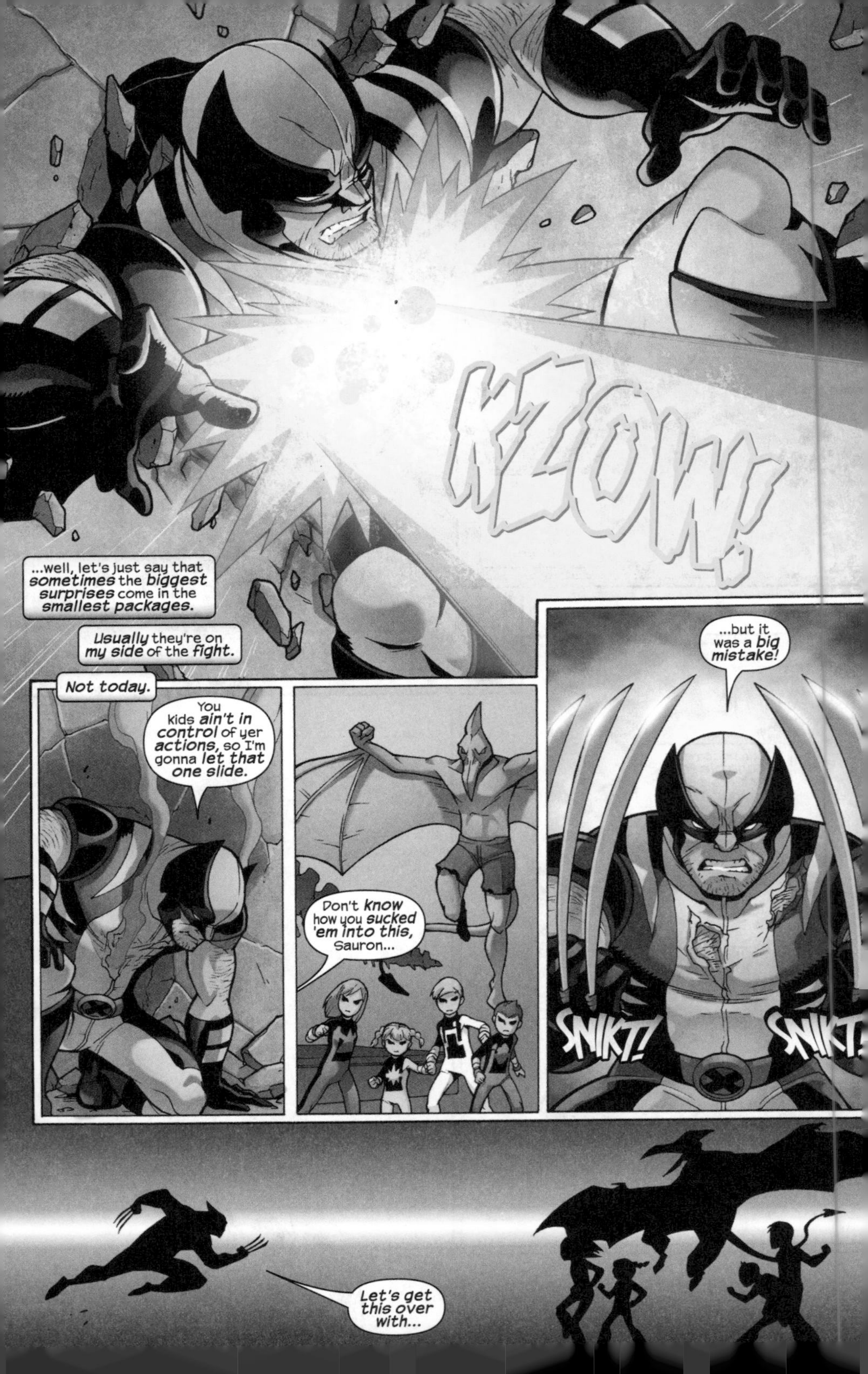
KZOW!
...well, let's just say that sometimes the biggest surprises come in the smallest packages.
Usually they're on my side of the fight.
Not today.
You kids ain't in control of yer actions, so I'm gonna let that one slide.
Don't know how you sucked 'em into this, Sauron...
...but it was a big mistake!
SNIKT!
SNIKT!
Let's get this over with...

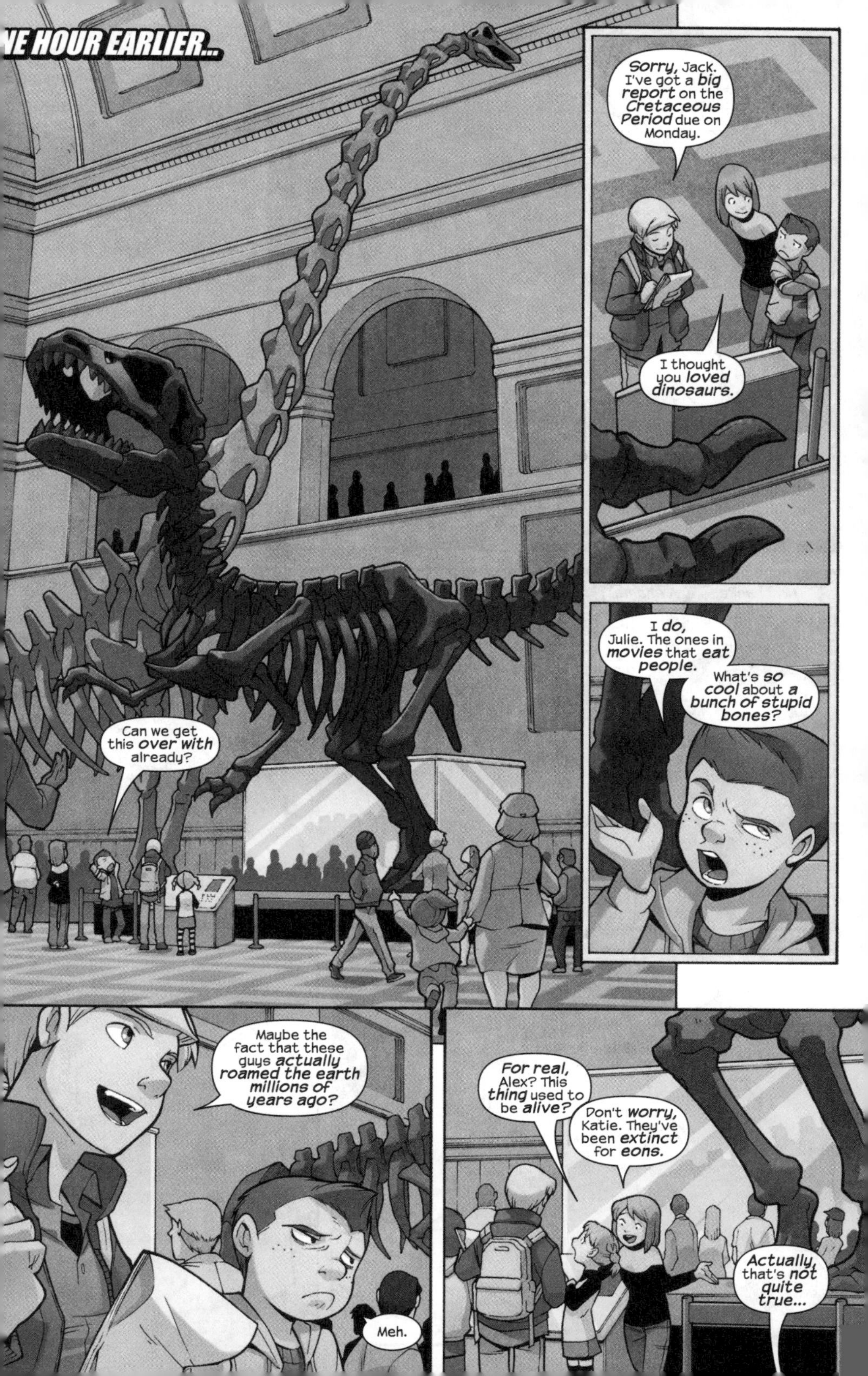
NE HOUR EARLIER...
Sorry, Jack. I've got a big report on the Cretaceous Period due on Monday.
I thought you loved dinosaurs.
I do, Julie. The ones in movies that eat people.
What's so cool about a bunch of stupid bones?
Can we get this over with already?
Maybe the fact that these guys actually roamed the earth millions of years ago?
Meh.
For real, Alex? This thing used to be alive?
Don't worry, Katie. They've been extinct for eons.
Actually, that's not quite true...

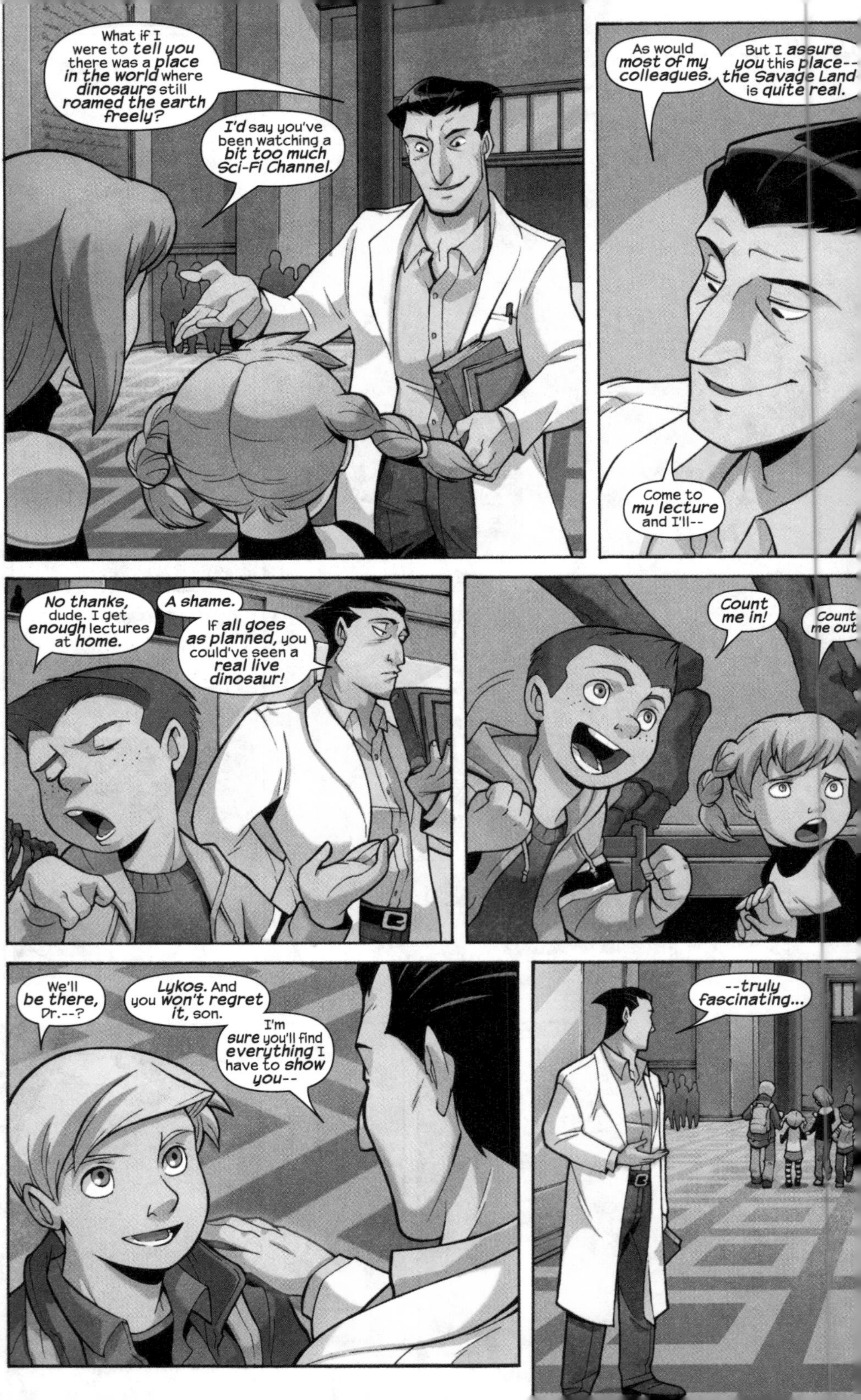
What if I were to tell you there was a place in the world where dinosaurs still roamed the earth freely?
I'd say you've been watching a bit too much Sci-Fi Channel.
As would most of my colleagues.
But I assure you this place--the Savage Land--is quite real.
Come to my lecture and I'll--
No thanks, dude. I get enough lectures at home.
A shame.
If all goes as planned, you could've seen a real live dinosaur!
Count me in!
Count me out
We'll be there, Dr.--?
Lykos. And you won't regret it, son.
I'm sure you'll find everything I have to show you--
--truly fascinating...

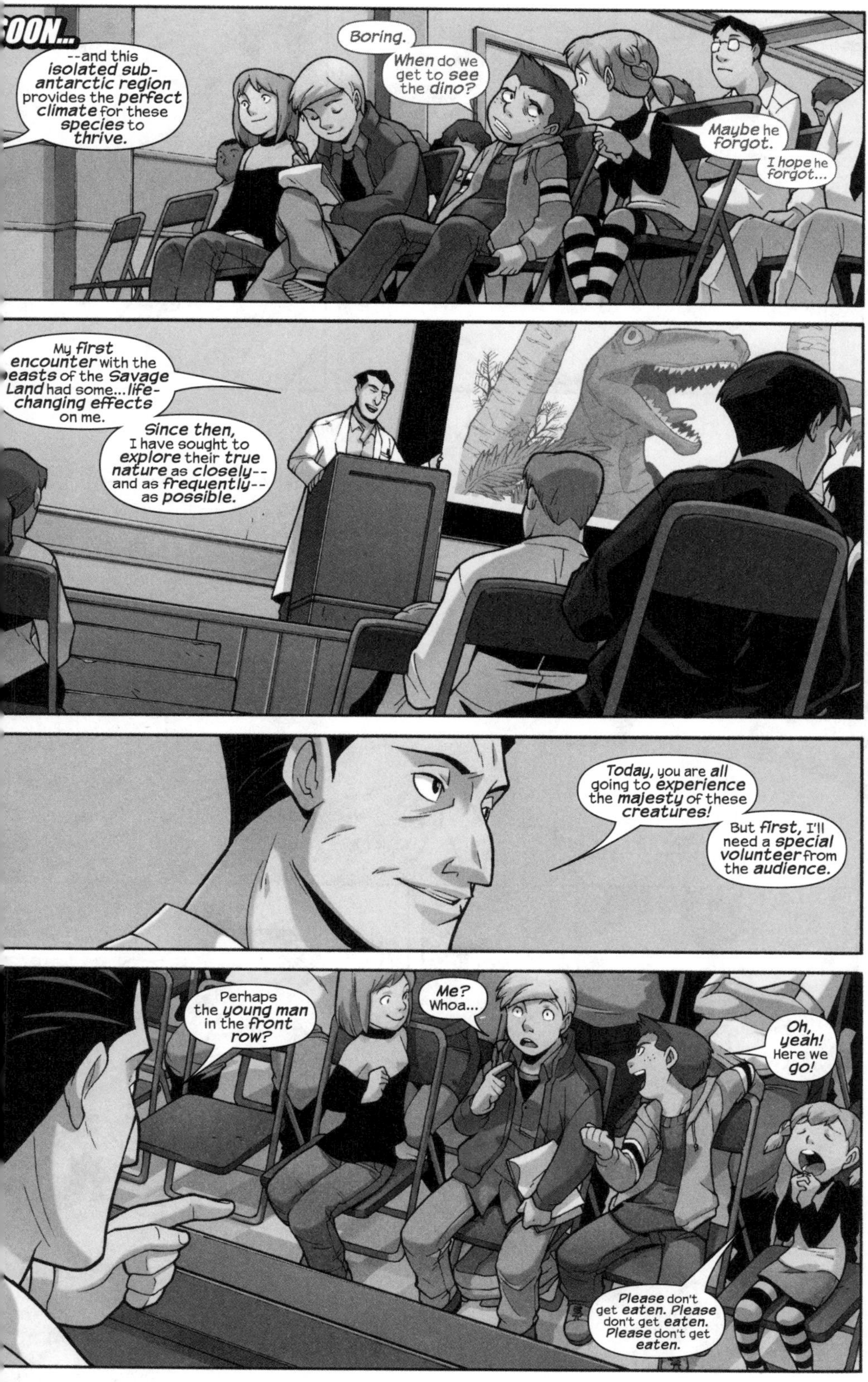
OON...
--and this isolated sub-antarctic region provides the perfect climate for these species to thrive.
Boring.
When do we get to see the dino?
Maybe he forgot.
I hope he forgot...
My first encounter with the easts of the Savage Land had some... life-changing effects on me.
Since then, I have sought to explore their true nature as closely--and as frequently--as possible.
Today, you are all going to experience the majesty of these creatures!
But first, I'll need a special volunteer from the audience.
Perhaps the young man in the front row?
Me? Whoa...
Oh, yeah! Here we go!
Please don't get eaten. Please don't get eaten. Please don't get eaten.

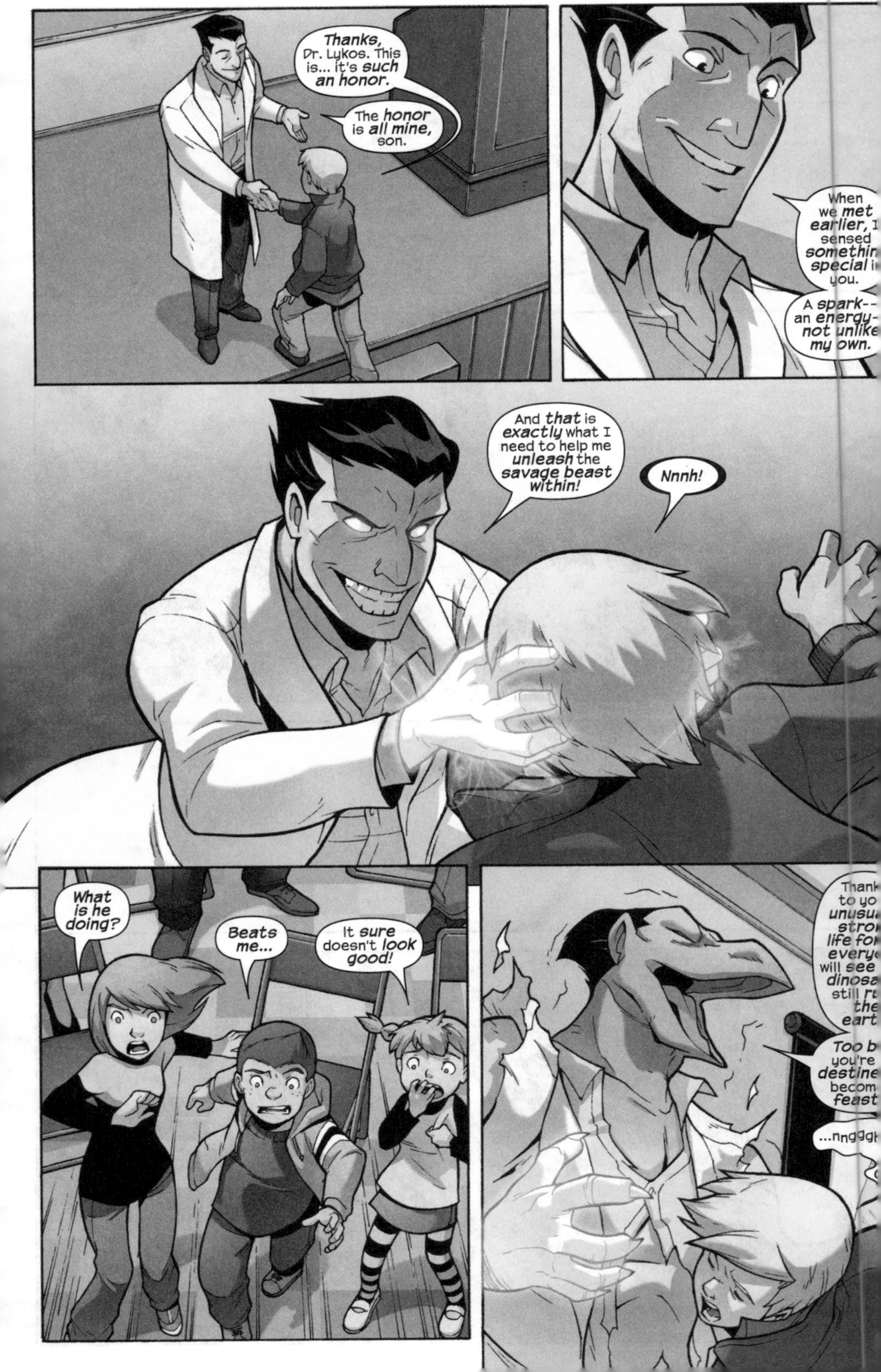

Thanks, Dr. Lykos. This is... it's such an honor.
The honor is all mine, son.
When we met earlier, I sensed somethin special i you.
A spark-- an energy- not unlike my own.
And that is exactly what I need to help me unleash the savage beast within!
Nnnh!
What is he doing?
Beats me...
It sure doesn't look good!
Thank to yo unusu stro life fo every will see dinosa still r the eart
Too b you're destine becom feast
...nngg

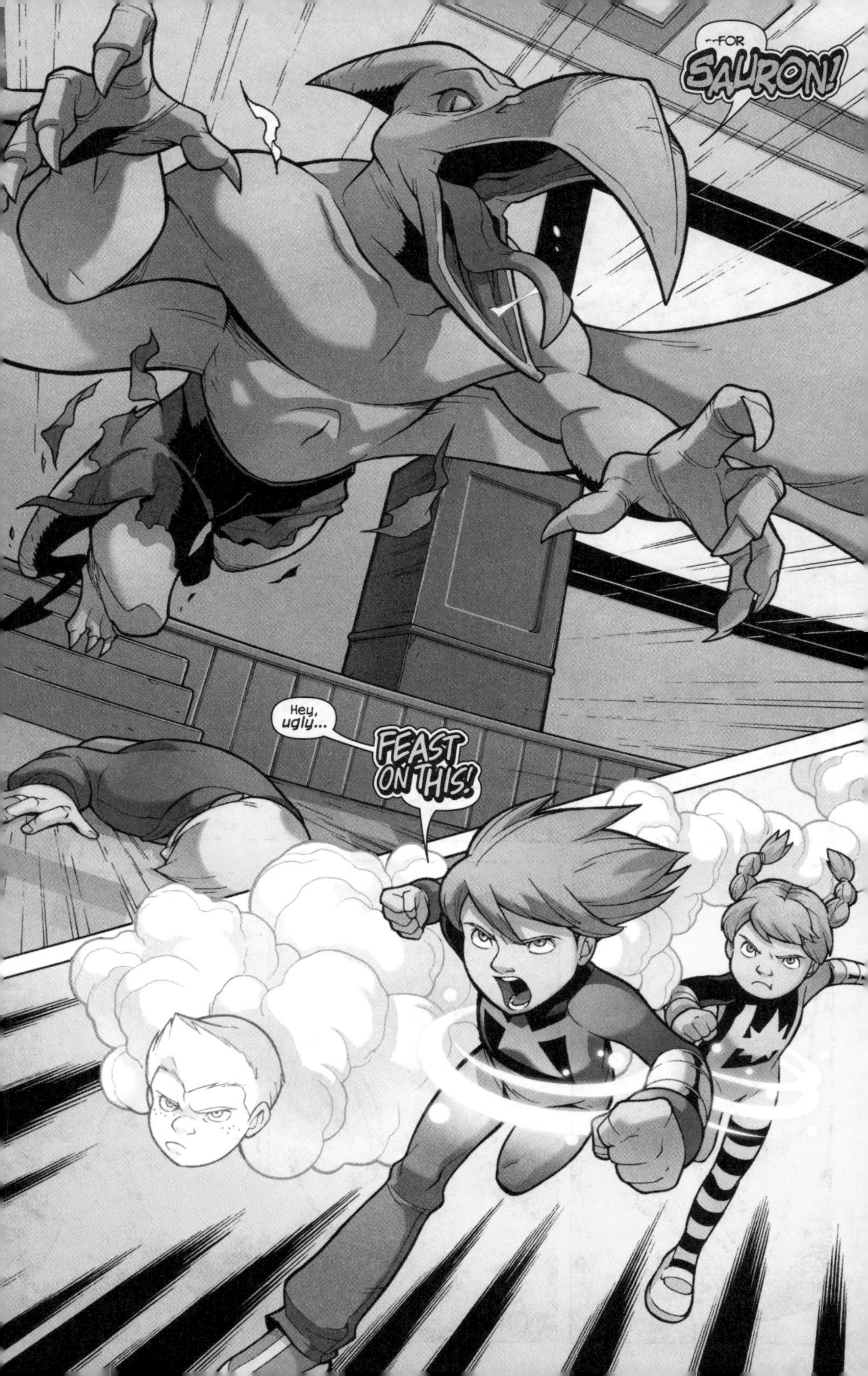
--FOR SAURON!
Hey, ugly...
FEAST ON THIS!

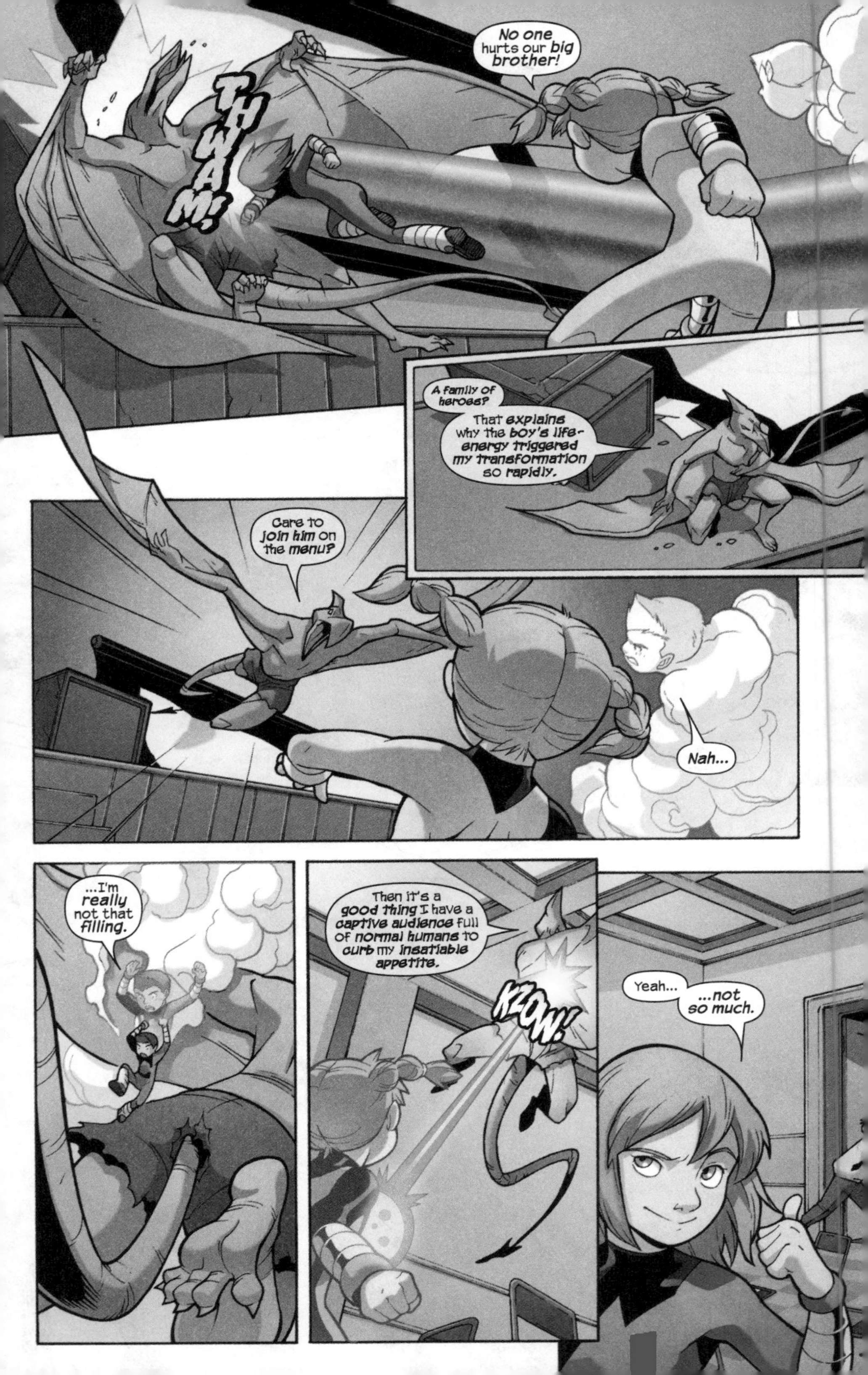
No one hurts our big brother!
THWAM!
A family of heroes?
That explains why the boy's life-energy triggered my transformation so rapidly.
Care to join him on the menu?
Nah...
...I'm really not that filling.
Then it's a good thing I have a captive audience full of normal humans to curb my insatiable appetite.
KZOW!
Yeah...
...not so much.

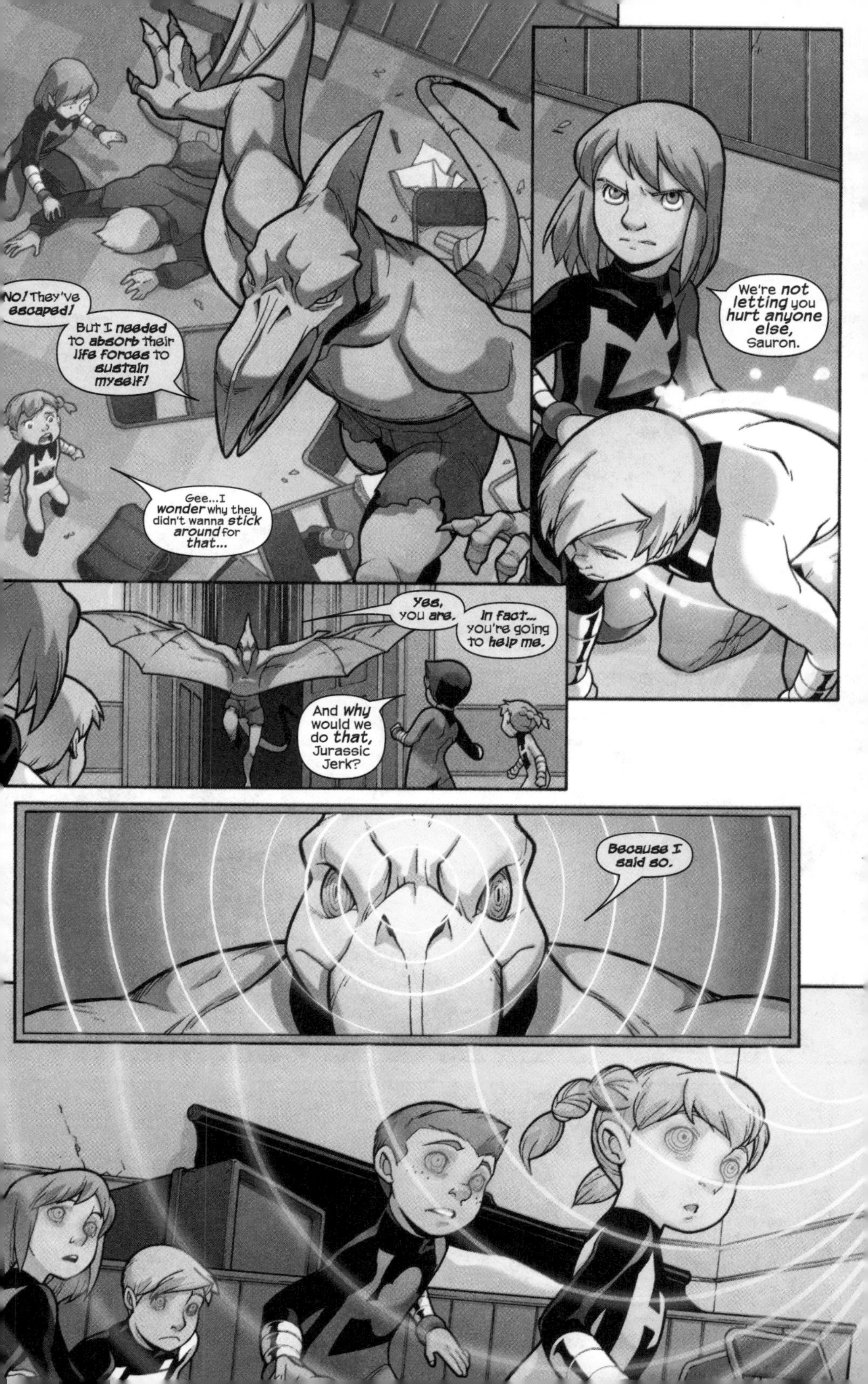
NO! They've escaped!
But I needed to absorb their life forces to sustain myself!
Gee...I wonder why they didn't wanna stick around for that...
We're not letting you hurt anyone else, Sauron.
Yes, you are.
In fact... you're going to help me.
And why would we do that, Jurassic Jerk?
Because I said so.

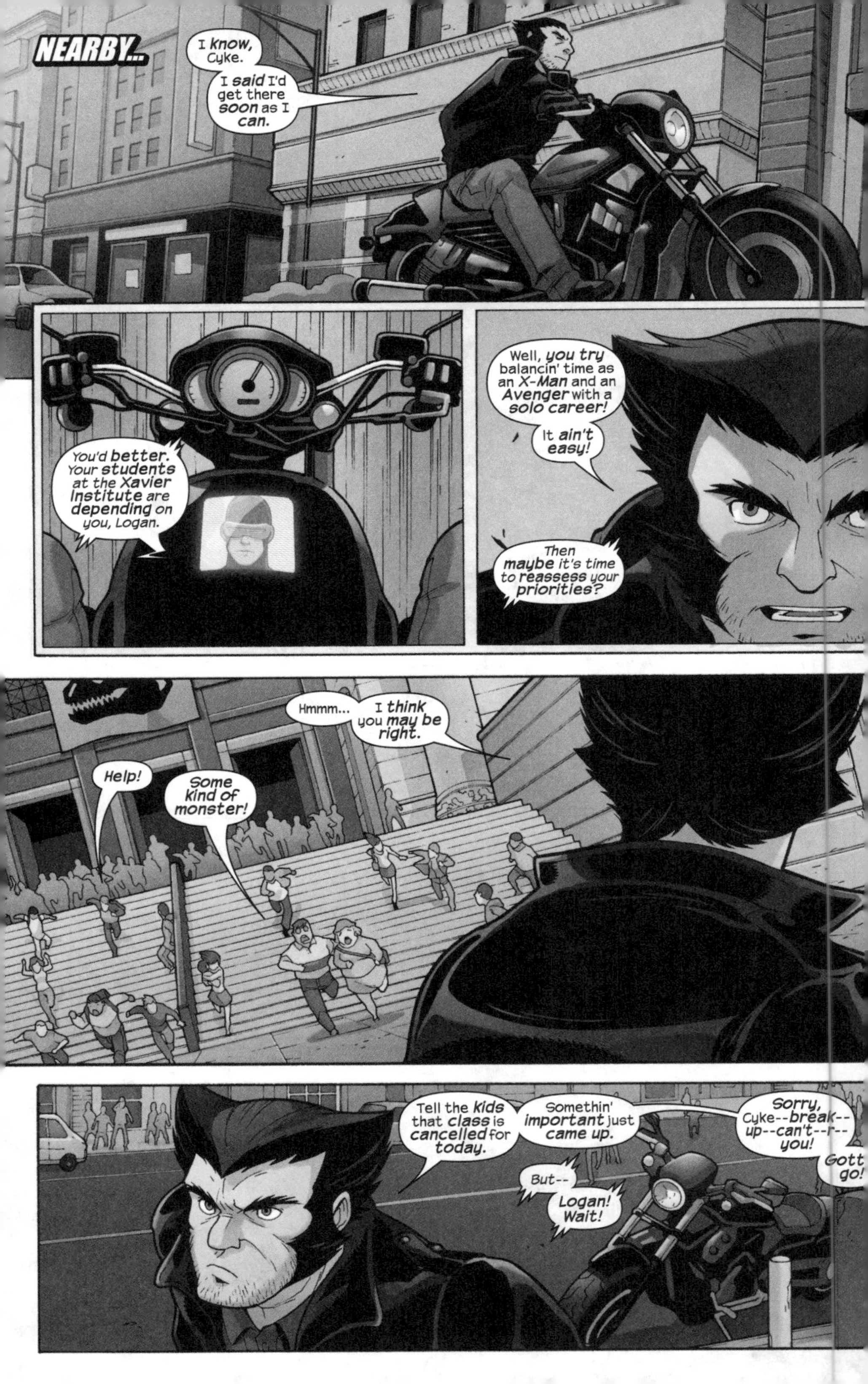
NEARBY...
I know, Cyke.
I said I'd get there soon as I can.
You'd better. Your students at the Xavier Institute are depending on you, Logan.
Well, you try balancin' time as an X-Man and an Avenger with a solo career!
It ain't easy!
Then maybe it's time to reassess your priorities?
Hmmm... I think you may be right.
Help!
Some kind of monster!
Tell the kids that class is cancelled for today.
Somethin' important just came up.
Sorry, Cyke--break--up--can't--r--you!
Gott go!
But--
Logan! Wait!

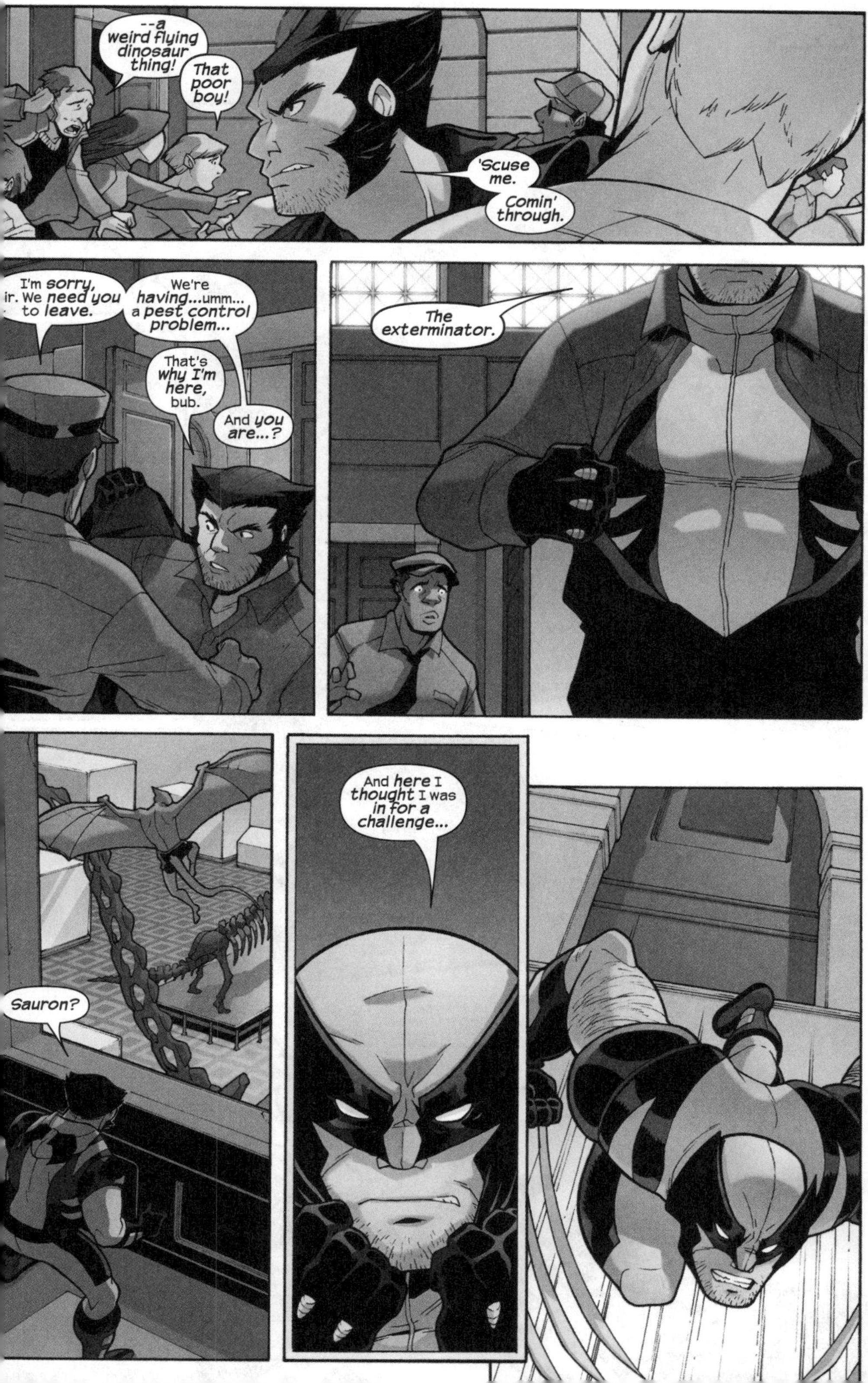

--a weird flying dinosaur thing!
That poor boy!
'Scuse me.
Comin' through.
I'm sorry, ir. We need you to leave.
We're having...umm... a pest control problem...
That's why I'm here, bub.
And you are...?
The exterminator.
Sauron?
And here I thought I was in for a challenge...

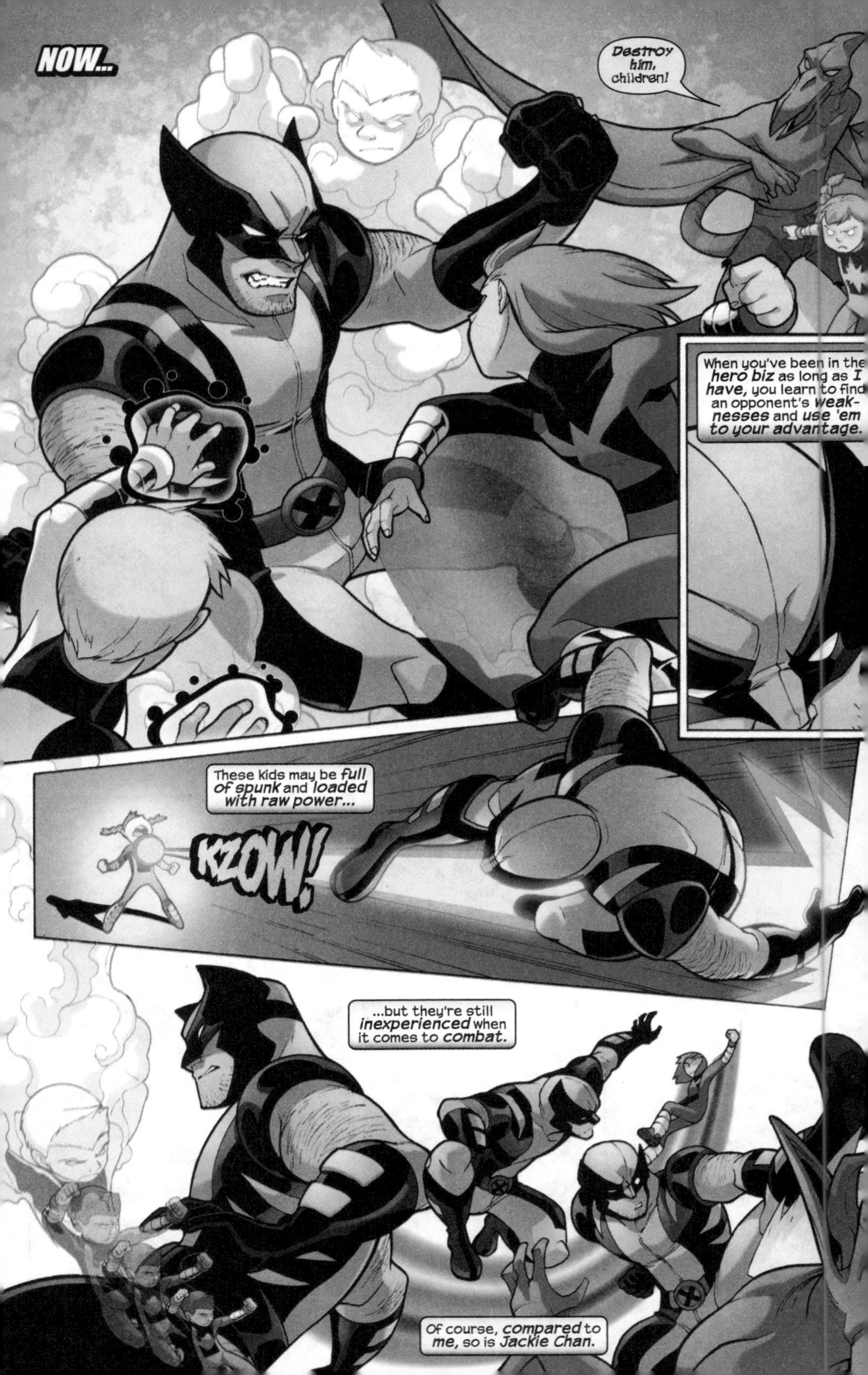
NOW...
Destroy him, children!
When you've been in the hero biz as long as I have, you learn to find an opponent's weak-nesses and use 'em to your advantage.
These kids may be full of spunk and loaded with raw power...
KZOW!
...but they're still inexperienced when it comes to combat.
Of course, compared to me, so is Jackie Chan.

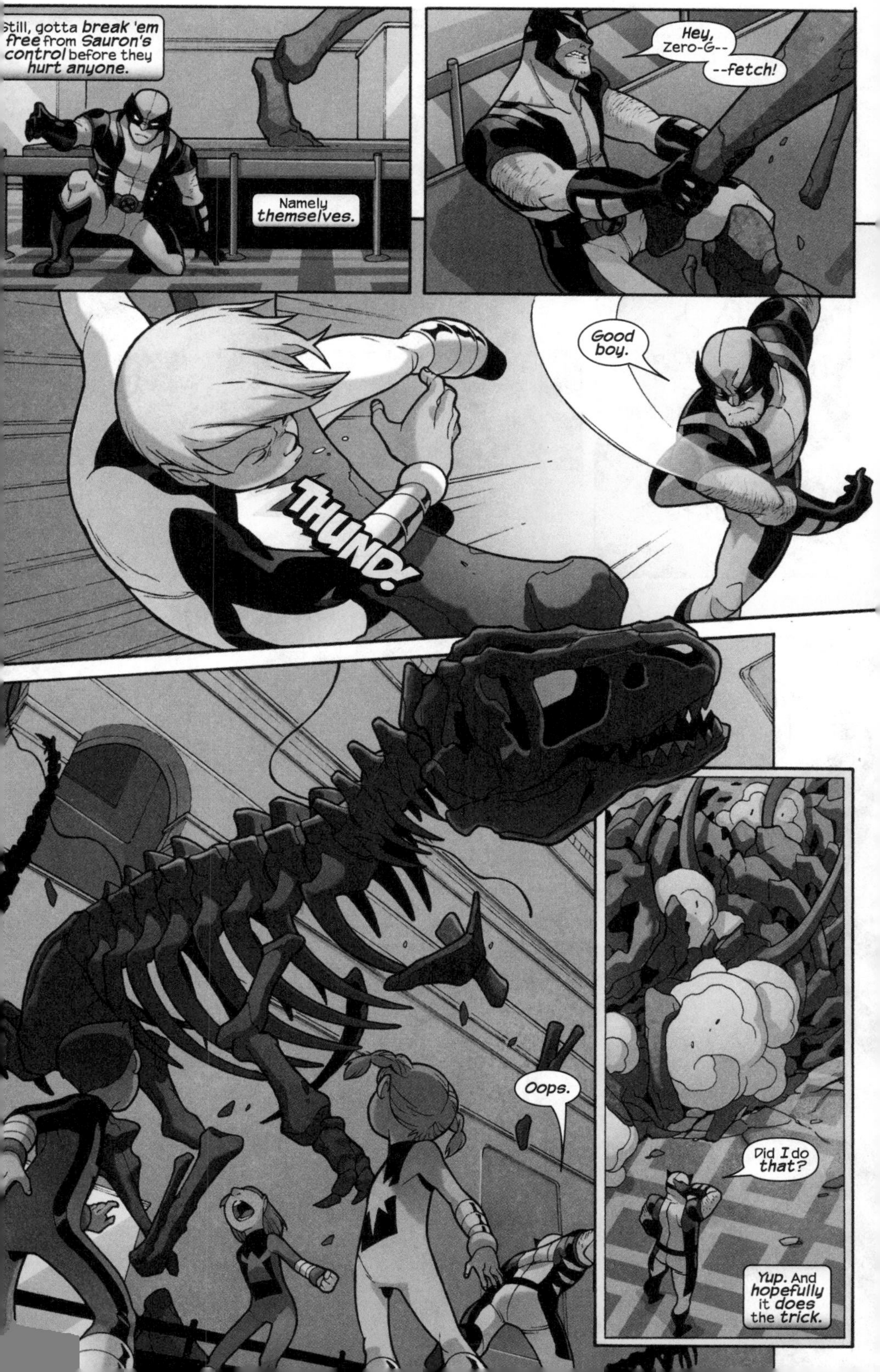
Still, gotta break 'em free from Sauron's control before they hurt anyone.
Namely themselves.
Hey, Zero-G--
--fetch!
Good boy.
THUND!
Oops.
Did I do that?
Yup. And hopefully it does the trick.

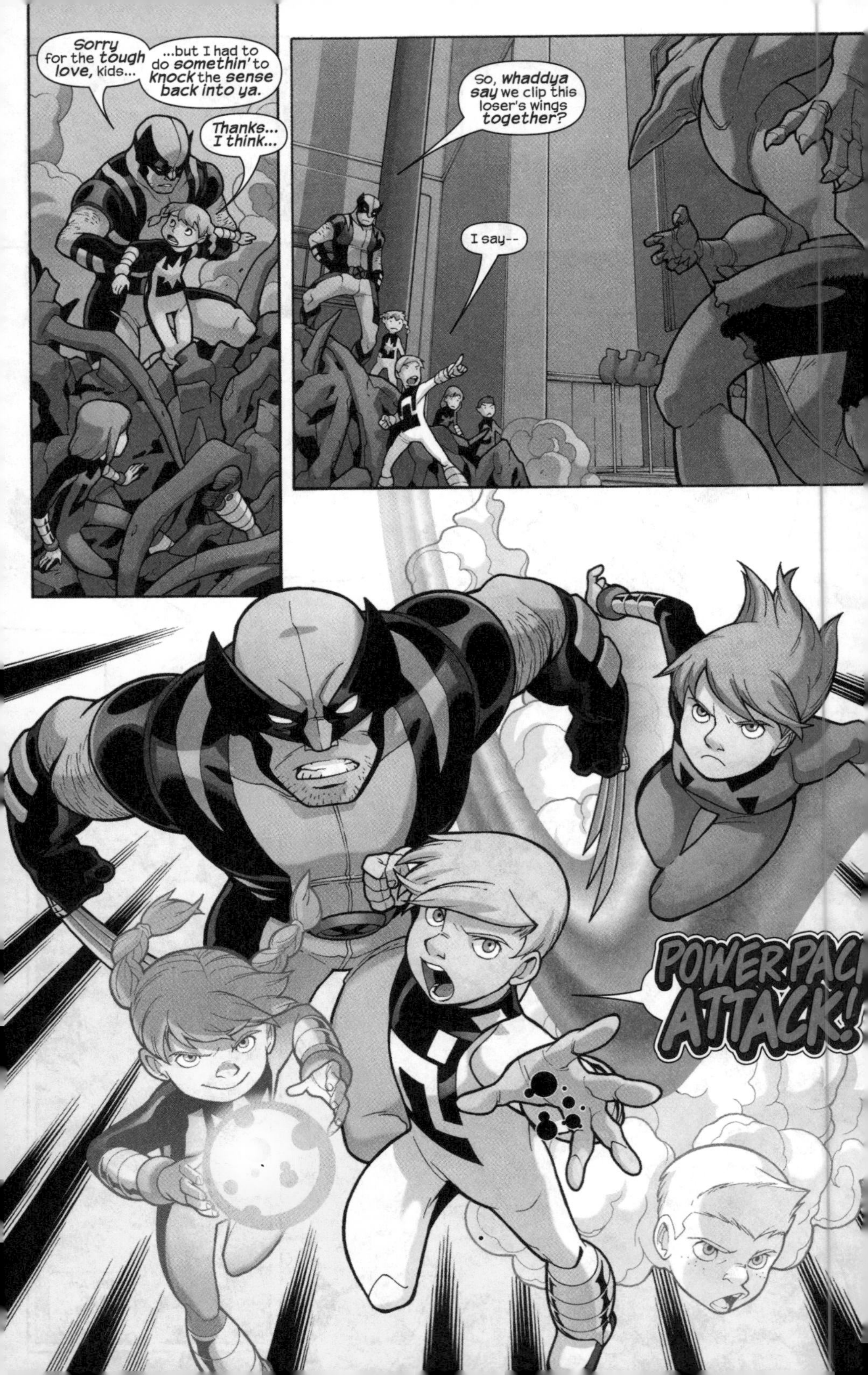

Sorry for the tough love, kids...
...but I had to do somethin' to knock the sense back into ya.
Thanks... I think...
So, whaddya say we clip this loser's wings together?
I say--
POWER PAC ATTACK!

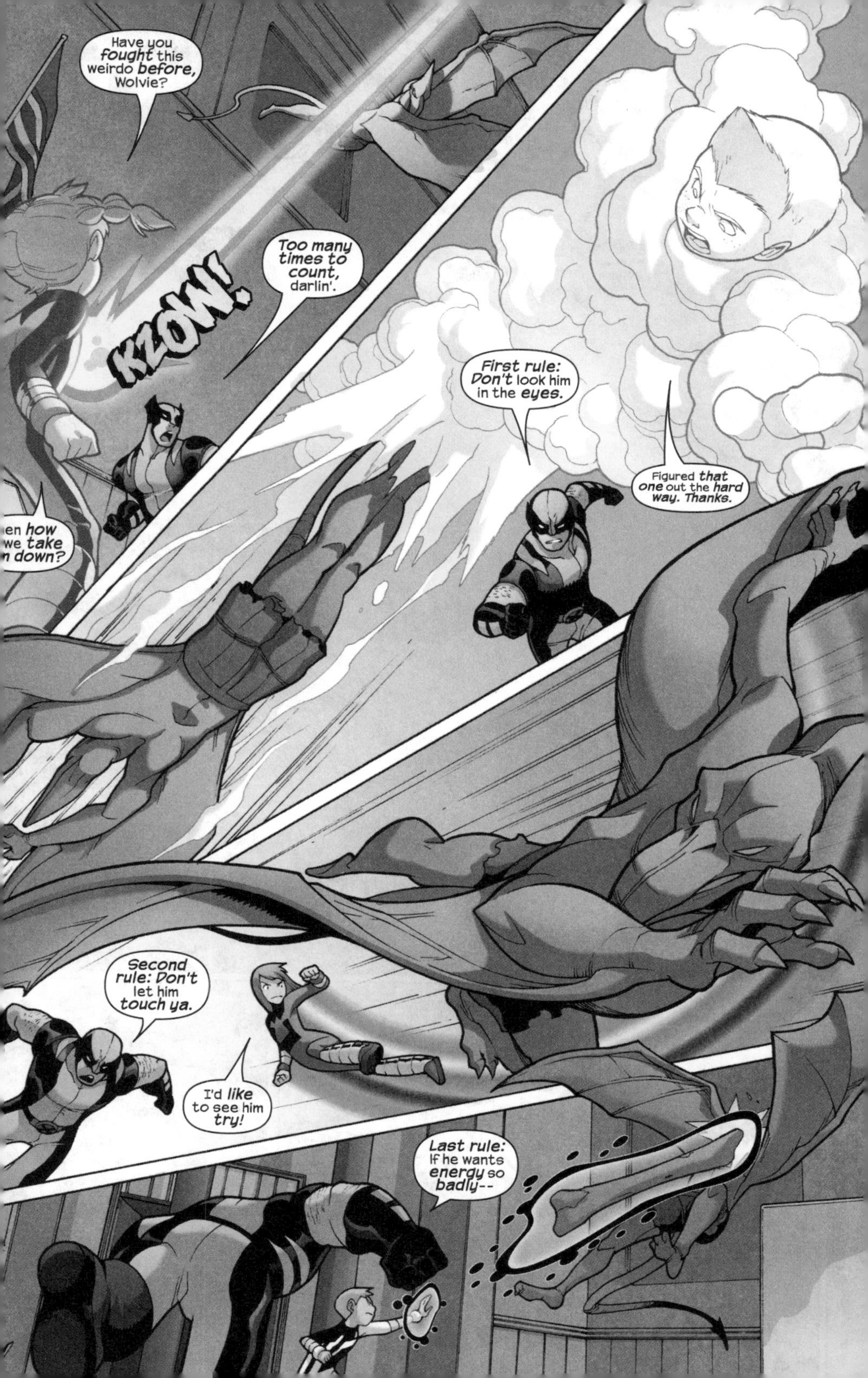
Have you fought this weirdo before, Wolvie?
KZOW!
Too many times to count, darlin'.
First rule: Don't look him in the eyes.
Figured that one out the hard way. Thanks.
Second rule: Don't let him touch ya.
I'd like to see him try!
Last rule: If he wants energy so badly--

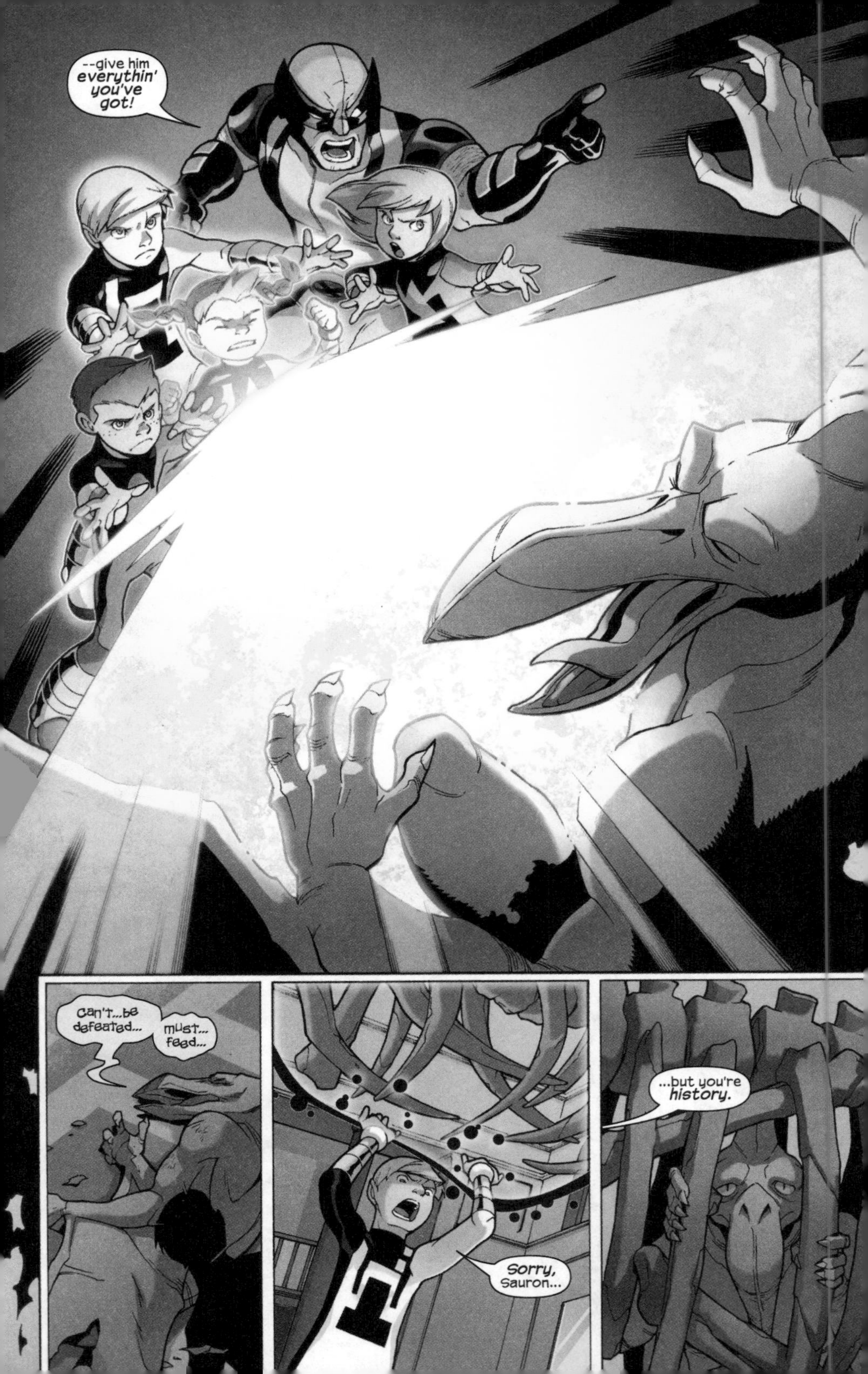
--give him everythin' you've got!
Can't...be defeated...
must... feed...
Sorry, Sauron...
...but you're history.

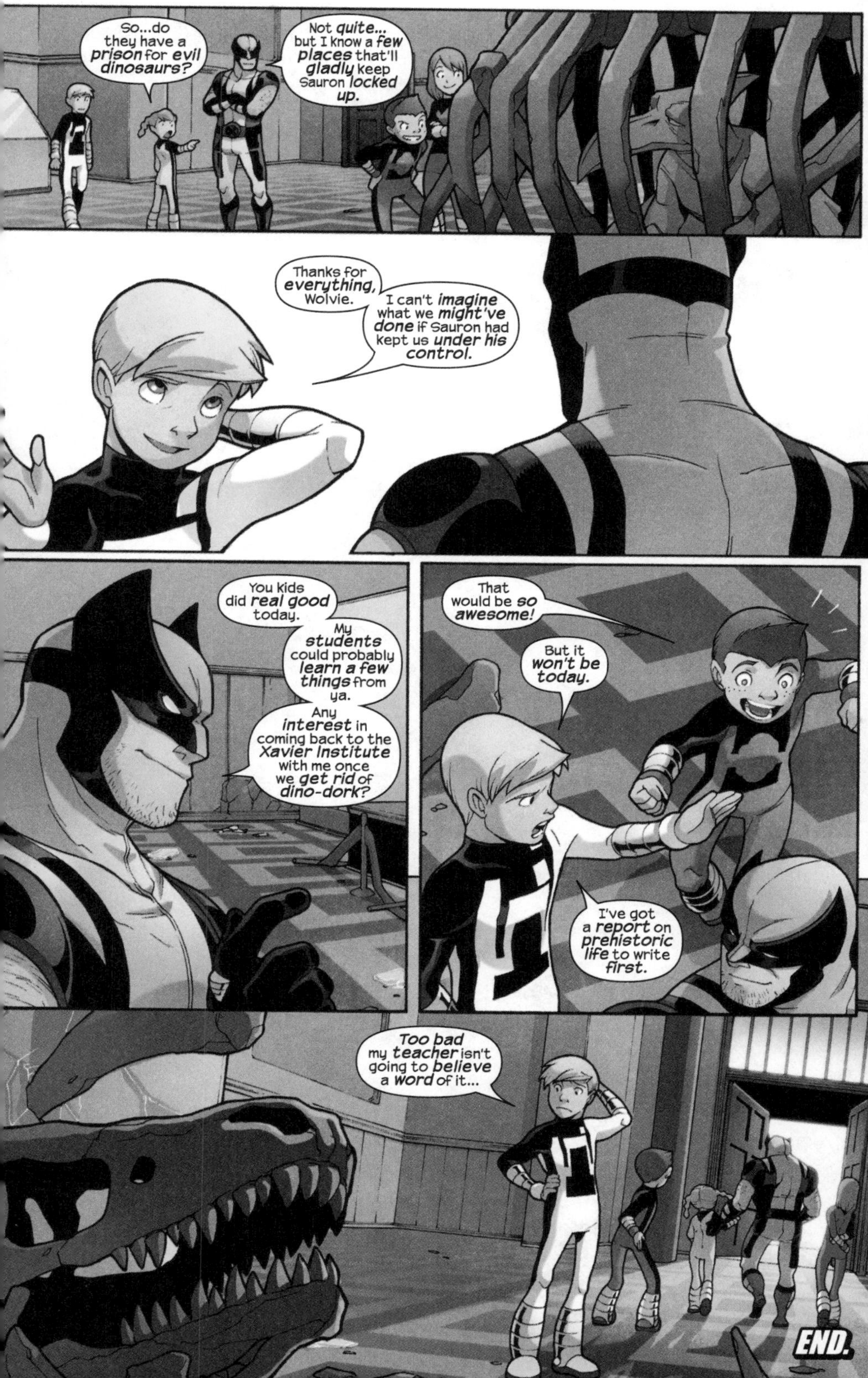
So...do they have a prison for evil dinosaurs?
Not quite... but I know a few places that'll gladly keep Sauron locked up.
Thanks for everything, Wolvie.
I can't imagine what we might've done if Sauron had kept us under his control.
You kids did real good today.
My students could probably learn a few things from ya.
Any interest in coming back to the Xavier Institute with me once we get rid of dino-dork?
That would be so awesome!
But it won't be today.
I've got a report on prehistoric life to write first.
Too bad my teacher isn't going to believe a word of it...
END.

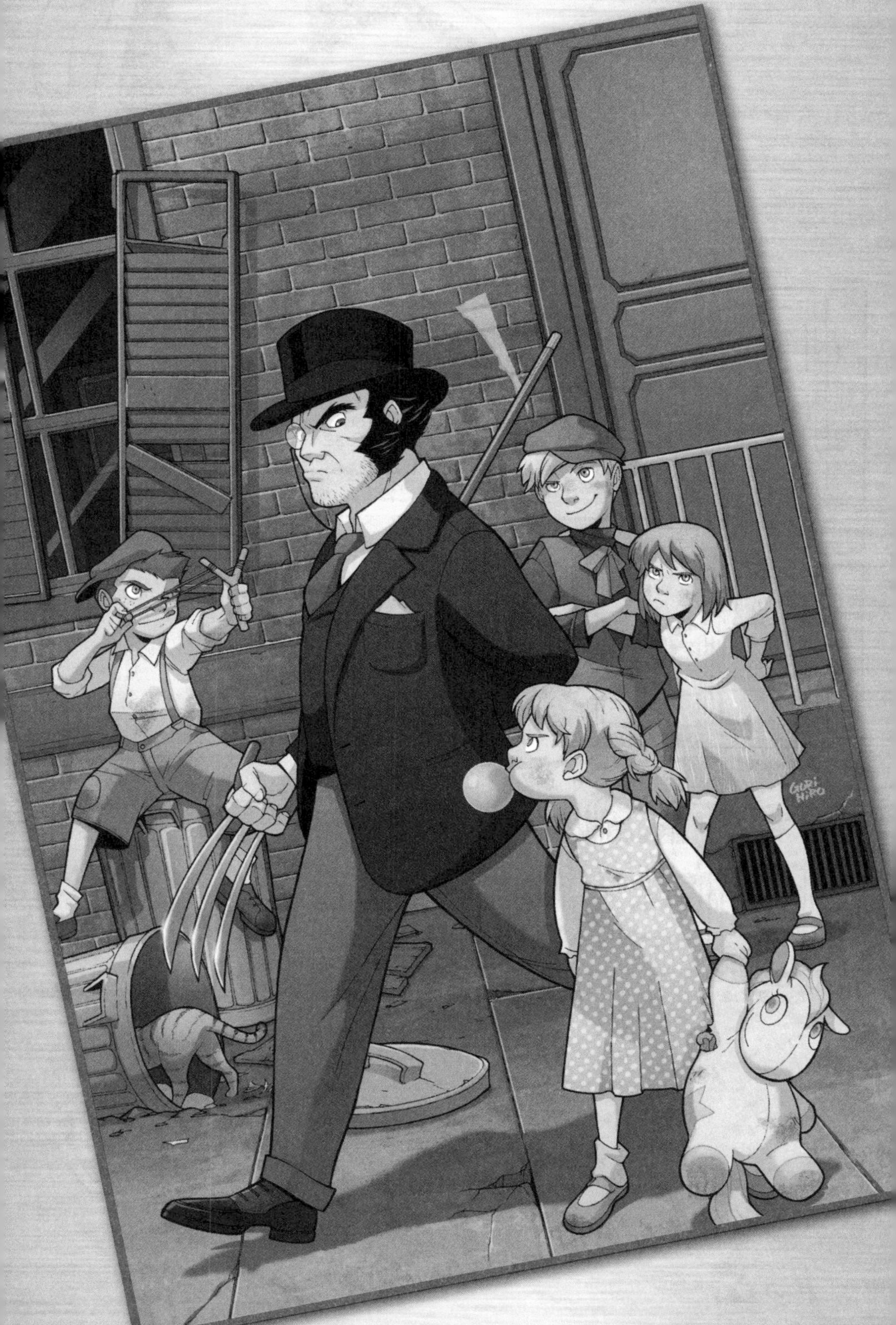

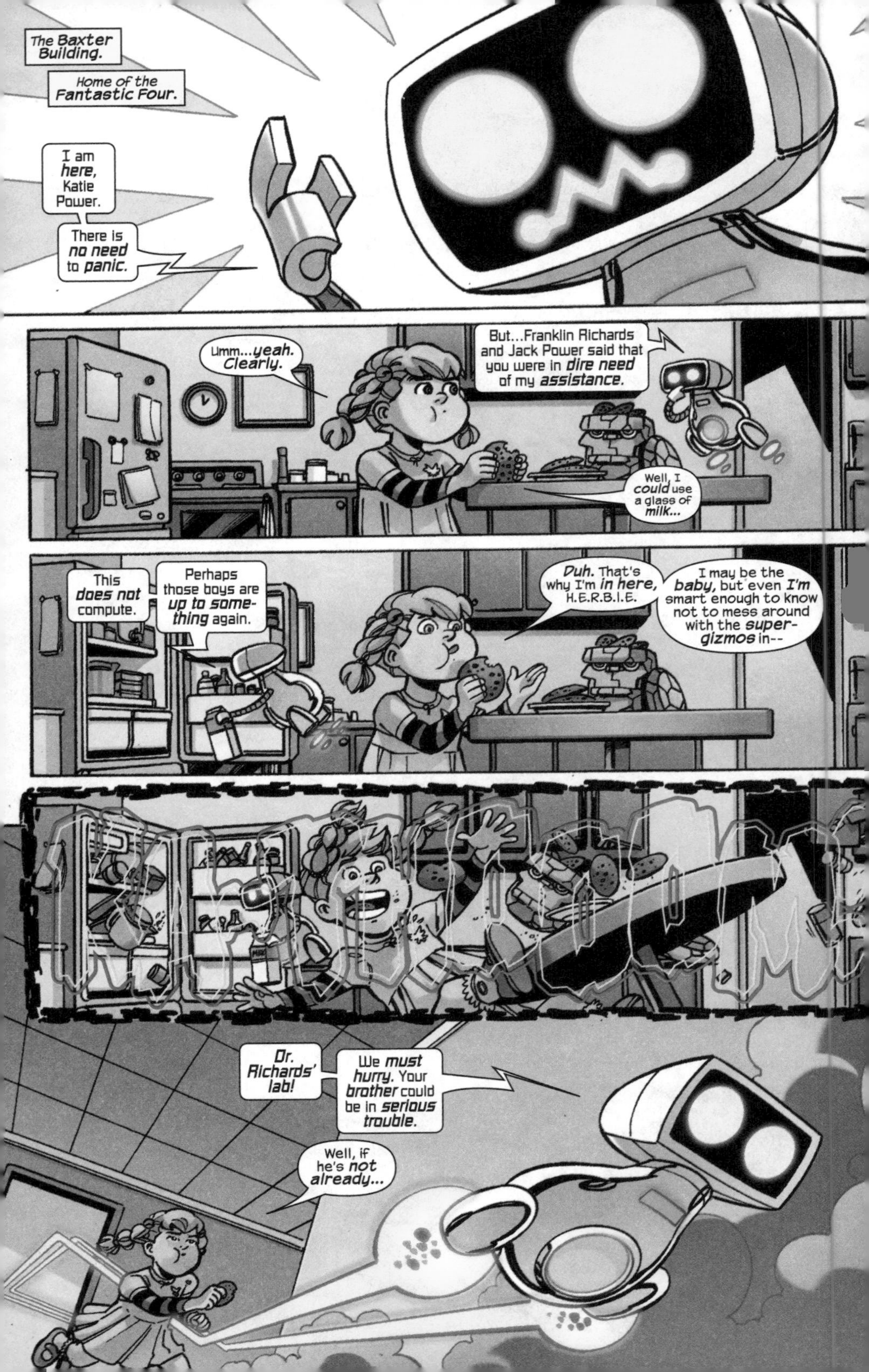
The Baxter Building.
Home of the Fantastic Four.
I am here, Katie Power.
There is no need to panic.
Umm...yeah. Clearly.
But...Franklin Richards and Jack Power said that you were in dire need of my assistance.
Well, I could use a glass of milk...
This does not compute.
Perhaps those boys are up to something again.
Duh. That's why I'm in here, H.E.R.B.I.E.
I may be the baby, but even I'm smart enough to know not to mess around with the super-gizmos in--
Dr. Richards' lab!
We must hurry. Your brother could be in serious trouble.
Well, if he's not already...

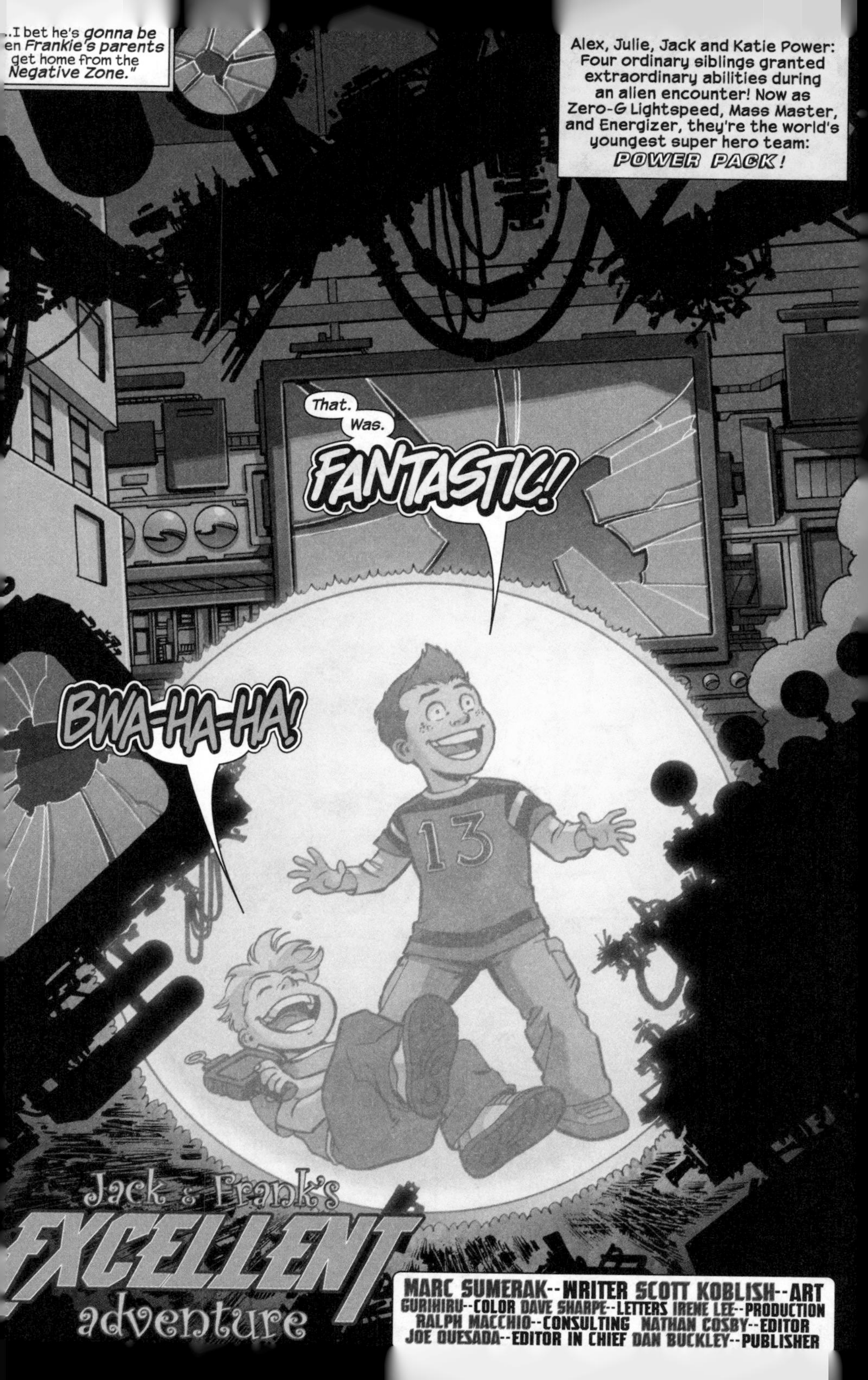
...I bet he's gonna be ...en Frankie's parents get home from the Negative Zone."
Alex, Julie, Jack and Katie Power: Four ordinary siblings granted extraordinary abilities during an alien encounter! Now as Zero-G Lightspeed, Mass Master, and Energizer, they're the world's youngest super hero team: POWER PACK!
That. Was. FANTASTIC!
BWA-HA-HA!
13
Jack & Frank's EXCELLENT adventure
MARC SUMERAK--WRITER SCOTT KOBLISH--ART
GURIHIRU--COLOR DAVE SHARPE--LETTERS IRENE LEE--PRODUCTION
RALPH MACCHIO--CONSULTING NATHAN COSBY--EDITOR
JOE QUESADA--EDITOR IN CHIEF DAN BUCKLEY--PUBLISHER

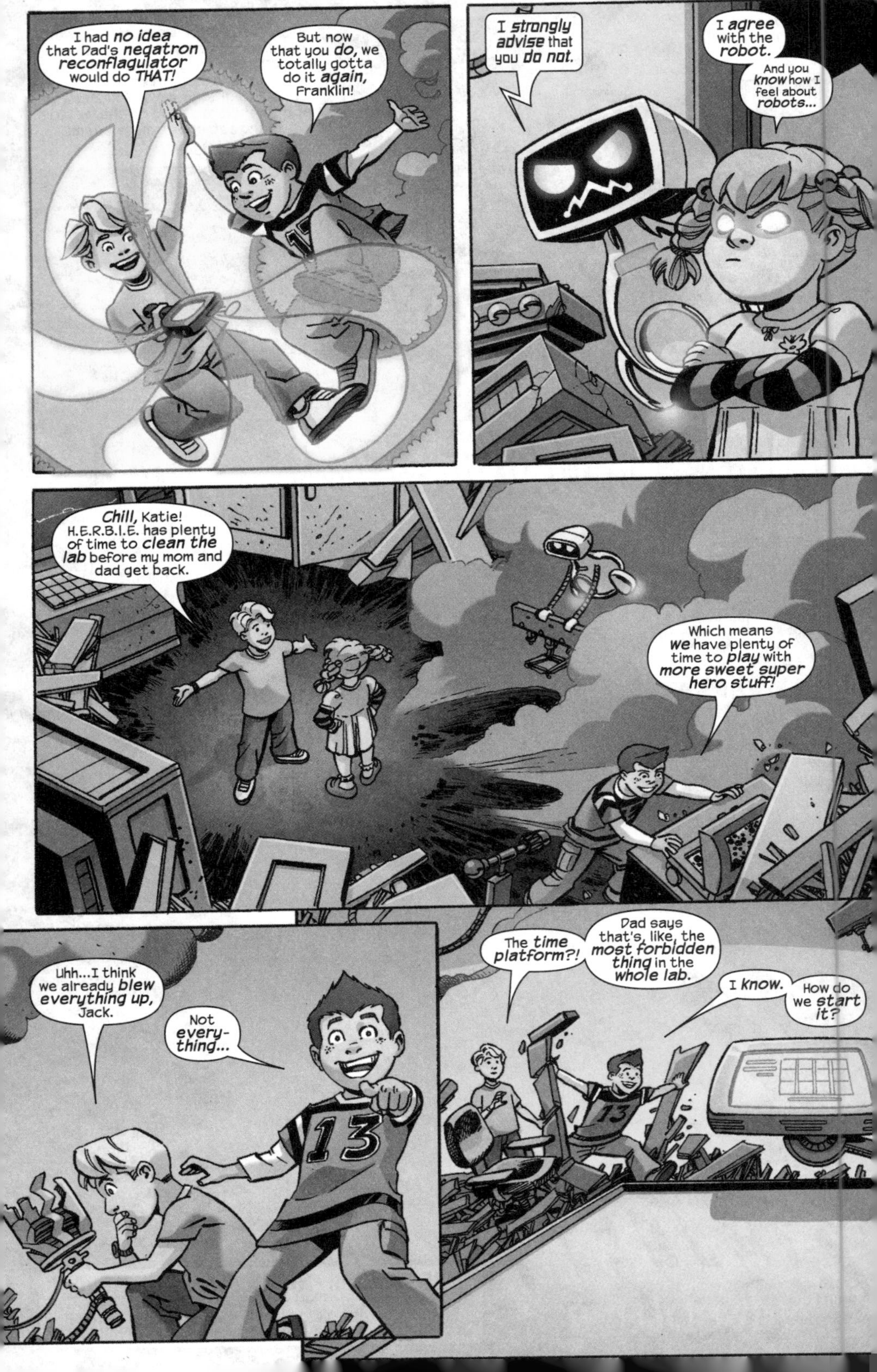

I had no idea that Dad's negatron reconflagulator would do THAT!
But now that you do, we totally gotta do it again, Franklin!
I strongly advise that you do not.
I agree with the robot.
And you know how I feel about robots...
Chill, Katie! H.E.R.B.I.E. has plenty of time to clean the lab before my mom and dad get back.
Which means we have plenty of time to play with more sweet super hero stuff!
Uhh...I think we already blew everything up, Jack.
Not every-thing...
The time platform?!
Dad says that's, like, the most forbidden thing in the whole lab.
I know.
How do we start it?

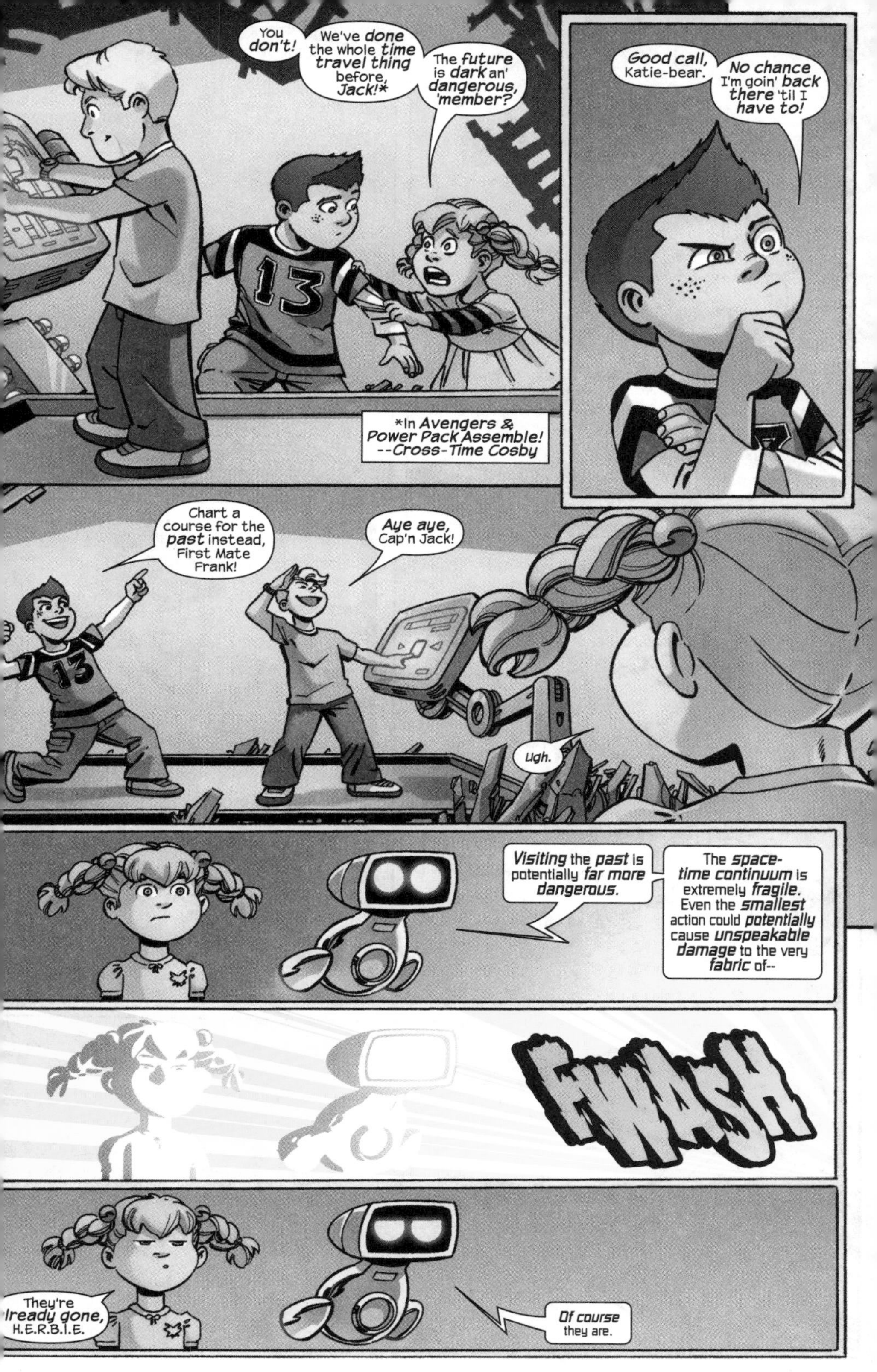

You don't!
We've done the whole time travel thing before, Jack!*
The future is dark an' dangerous, 'member?
*In Avengers & Power Pack Assemble! --Cross-Time Cosby
Good call, Katie-bear.
No chance I'm goin' back there 'til I have to!
Chart a course for the past instead, First Mate Frank!
Aye aye, Cap'n Jack!
Ugh.
Visiting the past is potentially far more dangerous.
The space-time continuum is extremely fragile. Even the smallest action could potentially cause unspeakable damage to the very fabric of--
FWASH
They're lready gone, H.E.R.B.I.E.
Of course they are.

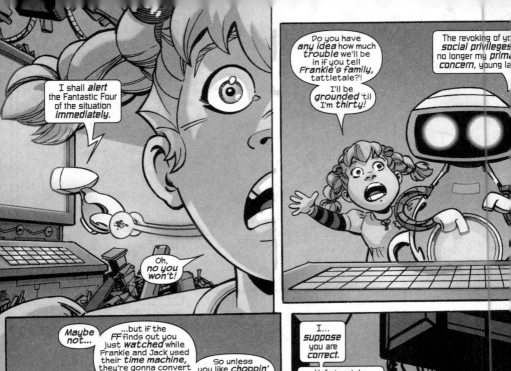

I shall *alert* the Fantastic Four of the situation *immediately*.

Oh, no you won't!

Do you have *any idea* how much *trouble* we'll be in if you tell *Frankie's family*, tattletale?!

I'll be *grounded* 'til I'm *thirty!*

The revoking of yo *social privileges* no longer my *prim. concern*, young la

Maybe not...

...but if the *FF* finds out you just *watched* while Frankie and Jack used their *time machine*, they're gonna convert *you* into a *food processor!*

So unless you like *choppin' onions*, we need a *better idea*.

I... *suppose* you are *correct*.

Unfortunately, *this* is not the kind of *dilemma* I was designed to *handle*.

No prob, H.E.R.B.I.E.

beep

I *know* people...

Calling: Jul...

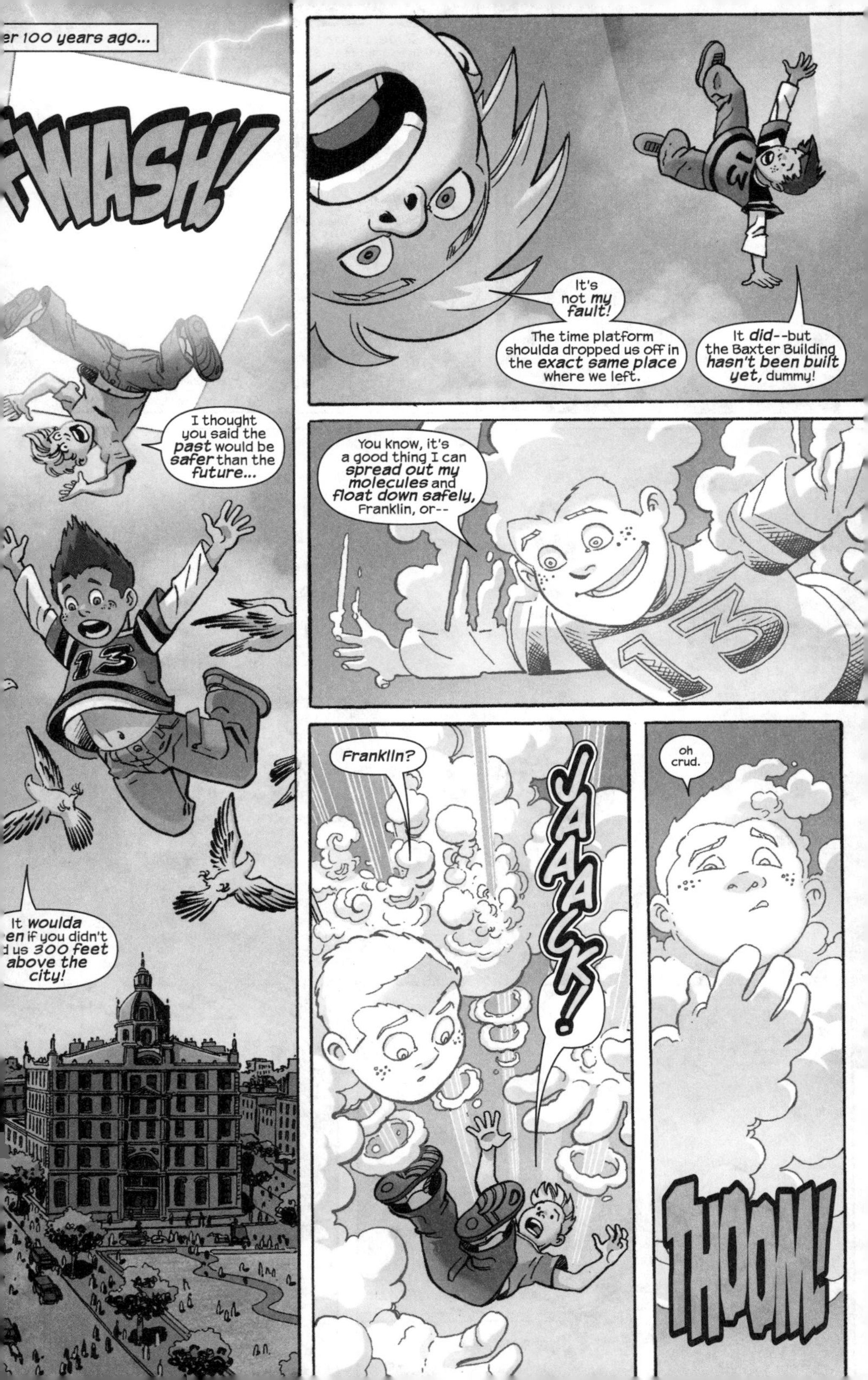

er 100 years ago...
WASH!
I thought you said the past would be safer than the future...
It woulda en if you didn't d us 300 feet above the city!
It's not my fault!
The time platform shoulda dropped us off in the exact same place where we left.
It did--but the Baxter Building hasn't been built yet, dummy!
You know, it's a good thing I can spread out my molecules and float down safely, Franklin, or--
Franklin?
JAAAACK!
oh crud.
THOOM!

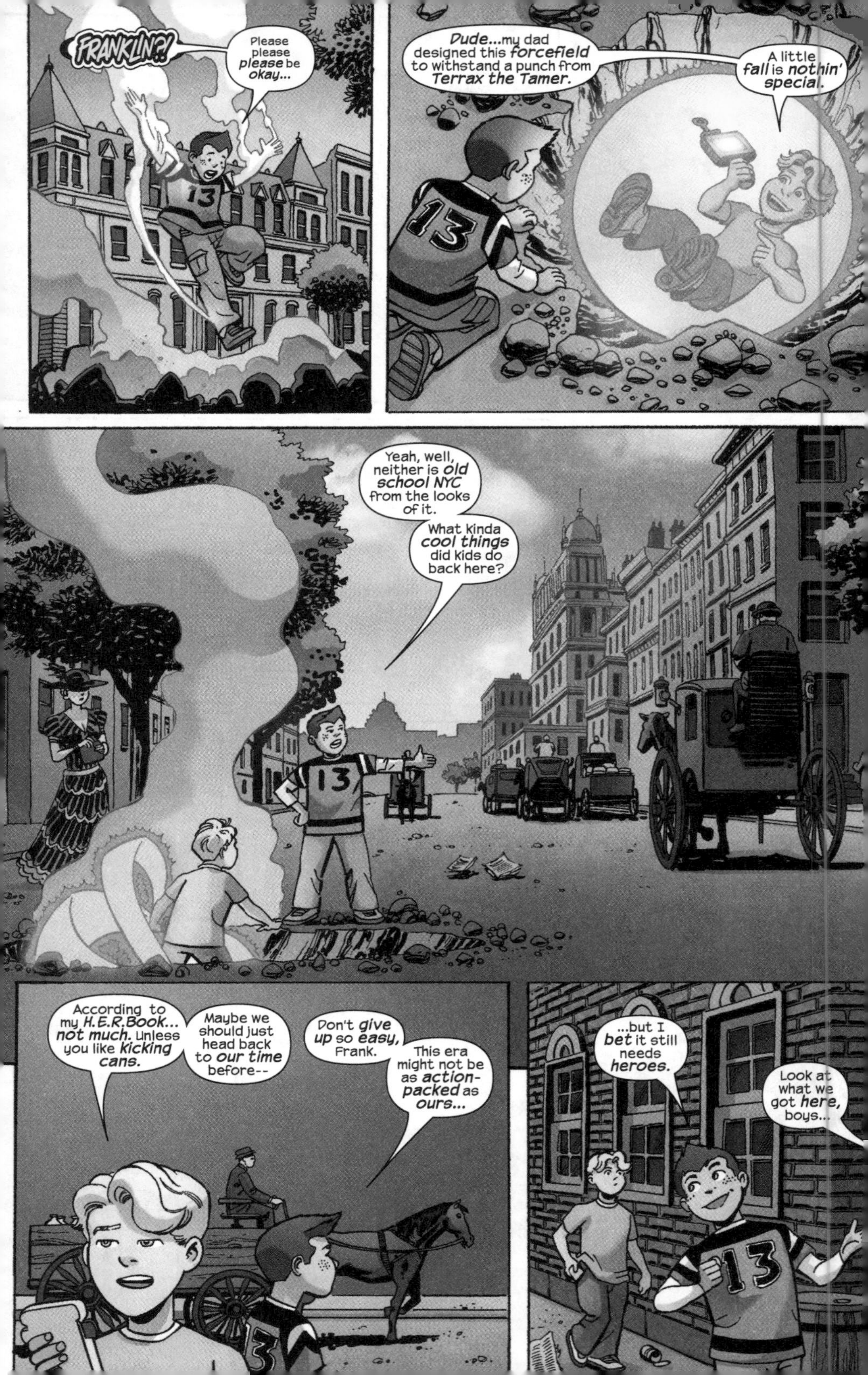
FRANKLIN?!
Please please please be okay...
Dude...my dad designed this forcefield to withstand a punch from Terrax the Tamer.
A little fall is nothin' special.
Yeah, well, neither is old school NYC from the looks of it.
What kinda cool things did kids do back here?
According to my H.E.R.Book... not much. Unless you like kicking cans.
Maybe we should just head back to our time before--
Don't give up so easy, Frank.
This era might not be as action-packed as ours...
...but I bet it still needs heroes.
Look at what we got here, boys...

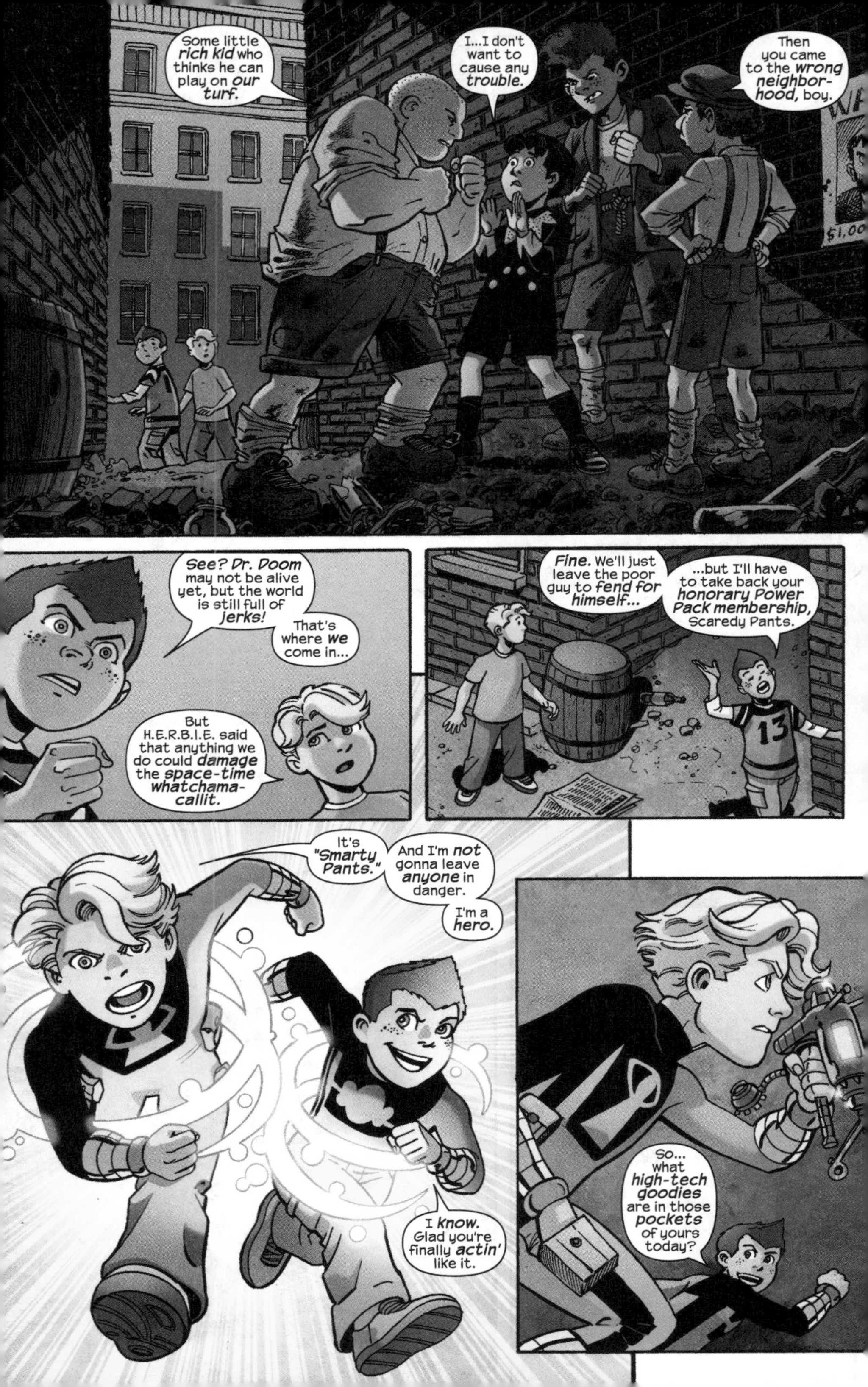
Some little rich kid who thinks he can play on our turf.
I...I don't want to cause any trouble.
Then you came to the wrong neighbor-hood, boy.
See? Dr. Doom may not be alive yet, but the world is still full of jerks!
That's where we come in...
But H.E.R.B.I.E. said that anything we do could damage the space-time whatchama-callit.
Fine. We'll just leave the poor guy to fend for himself...
...but I'll have to take back your honorary Power Pack membership, Scaredy Pants.
It's "Smarty Pants."
And I'm not gonna leave anyone in danger.
I'm a hero.
I know. Glad you're finally actin' like it.
So... what high-tech goodies are in those pockets of yours today?

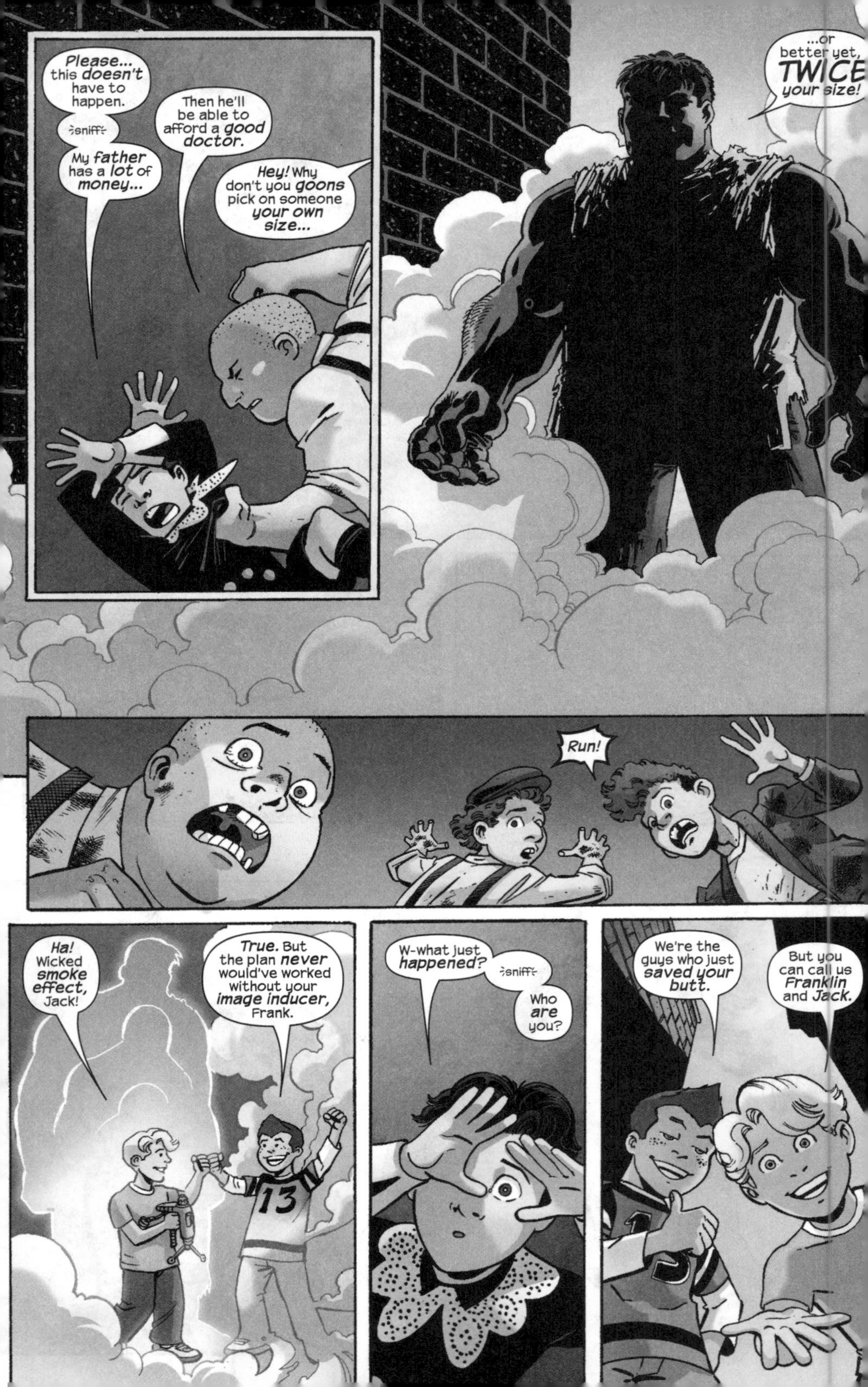
Please... this doesn't have to happen.
sniff
My father has a lot of money...
Then he'll be able to afford a good doctor.
Hey! Why don't you goons pick on someone your own size...
...or better yet, TWICE your size!
Run!
Ha! Wicked smoke effect, Jack!
True. But the plan never would've worked without your image inducer, Frank.
W-what just happened?
sniff
Who are you?
We're the guys who just saved your butt.
But you can call us Franklin and Jack.

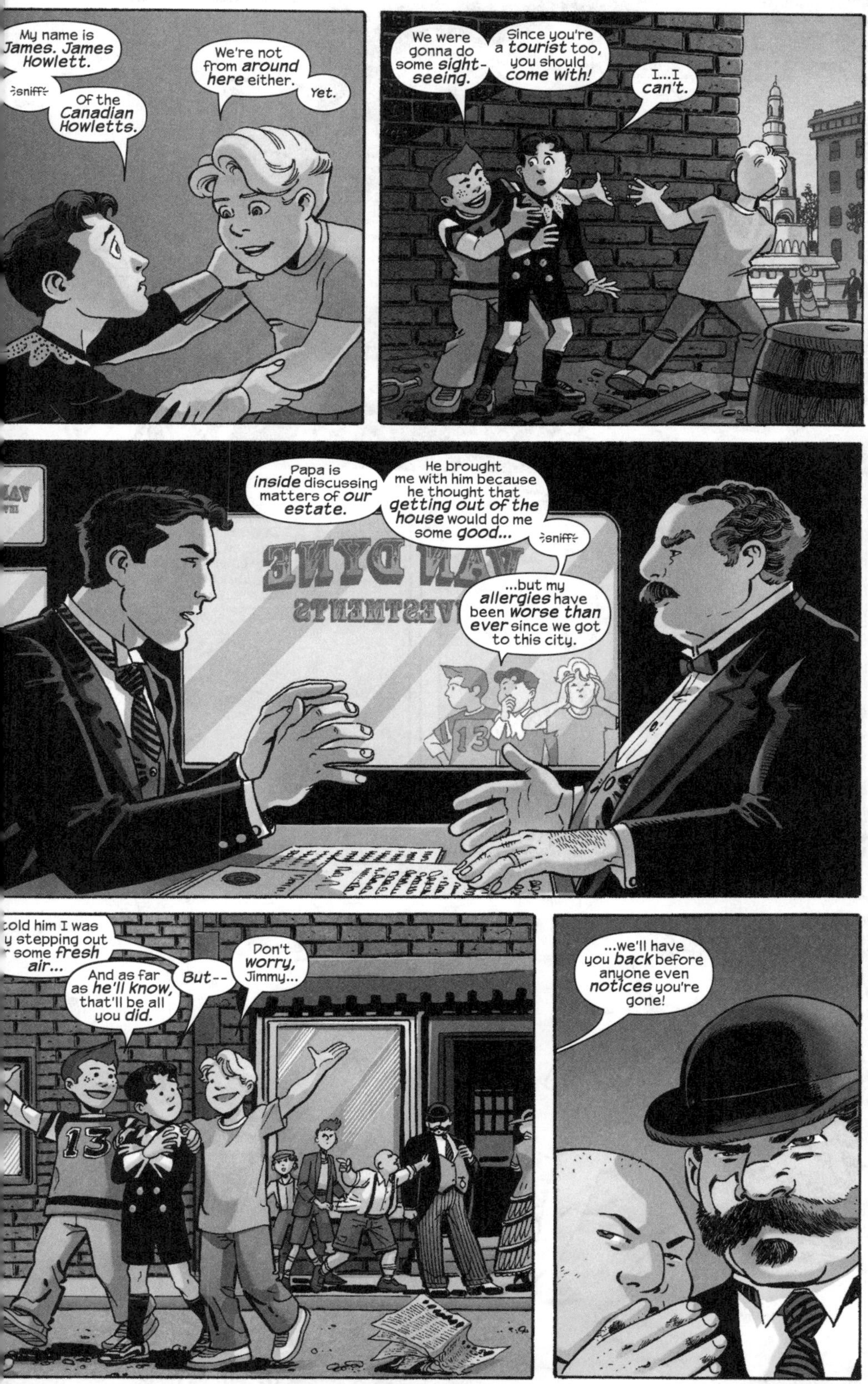

My name is James. James Howlett.
sniff
Of the Canadian Howletts.
We're not from around here either.
Yet.
We were gonna do some sight-seeing.
Since you're a tourist too, you should come with!
I...I can't.
Papa is inside discussing matters of our estate.
He brought me with him because he thought that getting out of the house would do me some good...
sniff
...but my allergies have been worse than ever since we got to this city.
VAN DYNE
INVESTMENTS
13
told him I was y stepping out r some fresh air...
But--
And as far as he'll know, that'll be all you did.
Don't worry, Jimmy...
13
...we'll have you back before anyone even notices you're gone!

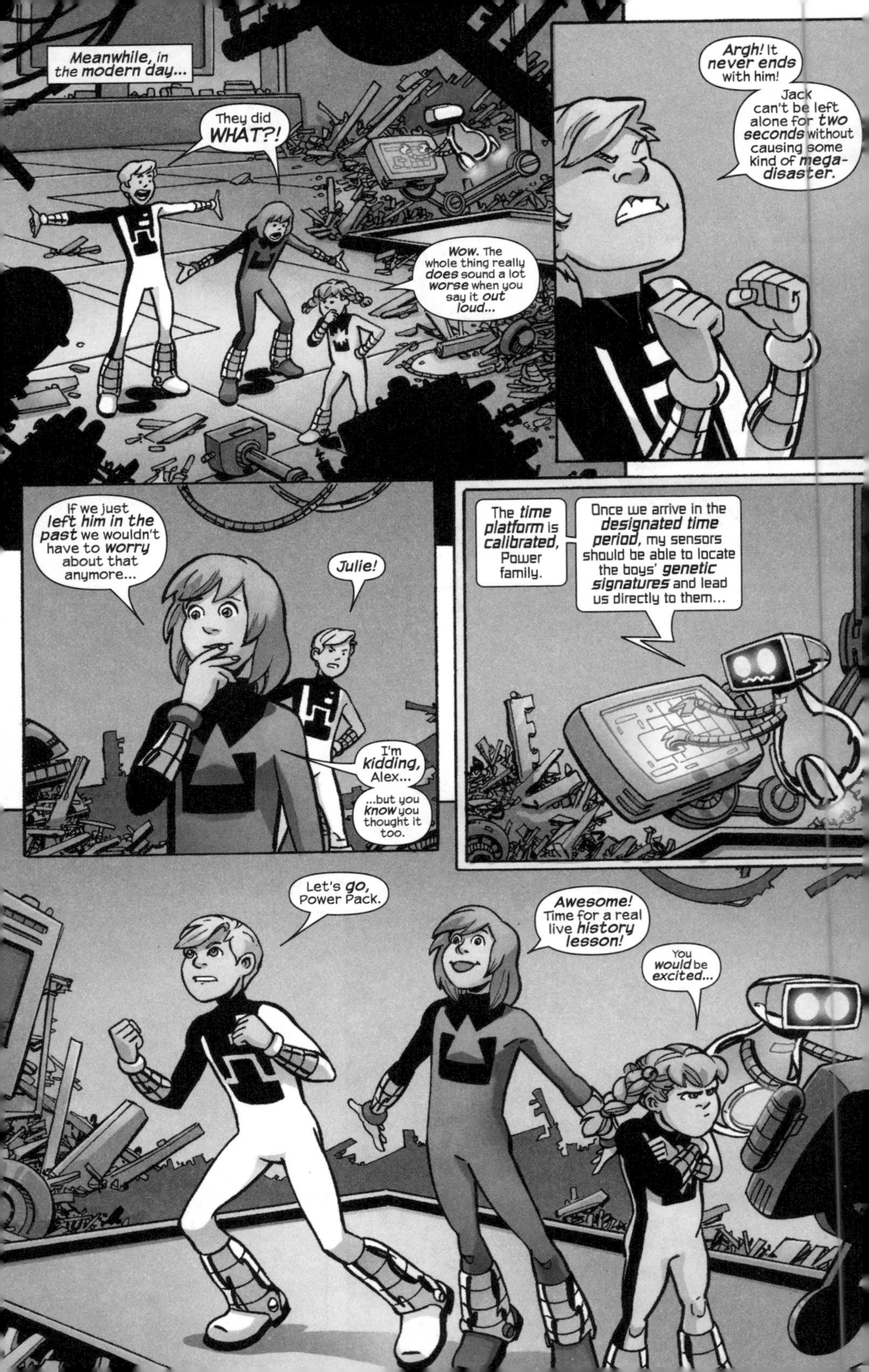

Meanwhile, in the modern day...
They did WHAT?!
Wow. The whole thing really does sound a lot worse when you say it out loud...
Argh! It never ends with him!
Jack can't be left alone for two seconds without causing some kind of mega-disaster.
If we just left him in the past we wouldn't have to worry about that anymore...
Julie!
I'm kidding, Alex...
...but you know you thought it too.
The time platform is calibrated, Power family.
Once we arrive in the designated time period, my sensors should be able to locate the boys' genetic signatures and lead us directly to them...
Let's go, Power Pack.
Awesome! Time for a real live history lesson!
You would be excited...

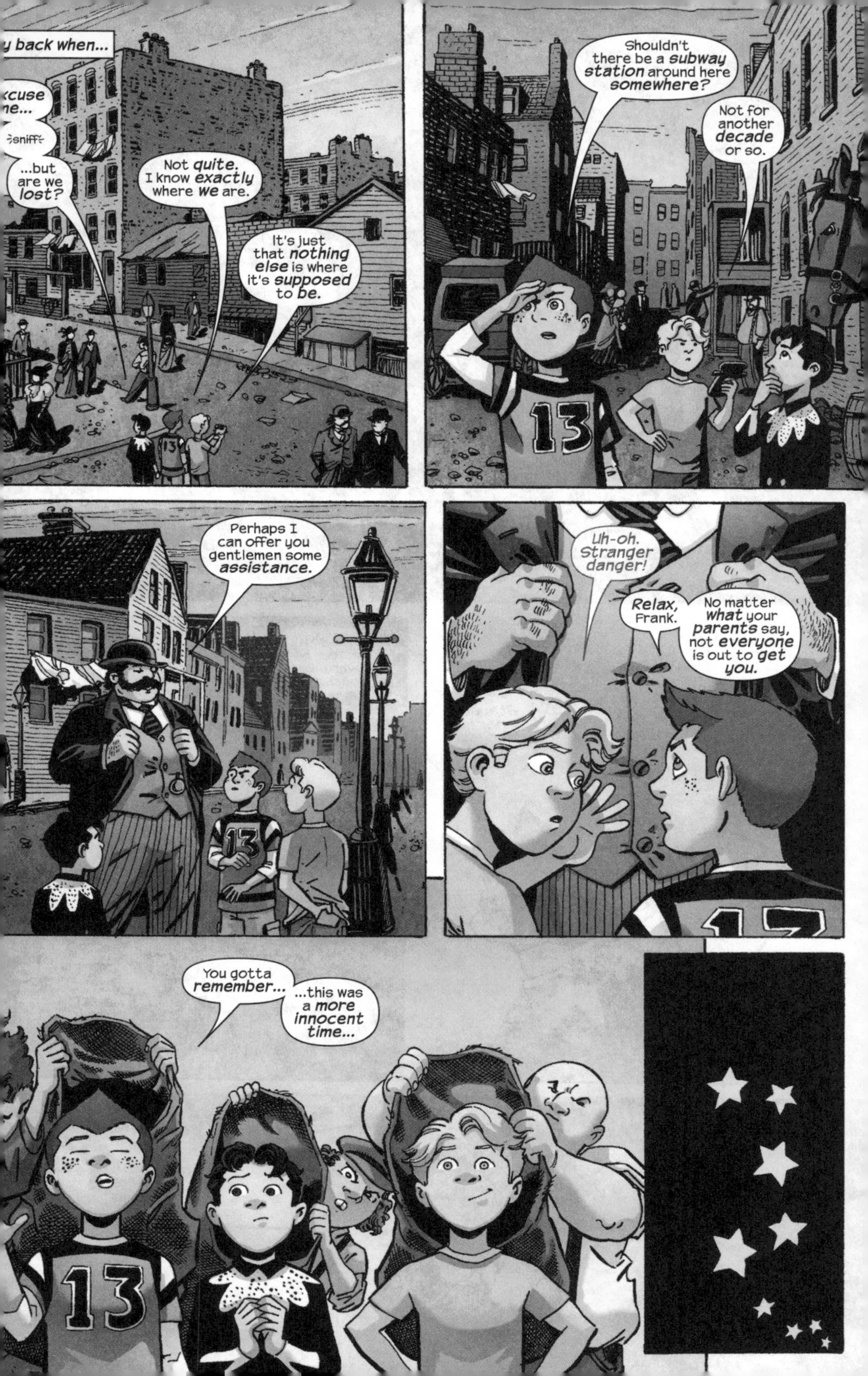

y back when...
xcuse
ne...
sniff
...but
are we
lost?
Not quite.
I know exactly
where we are.
It's just
that nothing
else is where
it's supposed
to be.
Shouldn't
there be a subway
station around here
somewhere?
Not for
another
decade
or so.
Perhaps I
can offer you
gentlemen some
assistance.
Uh-oh.
Stranger
danger!
Relax,
Frank.
No matter
what your
parents say,
not everyone
is out to get
you.
You gotta
remember...
...this was
a more
innocent
time...

Soon...

"A more innocent time," huh, Jack?

Hey, I got a "C" in history for a reason.

Well, you got super-powers for a reason, too.

So use 'em to get us outta these ropes already!

Not yet. First, we gotta find out what Fatty McHatty is after.

Standard super hero procedure: zip it and listen...

My boys tell me that your father is a very wealthy man, son.

One that would pay a handsome fee to make sure you are returned to him safely.

We plan to make certain that he does so...

...or you will be the one that pays the price!

:sniff:

You might wanna rethink your plan, fella.

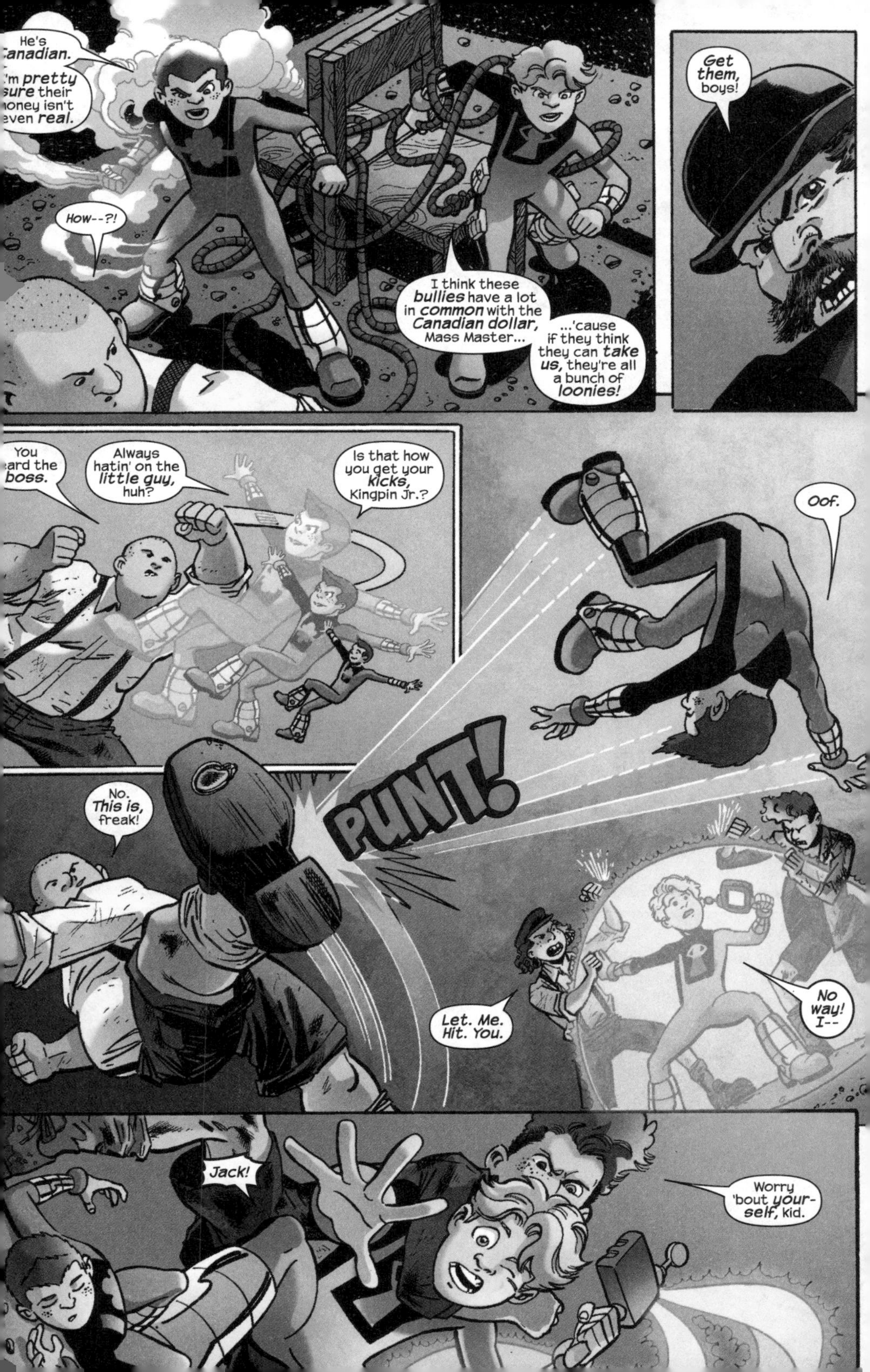

He's Canadian.
I'm pretty sure their money isn't even real.
How--?!
I think these bullies have a lot in common with the Canadian dollar, Mass Master...
...'cause if they think they can take us, they're all a bunch of loonies!
Get them, boys!
You heard the boss.
Always hatin' on the little guy, huh?
Is that how you get your kicks, Kingpin Jr.?
Oof.
PUNT!
No. This is, freak!
Let. Me. Hit. You.
No way! I--
Jack!
Worry 'bout yourself, kid.

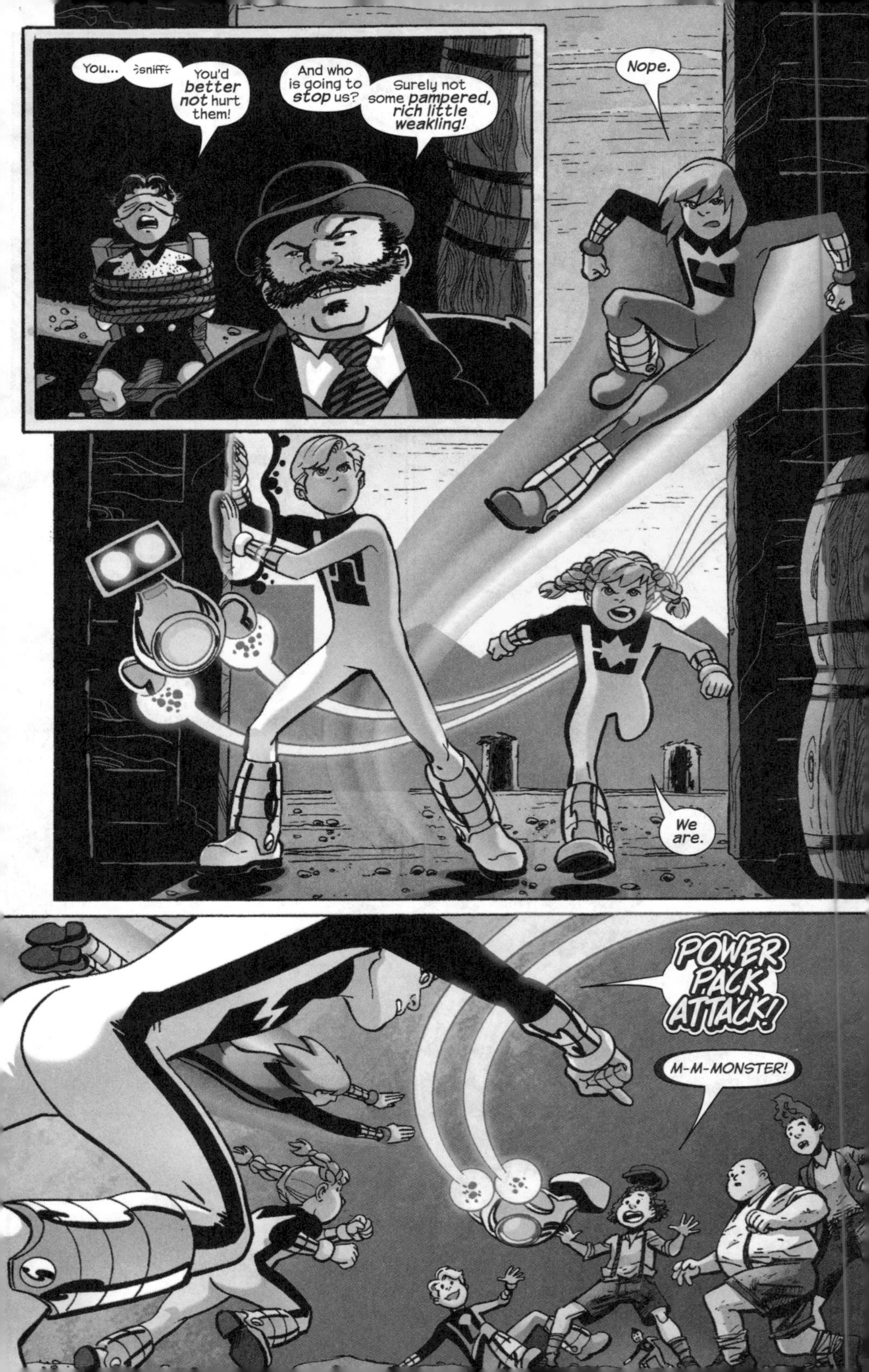
You...
~sniff~
You'd better not hurt them!
And who is going to stop us?
Surely not some pampered, rich little weakling!
Nope.
We are.
POWER PACK ATTACK!
M-M-MONSTER!

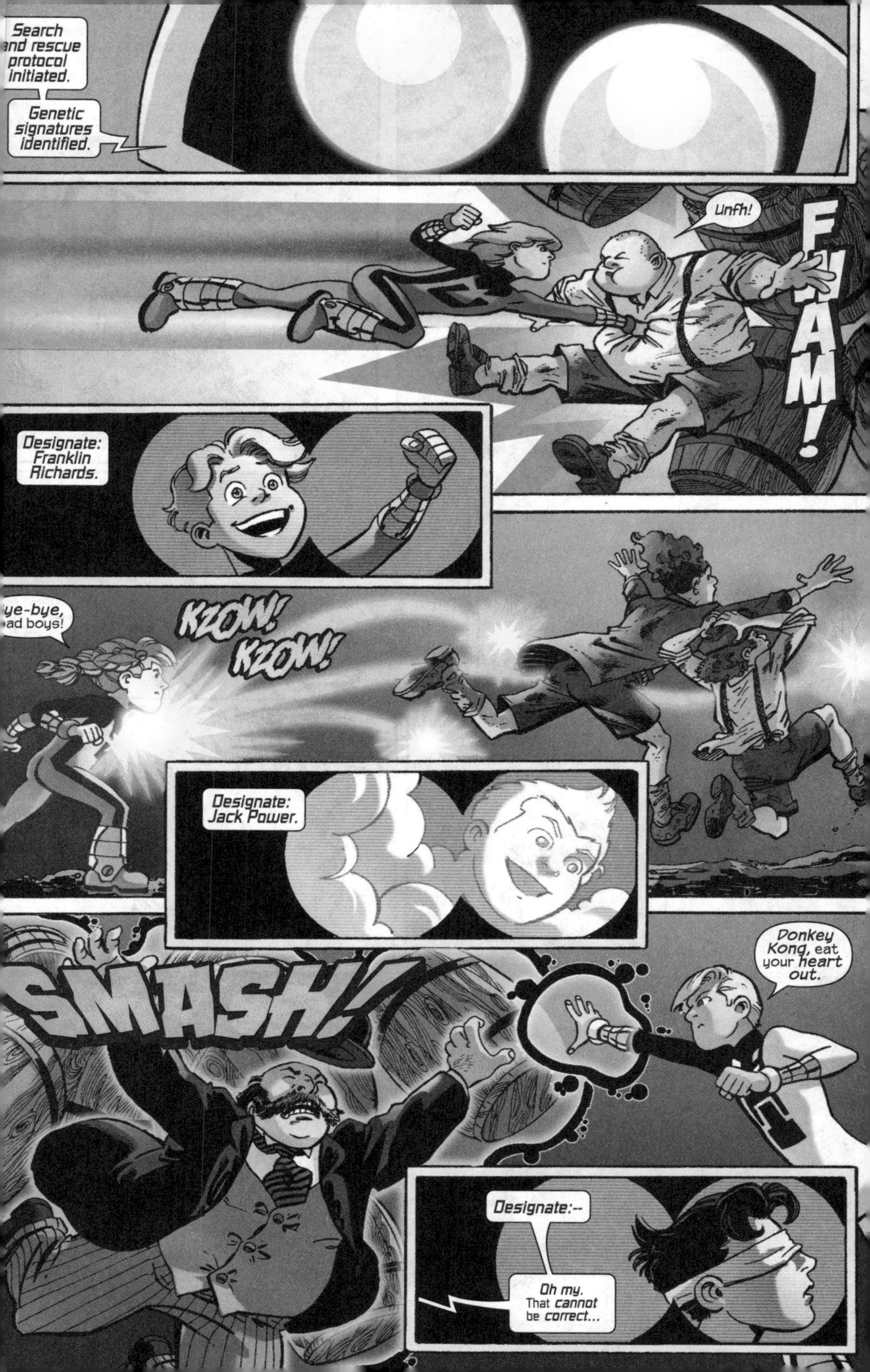
Search and rescue protocol initiated.
Genetic signatures identified.
Unfh!
FUDAM!
Designate: Franklin Richards.
ye-bye, ad boys!
KZOW! KZOW!
Designate: Jack Power.
SMASH!
Donkey Kong, eat your heart out.
Designate:--
Oh my. That cannot be correct...

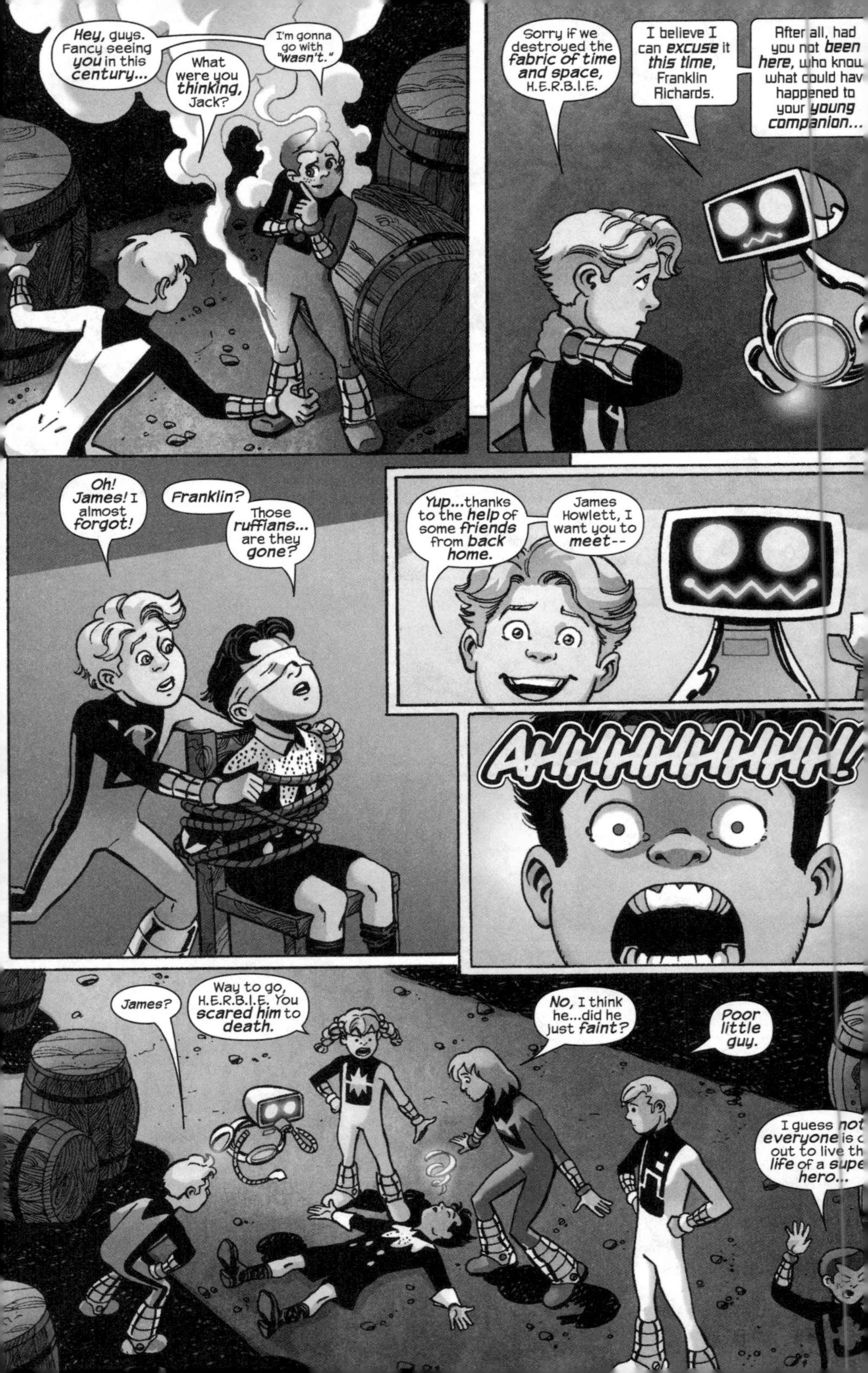
Hey, guys. Fancy seeing you in this century...
What were you thinking, Jack?
I'm gonna go with "wasn't."
Sorry if we destroyed the fabric of time and space, H.E.R.B.I.E.
I believe I can excuse it this time, Franklin Richards.
After all, had you not been here, who know what could hav happened to your young companion...
Oh! James! I almost forgot!
Franklin?
Those ruffians... are they gone?
Yup...thanks to the help of some friends from back home.
James Howlett, I want you to meet--
AHHHHHHHHH!
James?
Way to go, H.E.R.B.I.E. You scared him to death.
No, I think he...did he just faint?
Poor little guy.
I guess not everyone is c out to live th life of a supe hero...

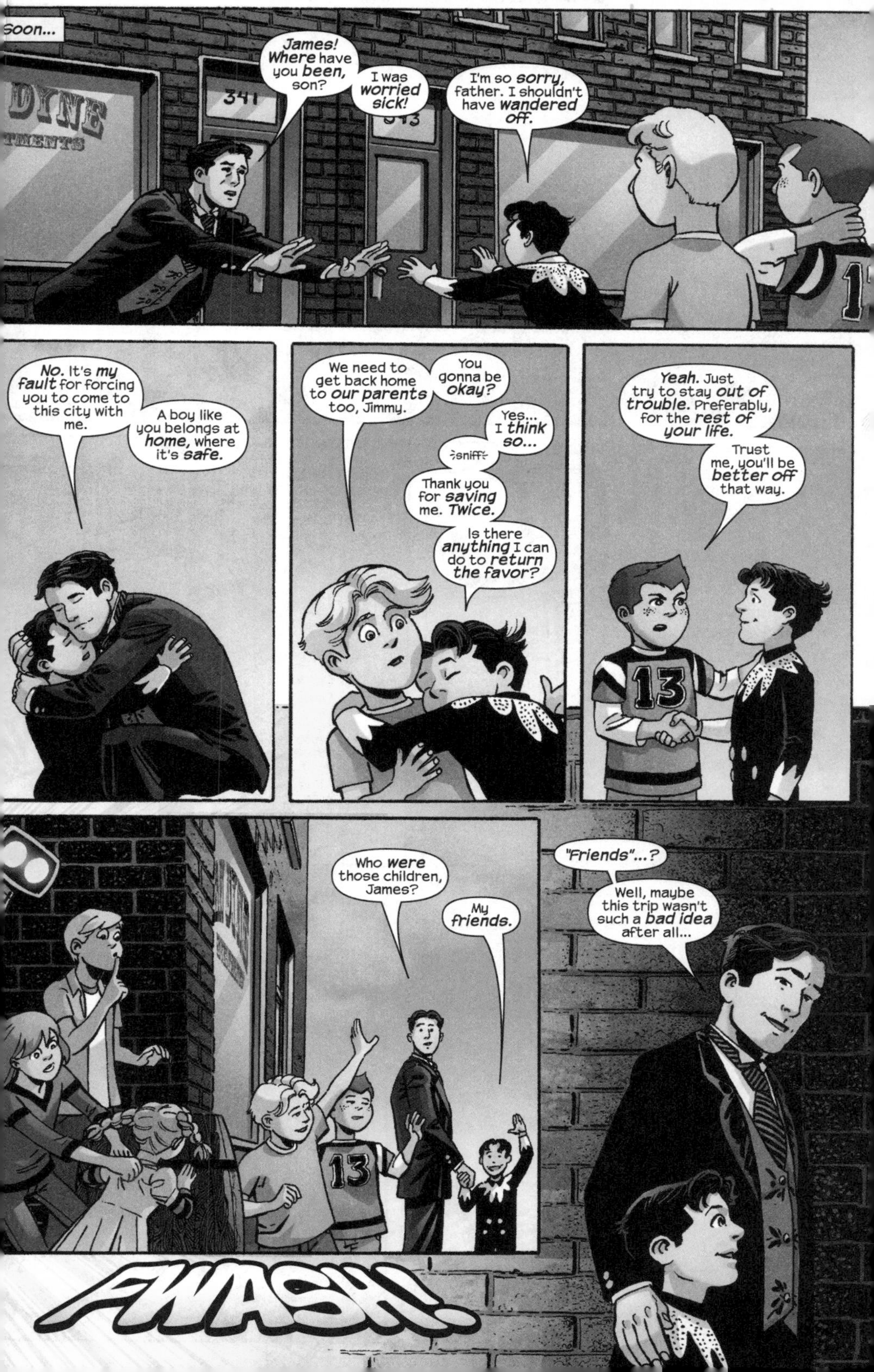
Soon...
James! Where have you been, son?
I was worried sick!
I'm so sorry, father. I shouldn't have wandered off.
No. It's my fault for forcing you to come to this city with me.
A boy like you belongs at home, where it's safe.
We need to get back home to our parents too, Jimmy.
You gonna be okay?
Yes... I think so...
sniff
Thank you for saving me. Twice.
Is there anything I can do to return the favor?
Yeah. Just try to stay out of trouble. Preferably, for the rest of your life.
Trust me, you'll be better off that way.
Who were those children, James?
My friends.
"Friends"...?
Well, maybe this trip wasn't such a bad idea after all...
FWASH!!

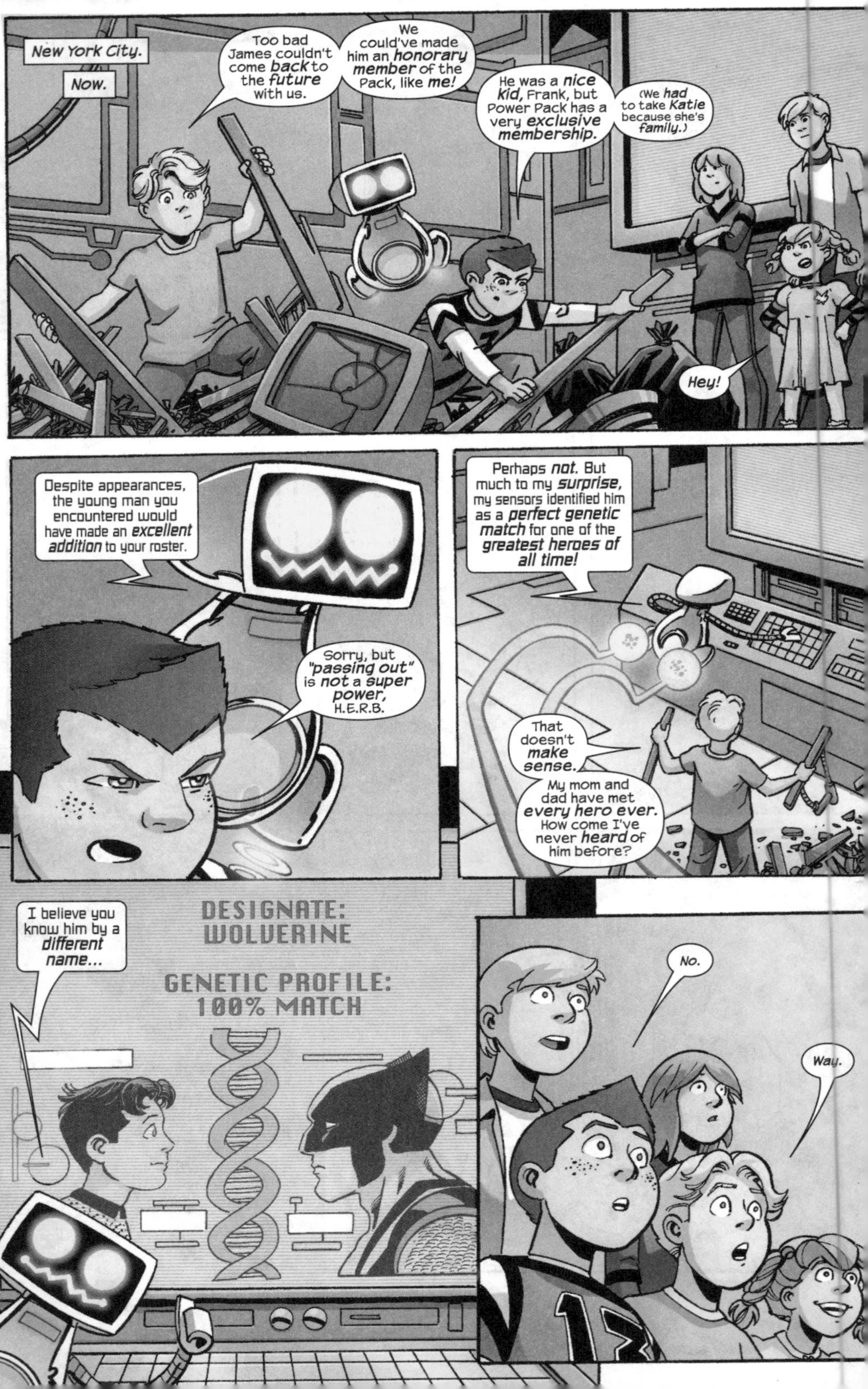
New York City.
Now.
Too bad James couldn't come back to the future with us.
We could've made him an honorary member of the Pack, like me!
He was a nice kid, Frank, but Power Pack has a very exclusive membership.
(We had to take Katie because she's family.)
Hey!
Despite appearances, the young man you encountered would have made an excellent addition to your roster.
Sorry, but "passing out" is not a super power, H.E.R.B.
Perhaps not. But much to my surprise, my sensors identified him as a perfect genetic match for one of the greatest heroes of all time!
That doesn't make sense.
My mom and dad have met every hero ever. How come I've never heard of him before?
I believe you know him by a different name...
DESIGNATE: WOLVERINE
GENETIC PROFILE: 100% MATCH
No.
Way.

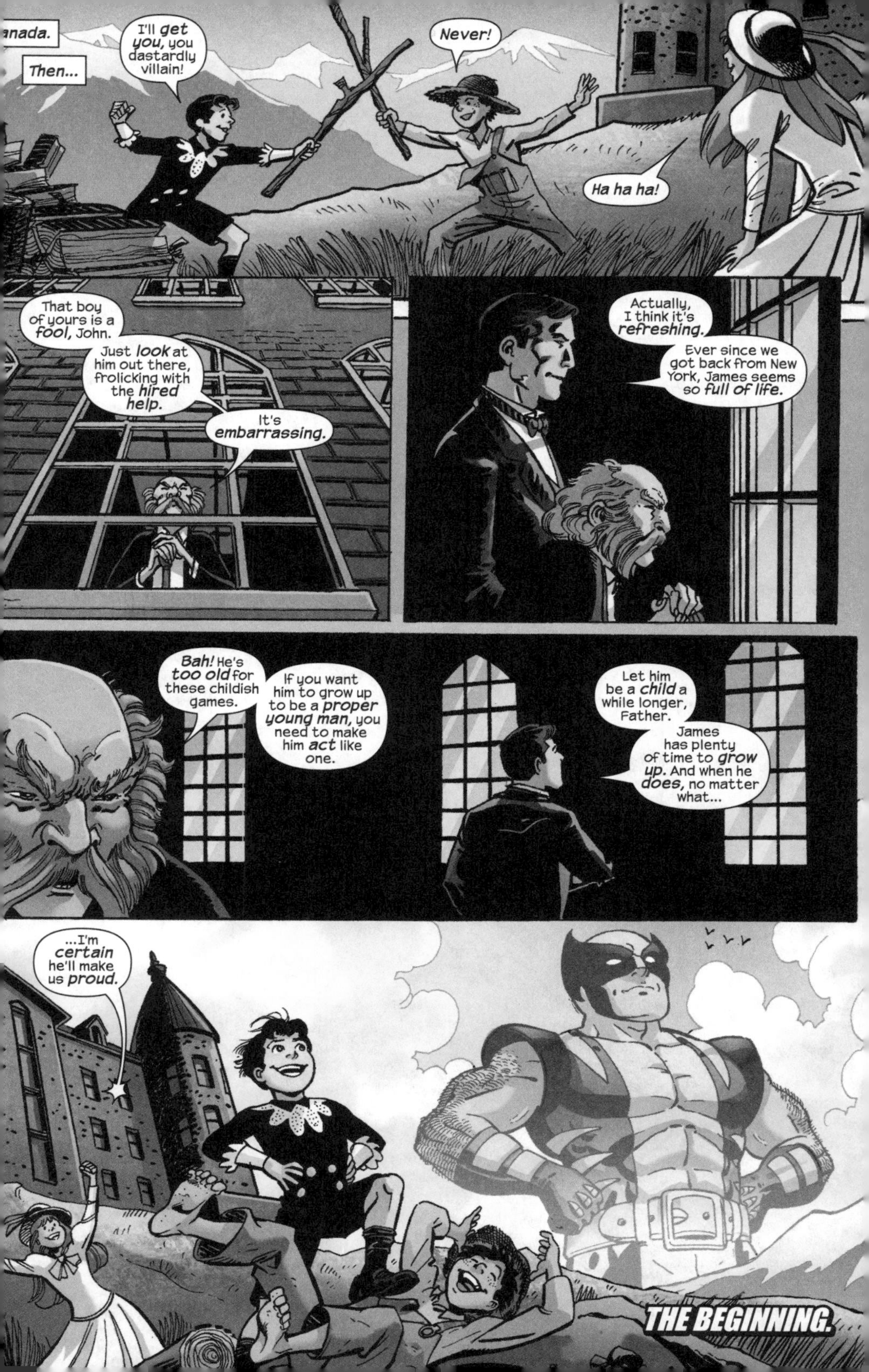
anada.
Then...
I'll get you, you dastardly villain!
Never!
Ha ha ha!
That boy of yours is a fool, John.
Just look at him out there, frolicking with the hired help.
It's embarrassing.
Actually, I think it's refreshing.
Ever since we got back from New York, James seems so full of life.
Bah! He's too old for these childish games.
If you want him to grow up to be a proper young man, you need to make him act like one.
Let him be a child a while longer, Father.
James has plenty of time to grow up. And when he does, no matter what...
...I'm certain he'll make us proud.
THE BEGINNING.

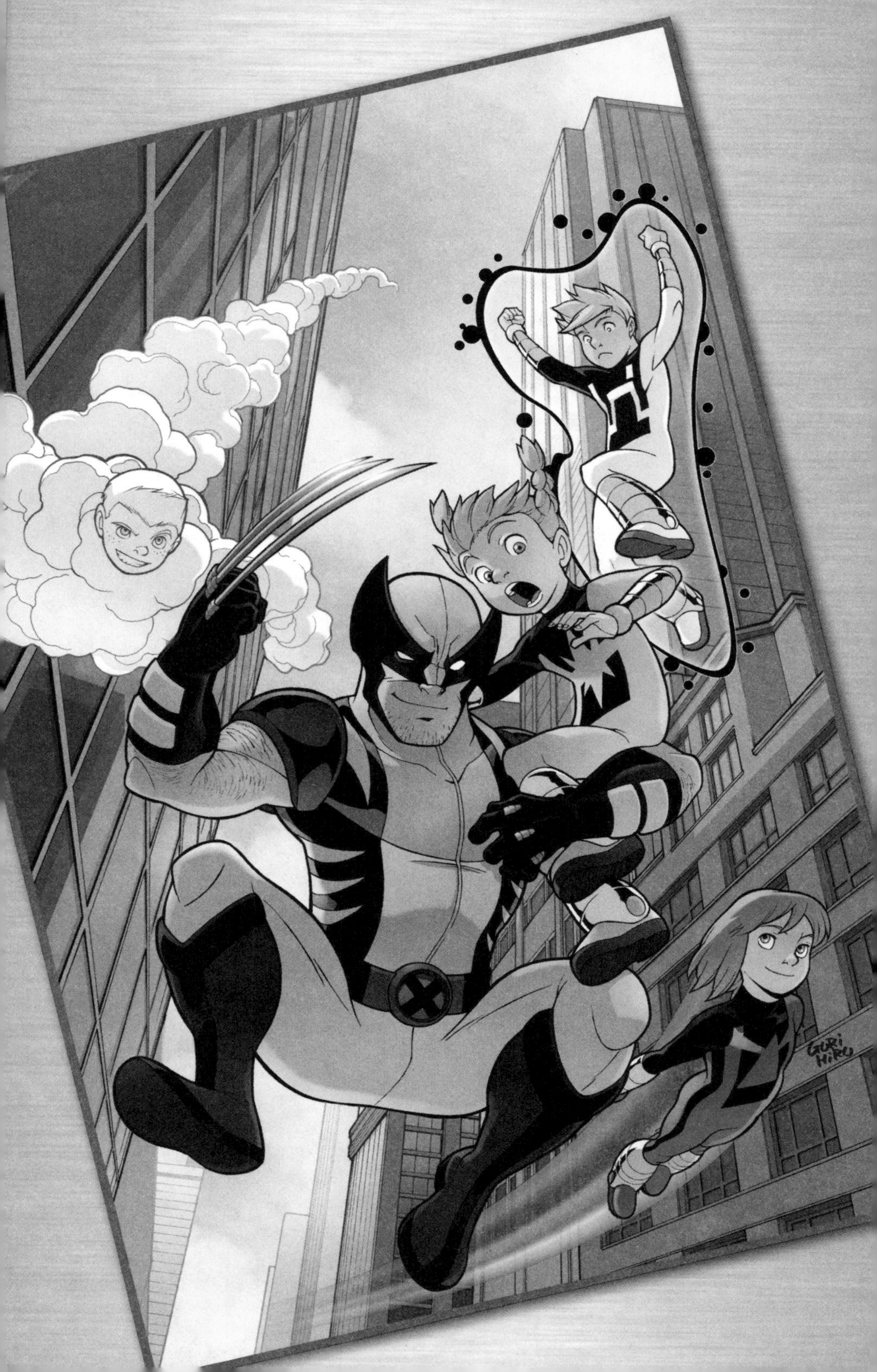
GURI HIRU

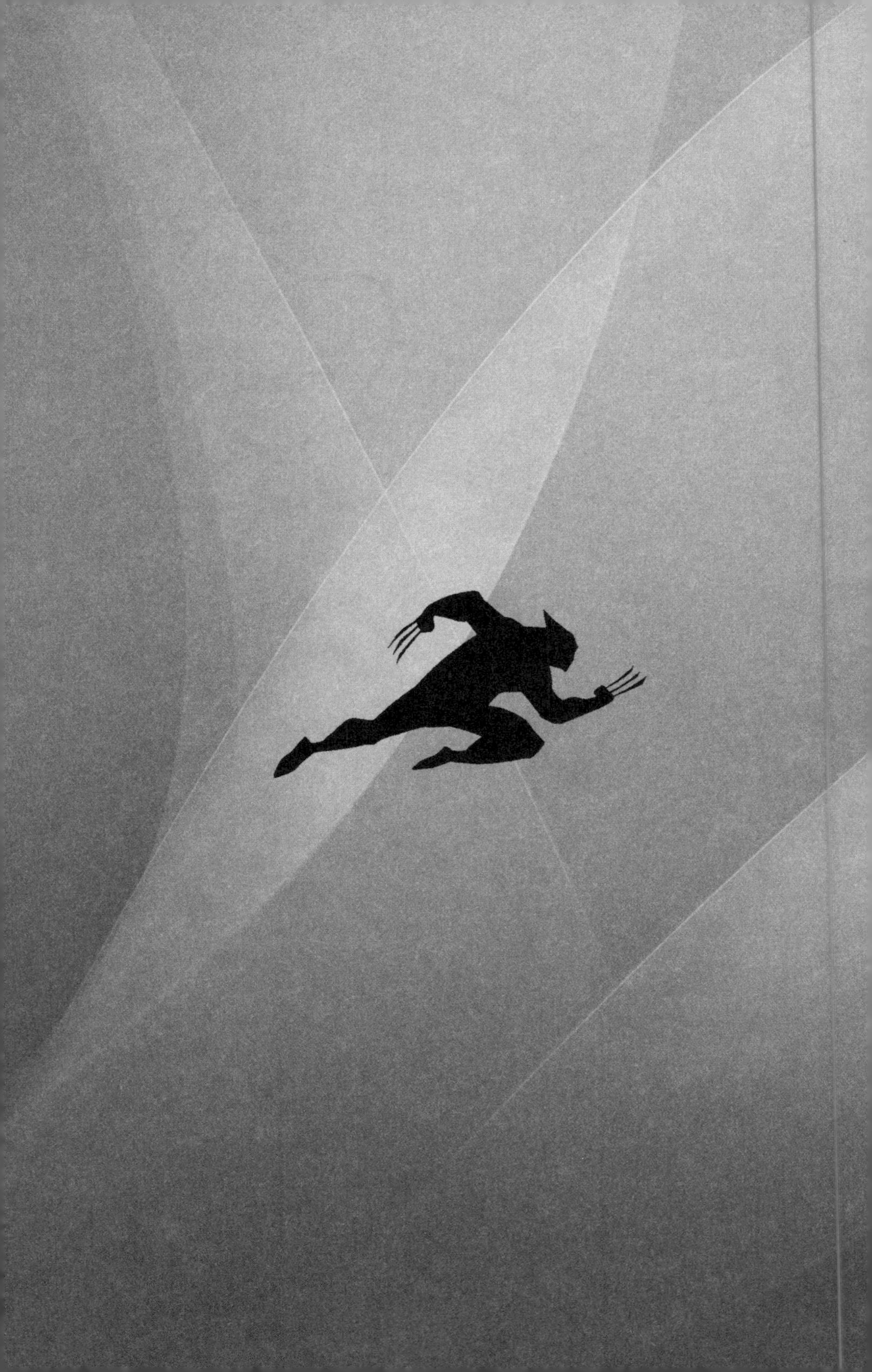

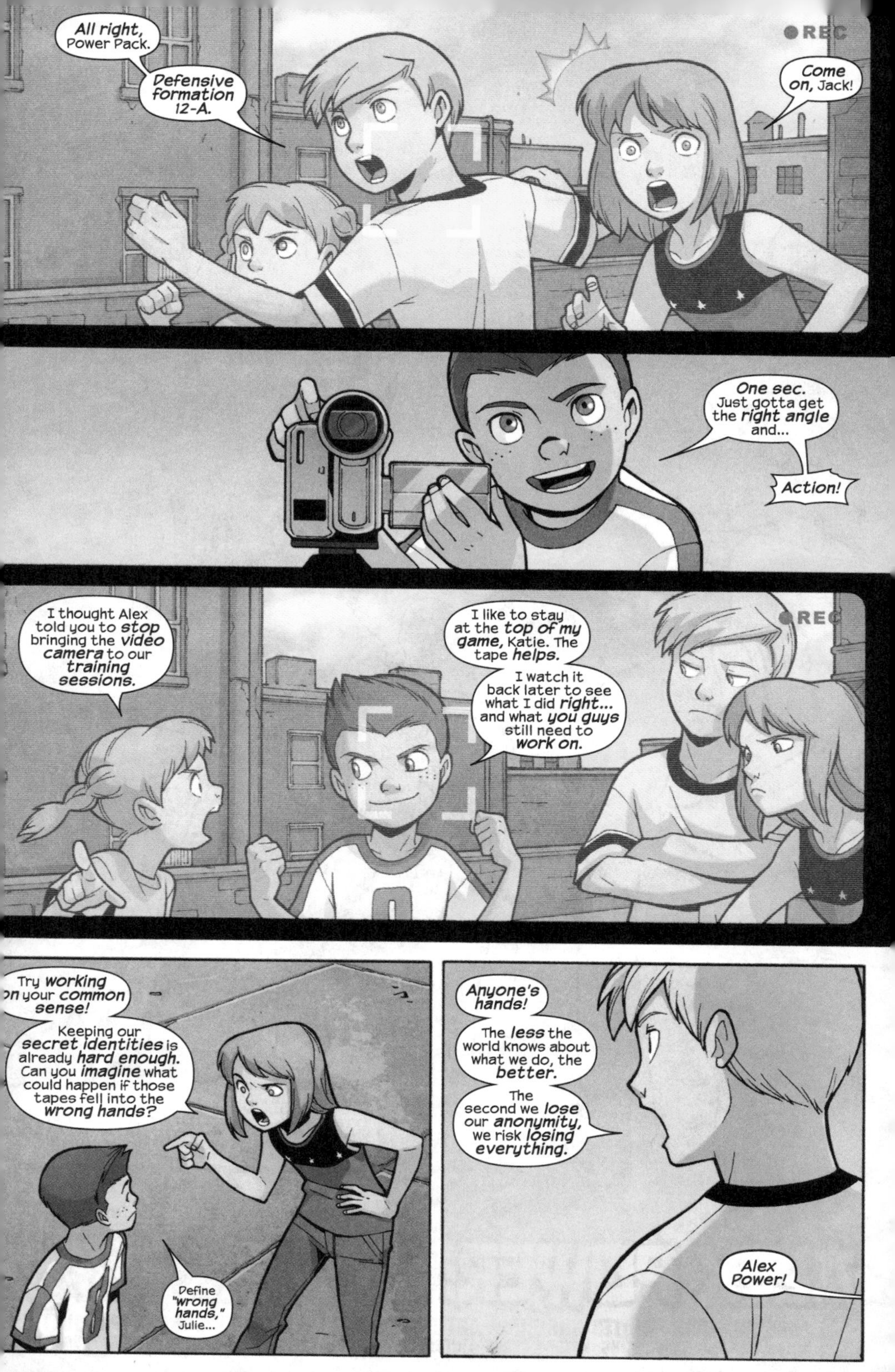

REC
All right, Power Pack.
Defensive formation 12-A.
Come on, Jack!
One sec. Just gotta get the right angle and...
Action!
REC
I thought Alex told you to stop bringing the video camera to our training sessions.
I like to stay at the top of my game, Katie. The tape helps.
I watch it back later to see what I did right... and what you guys still need to work on.
Try working on your common sense!
Keeping our secret identities is already hard enough. Can you imagine what could happen if those tapes fell into the wrong hands?
Define "wrong hands," Julie...
Anyone's hands!
The less the world knows about what we do, the better.
The second we lose our anonymity, we risk losing everything.
Alex Power!

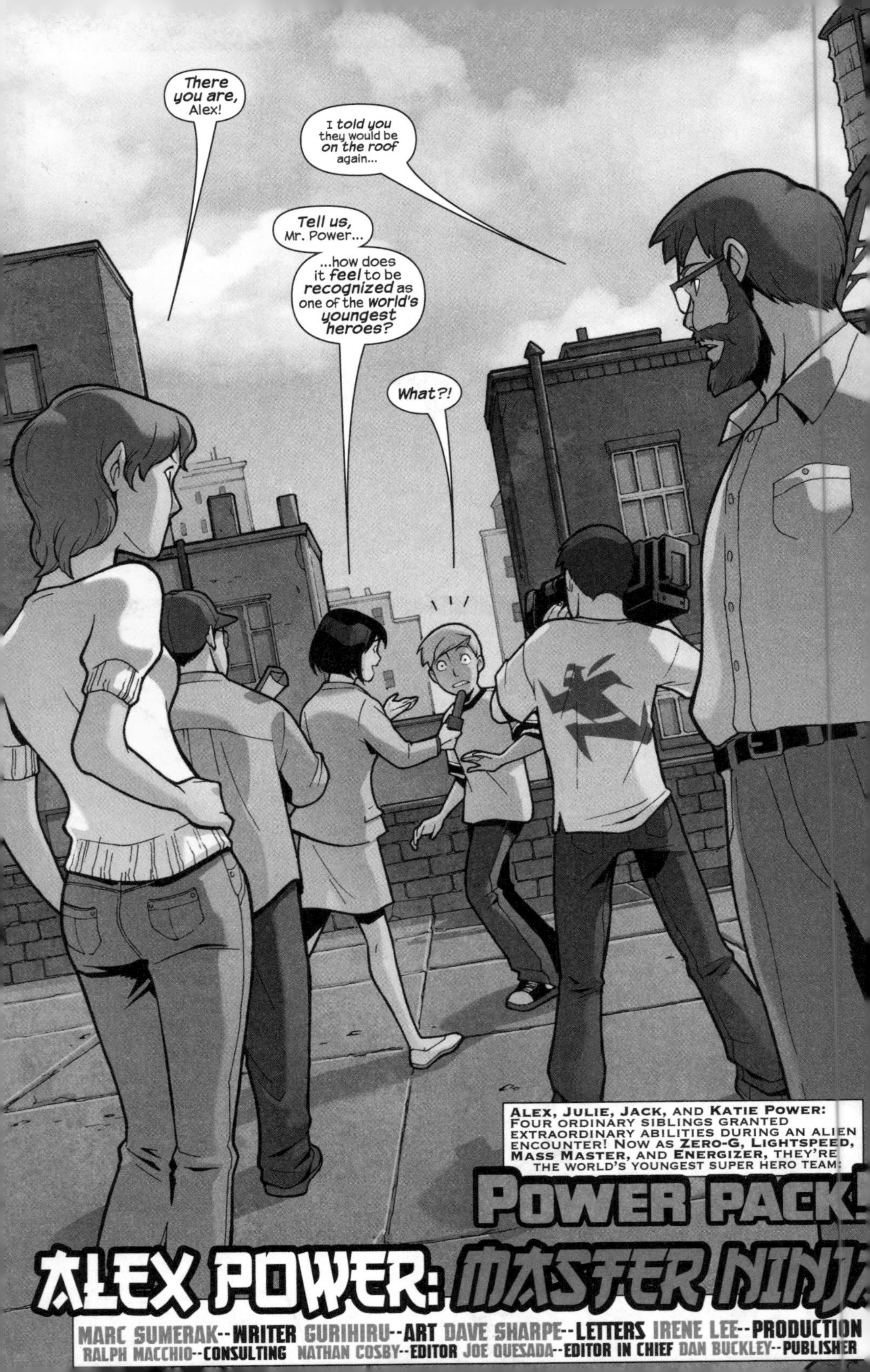

There you are, Alex!
I told you they would be on the roof again...
Tell us, Mr. Power...
...how does it feel to be recognized as one of the world's youngest heroes?
What?!
ALEX, JULIE, JACK, AND KATIE POWER: FOUR ORDINARY SIBLINGS GRANTED EXTRAORDINARY ABILITIES DURING AN ALIEN ENCOUNTER! NOW AS ZERO-G, LIGHTSPEED, MASS MASTER, AND ENERGIZER, THEY'RE THE WORLD'S YOUNGEST SUPER HERO TEAM:
POWER PACK!
ALEX POWER: MASTER NINJA
MARC SUMERAK--WRITER GURIHIRU--ART DAVE SHARPE--LETTERS IRENE LEE--PRODUCTION
RALPH MACCHIO--CONSULTING NATHAN COSBY--EDITOR JOE QUESADA--EDITOR IN CHIEF DAN BUCKLEY--PUBLISHER

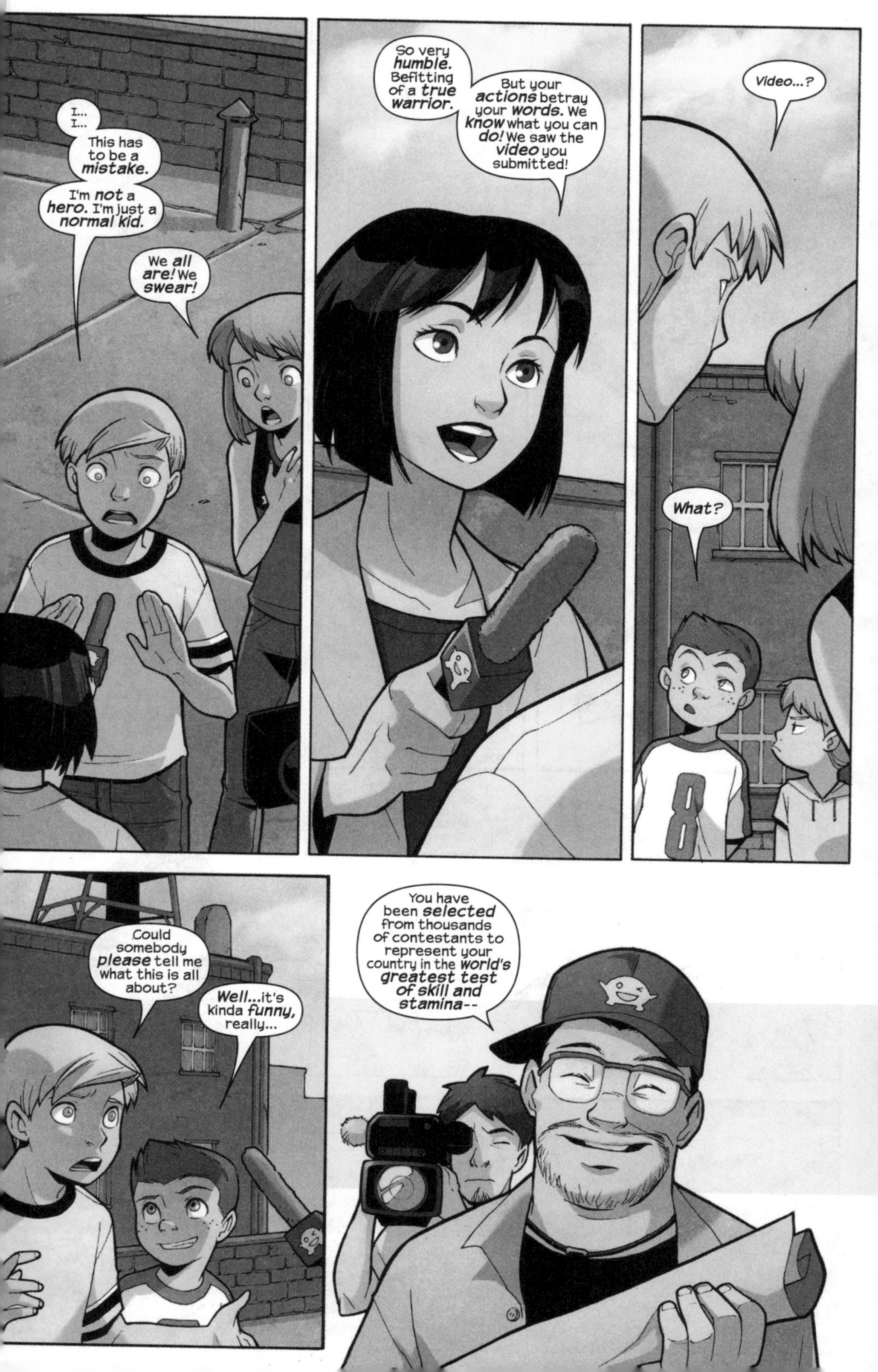
I...
I...
This has to be a mistake.
I'm not a hero. I'm just a normal kid.
We all are! We swear!
So very humble. Befitting of a true warrior.
But your actions betray your words. We know what you can do! We saw the video you submitted!
Video...?
What?
Could somebody please tell me what this is all about?
Well...it's kinda funny, really...
You have been selected from thousands of contestants to represent your country in the world's greatest test of skill and stamina--

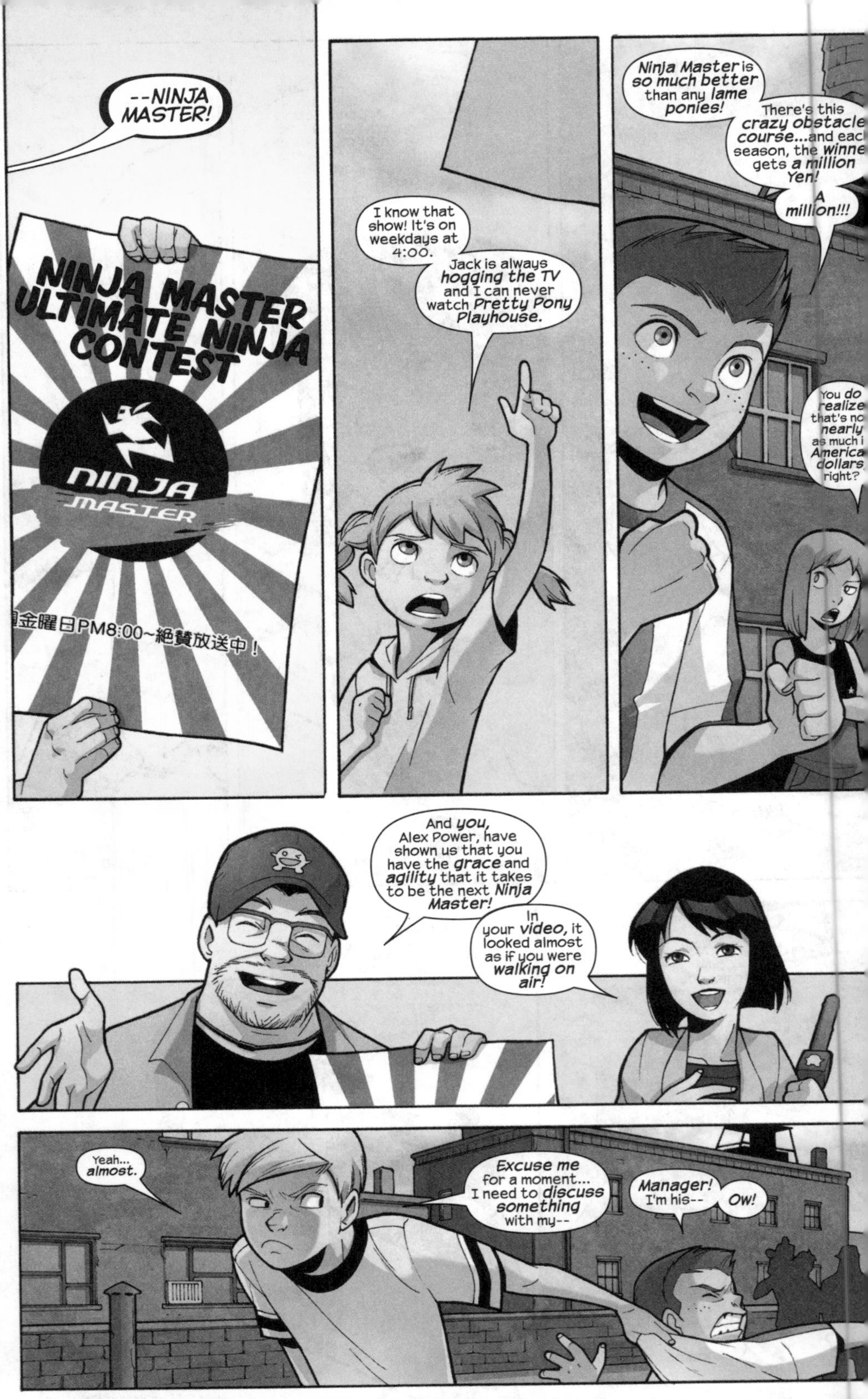
--NINJA MASTER!
NINJA MASTER ULTIMATE NINJA CONTEST
NINJA MASTER
金曜日PM8:00~絶賛放送中！
I know that show! It's on weekdays at 4:00.
Jack is always hogging the TV and I can never watch Pretty Pony Playhouse.
Ninja Master is so much better than any lame ponies!
There's this crazy obstacle course...and eac season, the winne gets a million Yen!
A million!!!
You do realize that's no nearly as much i America dollars right?
And you, Alex Power, have shown us that you have the grace and agility that it takes to be the next Ninja Master!
In your video, it looked almost as if you were walking on air!
Yeah... almost.
Excuse me for a moment... I need to discuss something with my--
Manager! I'm his--
Ow!

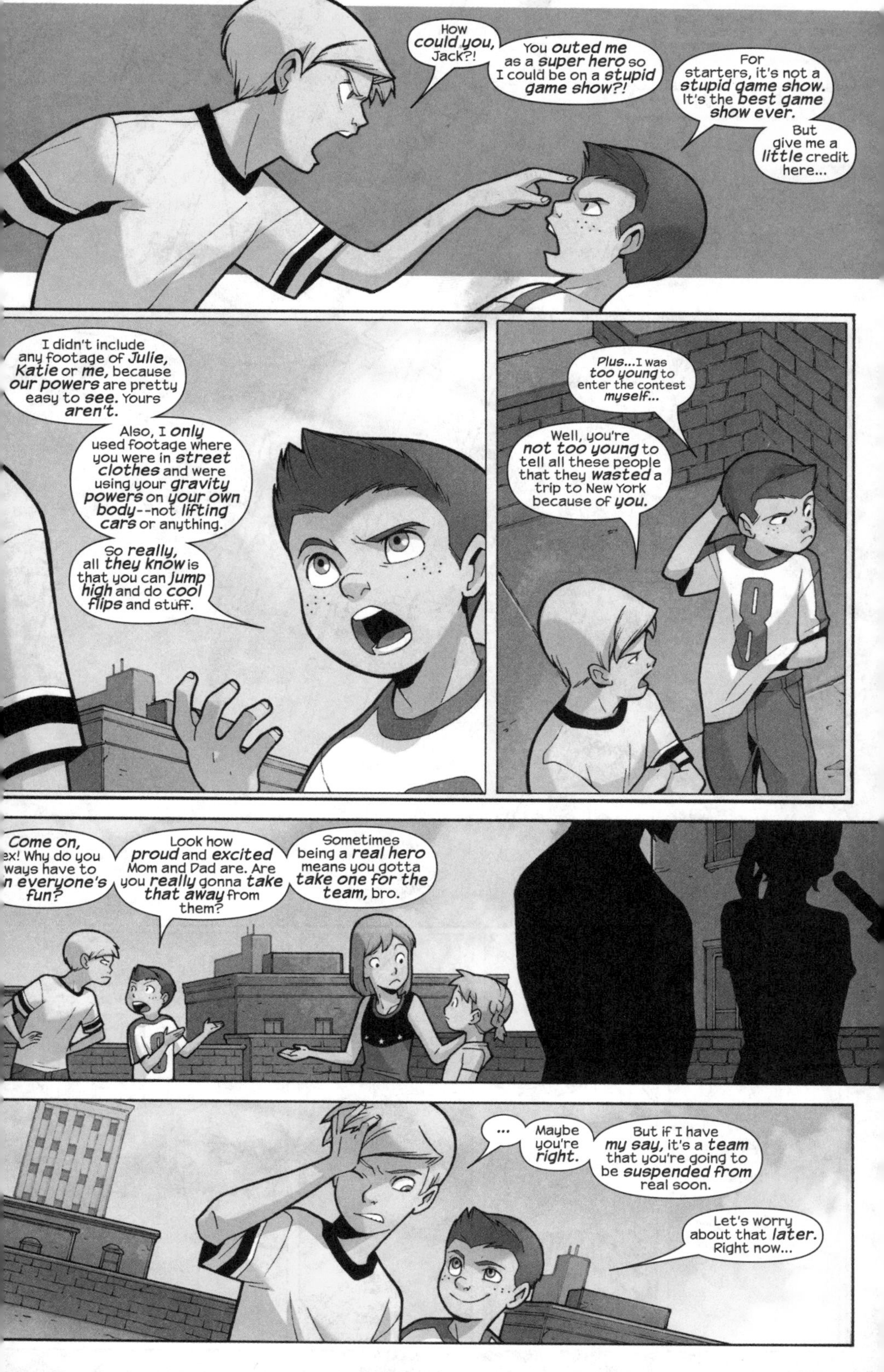
How could you, Jack?!
You outed me as a super hero so I could be on a stupid game show?!
For starters, it's not a stupid game show. It's the best game show ever.
But give me a little credit here...
I didn't include any footage of Julie, Katie or me, because our powers are pretty easy to see. Yours aren't.
Also, I only used footage where you were in street clothes and were using your gravity powers on your own body--not lifting cars or anything.
So really, all they know is that you can jump high and do cool flips and stuff.
Plus...I was too young to enter the contest myself...
Well, you're not too young to tell all these people that they wasted a trip to New York because of you.
Come on, ex! Why do you ways have to n everyone's fun?
Look how proud and excited Mom and Dad are. Are you really gonna take that away from them?
Sometimes being a real hero means you gotta take one for the team, bro.
...
Maybe you're right.
But if I have my say, it's a team that you're going to be suspended from real soon.
Let's worry about that later. Right now...

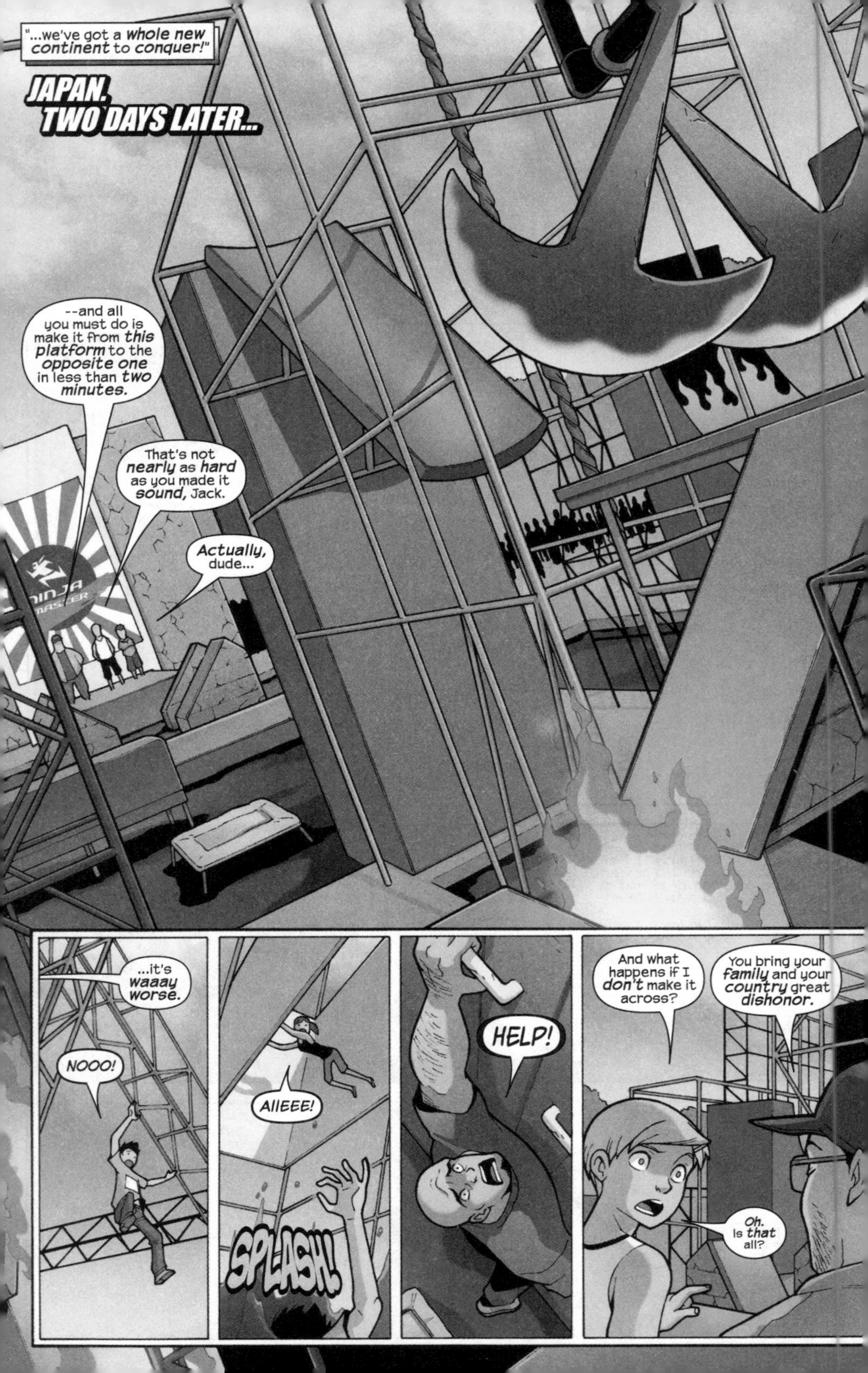
"...we've got a whole new continent to conquer!"
JAPAN. TWO DAYS LATER...
--and all you must do is make it from this platform to the opposite one in less than two minutes.
That's not nearly as hard as you made it sound, Jack.
Actually, dude...
NINJA MASTER
...it's waaay worse.
NOOO!
AIIEEE!
SPLASH!
HELP!
And what happens if I don't make it across?
You bring your family and your country great dishonor.
Oh. Is that all?

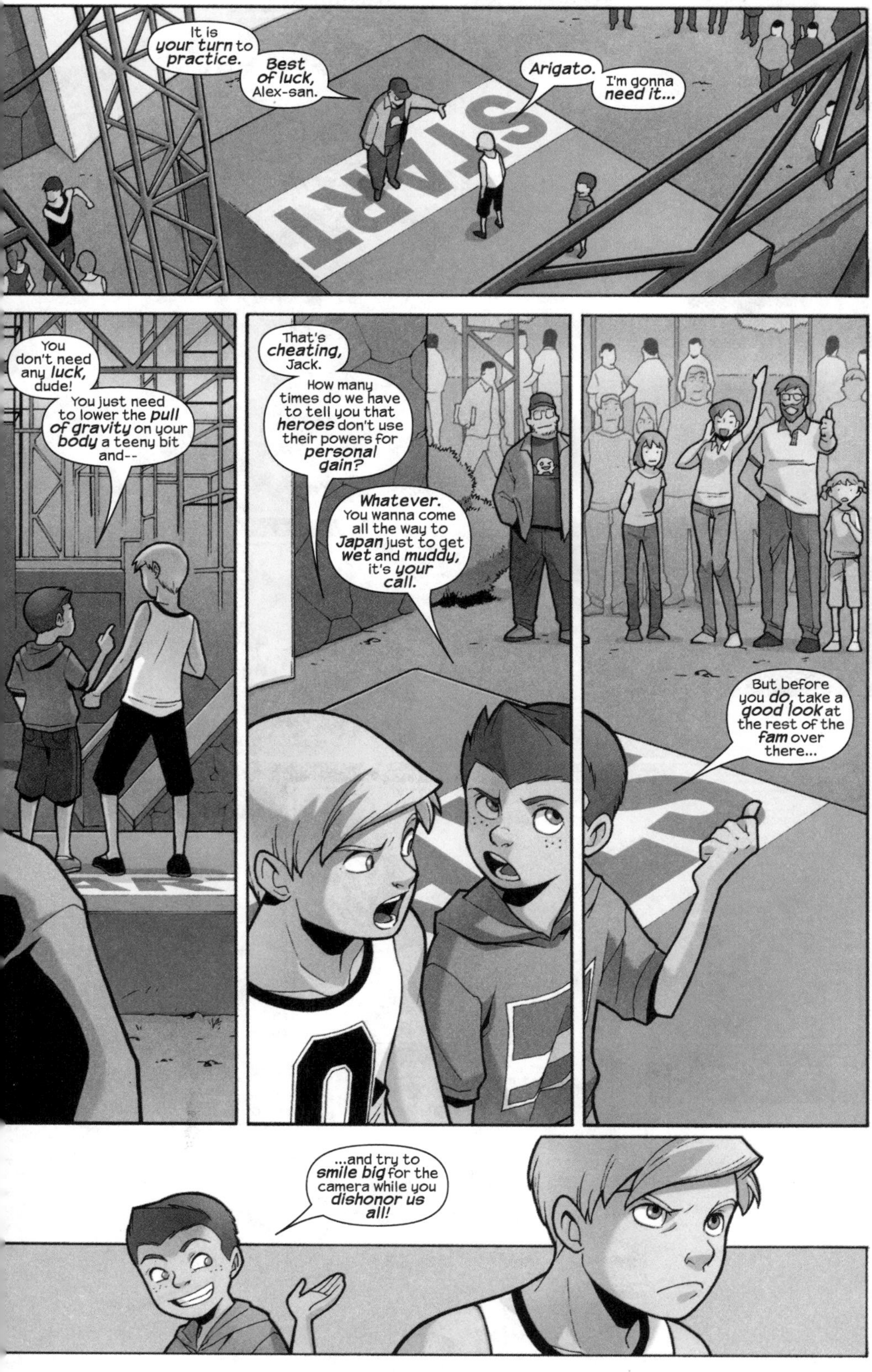
It is your turn to practice.
Best of luck, Alex-san.
Arigato.
I'm gonna need it...
START
You don't need any luck, dude!
You just need to lower the pull of gravity on your body a teeny bit and--
That's cheating, Jack.
How many times do we have to tell you that heroes don't use their powers for personal gain?
Whatever. You wanna come all the way to Japan just to get wet and muddy, it's your call.
But before you do, take a good look at the rest of the fam over there...
...and try to smile big for the camera while you dishonor us all!

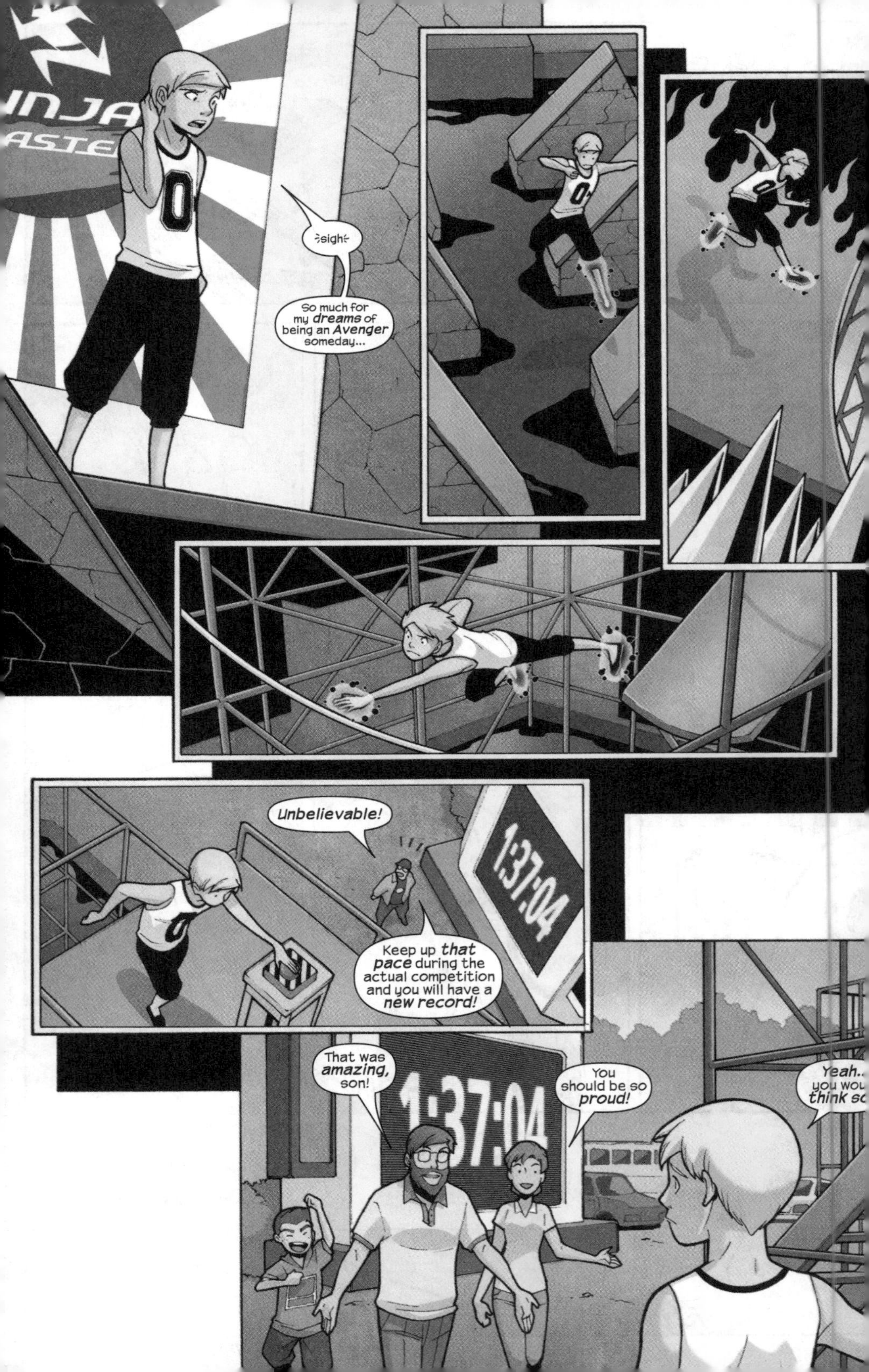

INJA
ASTE
-sigh-
So much for my dreams of being an Avenger someday...
Unbelievable!
1:37:04
Keep up that pace during the actual competition and you will have a new record!
That was amazing, son!
1:37:04
You should be so proud!
Yeah..

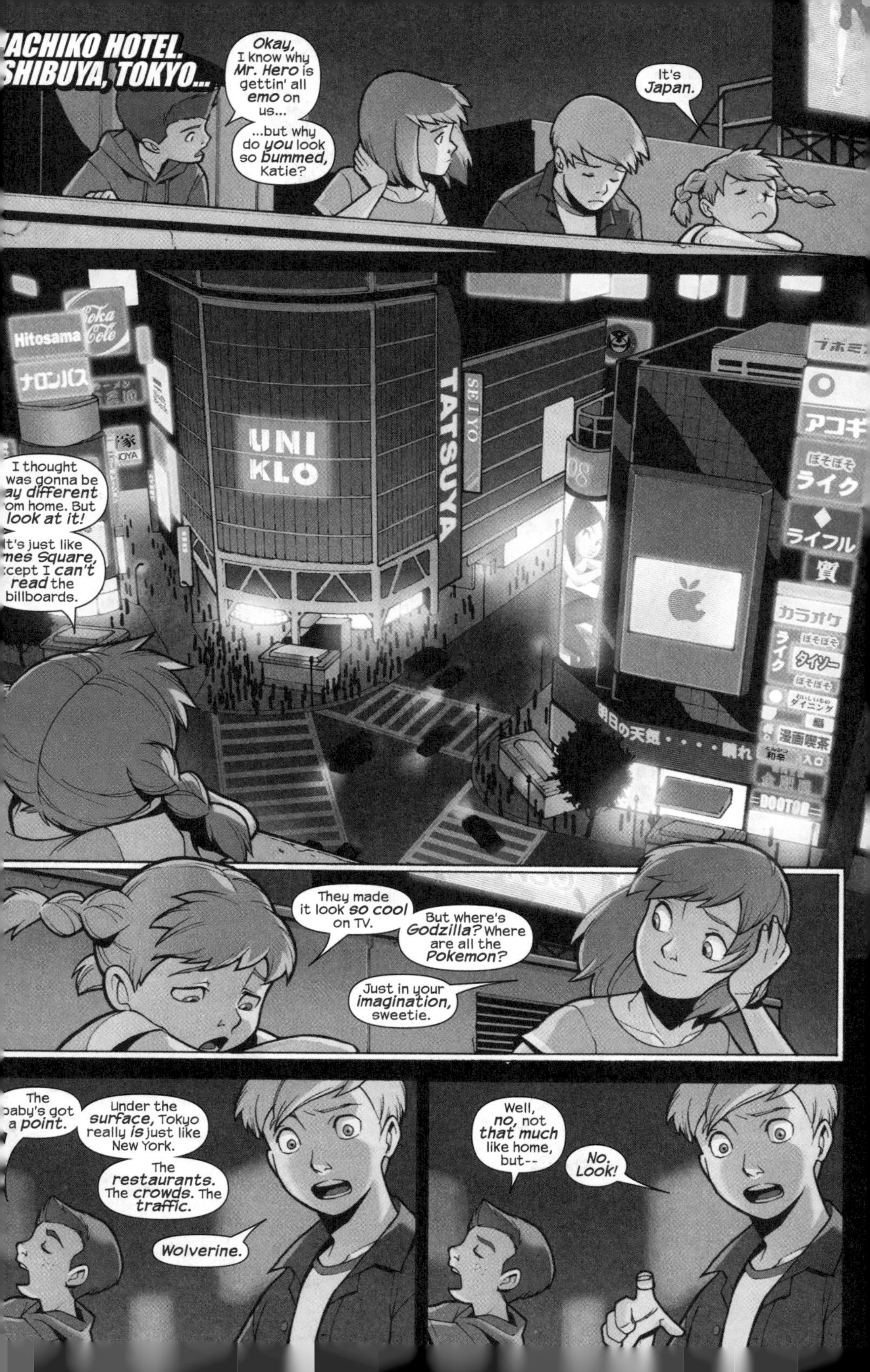

ACHIKO HOTEL. SHIBUYA, TOKYO...
Okay, I know why Mr. Hero is gettin' all emo on us...
...but why do you look so bummed, Katie?
It's Japan.
Hitosama
Coka Cola
UNI KLO
TATSUYA
SEIYO
I thought was gonna be ay different om home. But look at it!
It's just like mes Square, cept I can't read the billboards.
アコギ
ライク
ライフル
カラオケ
タイソー
明日の天気・・・・晴れ
漫画喫茶
DOOTOR
They made it look so cool on TV.
But where's Godzilla? Where are all the Pokemon?
Just in your imagination, sweetie.
The baby's got a point.
Under the surface, Tokyo really is just like New York.
The restaurants. The crowds. The traffic.
Wolverine.
Well, no, not that much like home, but--
No. Look!

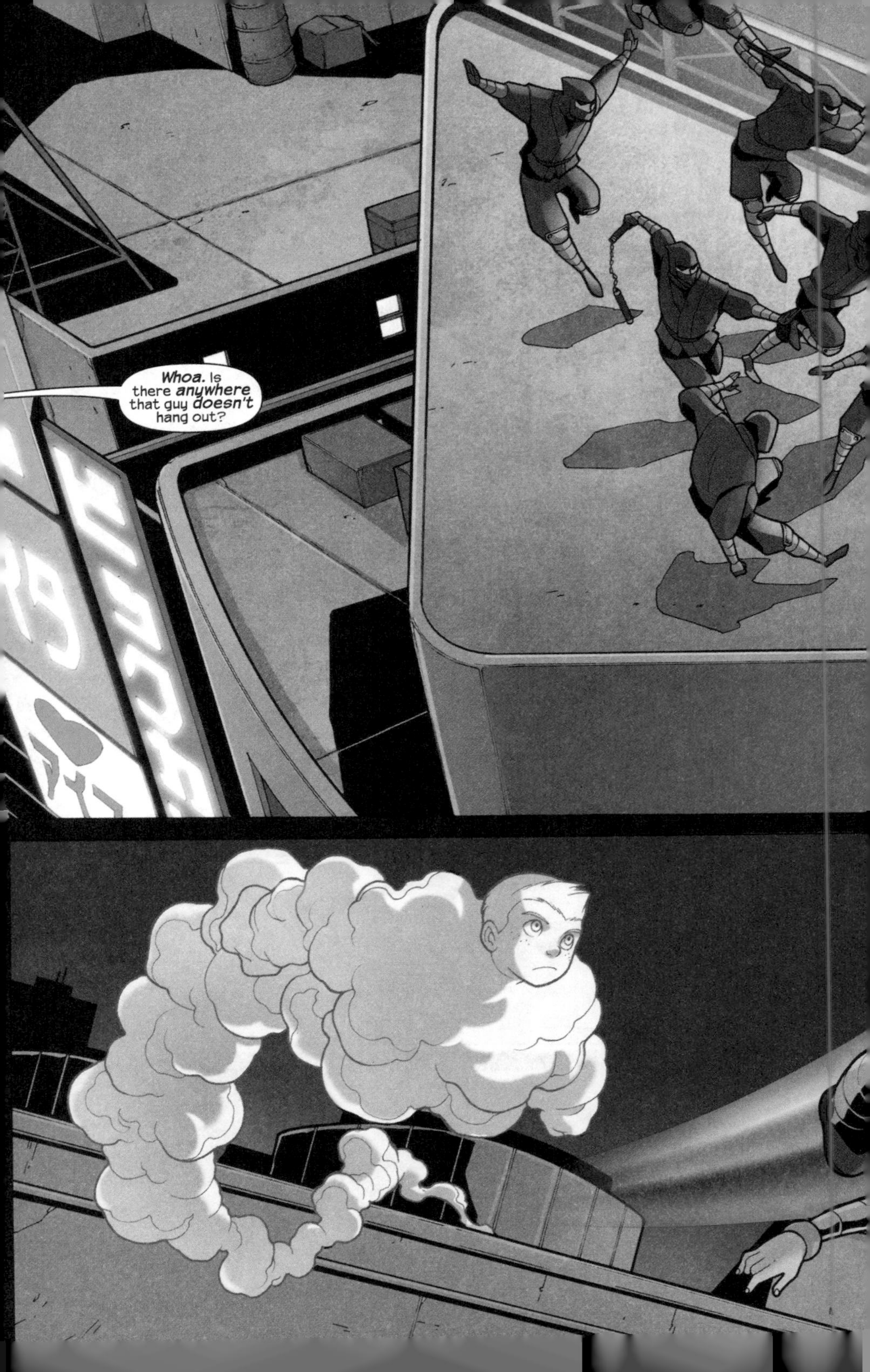
Whoa. Is there anywhere that guy doesn't hang out?

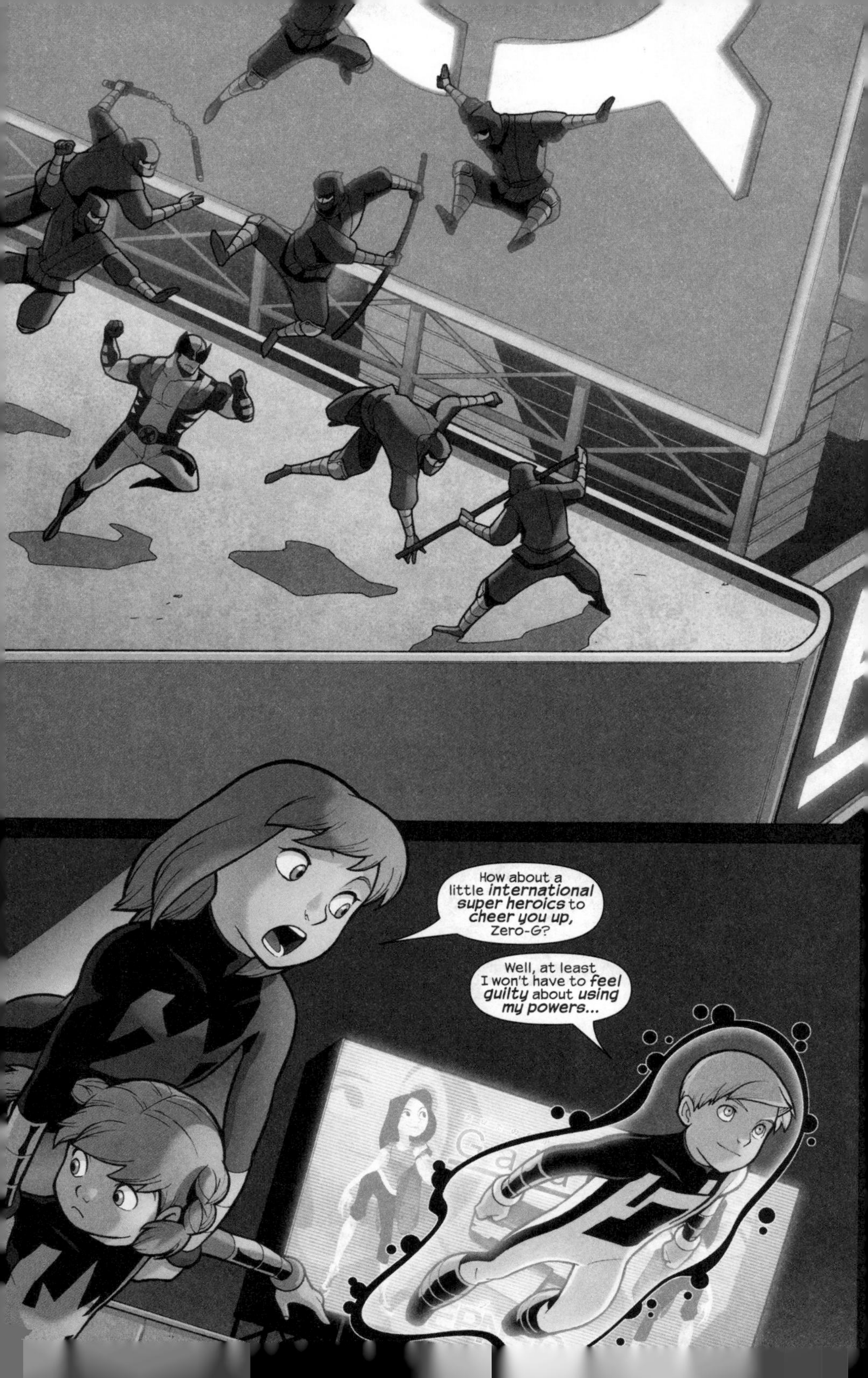
How about a little international super heroics to cheer you up, Zero-G?
Well, at least I won't have to feel guilty about using my powers...

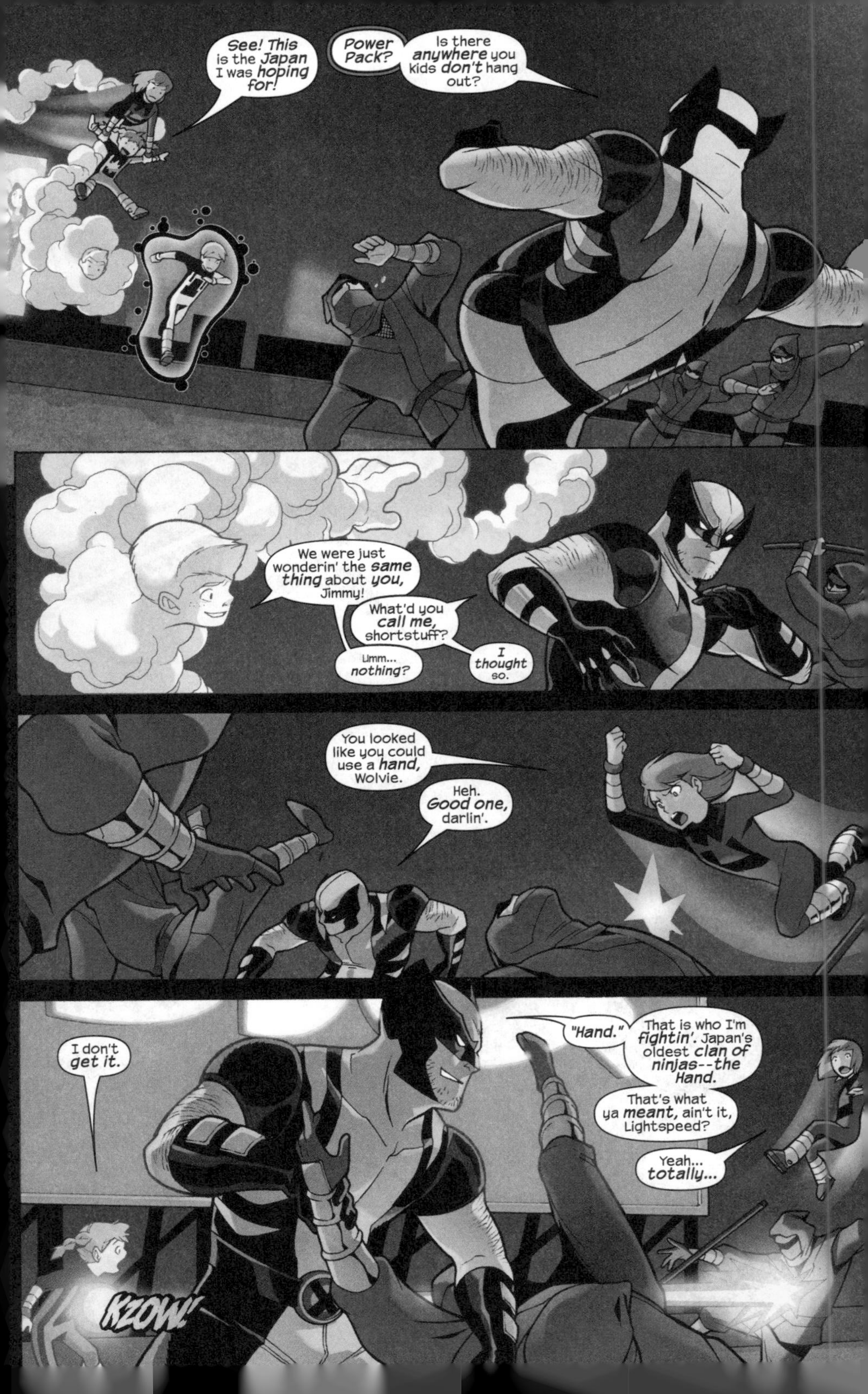
See! This is the Japan I was hoping for!
Power Pack?
Is there anywhere you kids don't hang out?
We were just wonderin' the same thing about you, Jimmy!
What'd you call me, shortstuff?
Umm... nothing?
I thought so.
You looked like you could use a hand, Wolvie.
Heh. Good one, darlin'.
I don't get it.
"Hand."
That is who I'm fightin'. Japan's oldest clan of ninjas--the Hand.
That's what ya meant, ain't it, Lightspeed?
Yeah... totally...
KZOW!

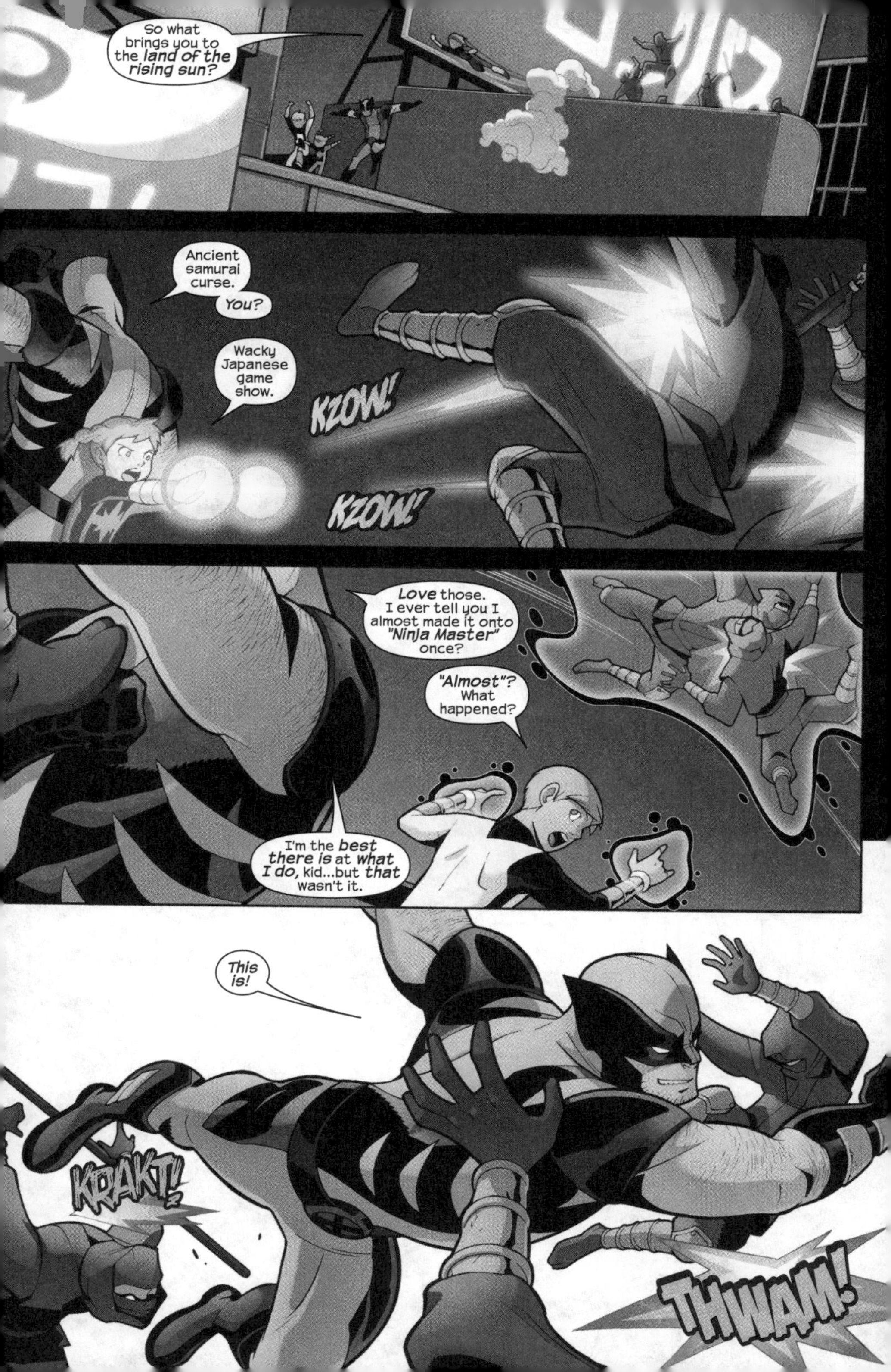
So what brings you to the *land of the rising sun?*
Ancient samurai curse.
You?
Wacky Japanese game show.
KZOW!
KZOW!
Love those. I ever tell you I almost made it onto *"Ninja Master"* once?
"Almost"? What happened?
I'm the *best there is* at *what I do,* kid...but *that* wasn't it.
This is!
KRAKT!
THWAM!

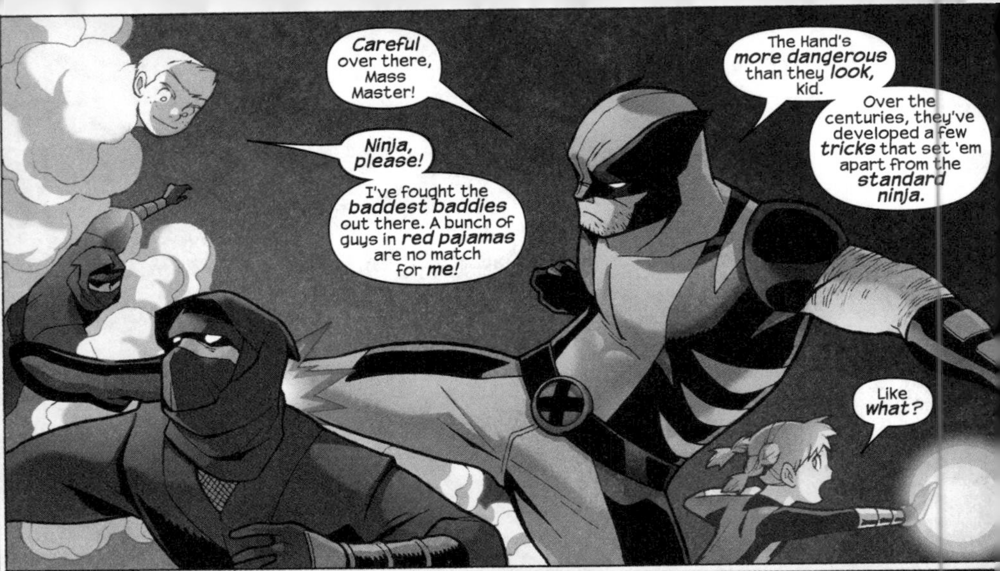
Careful over there, Mass Master!
Ninja, please!
I've fought the baddest baddies out there. A bunch of guys in red pajamas are no match for me!
The Hand's more dangerous than they look, kid.
Over the centuries, they've developed a few tricks that set 'em apart from the standard ninja.
Like what?

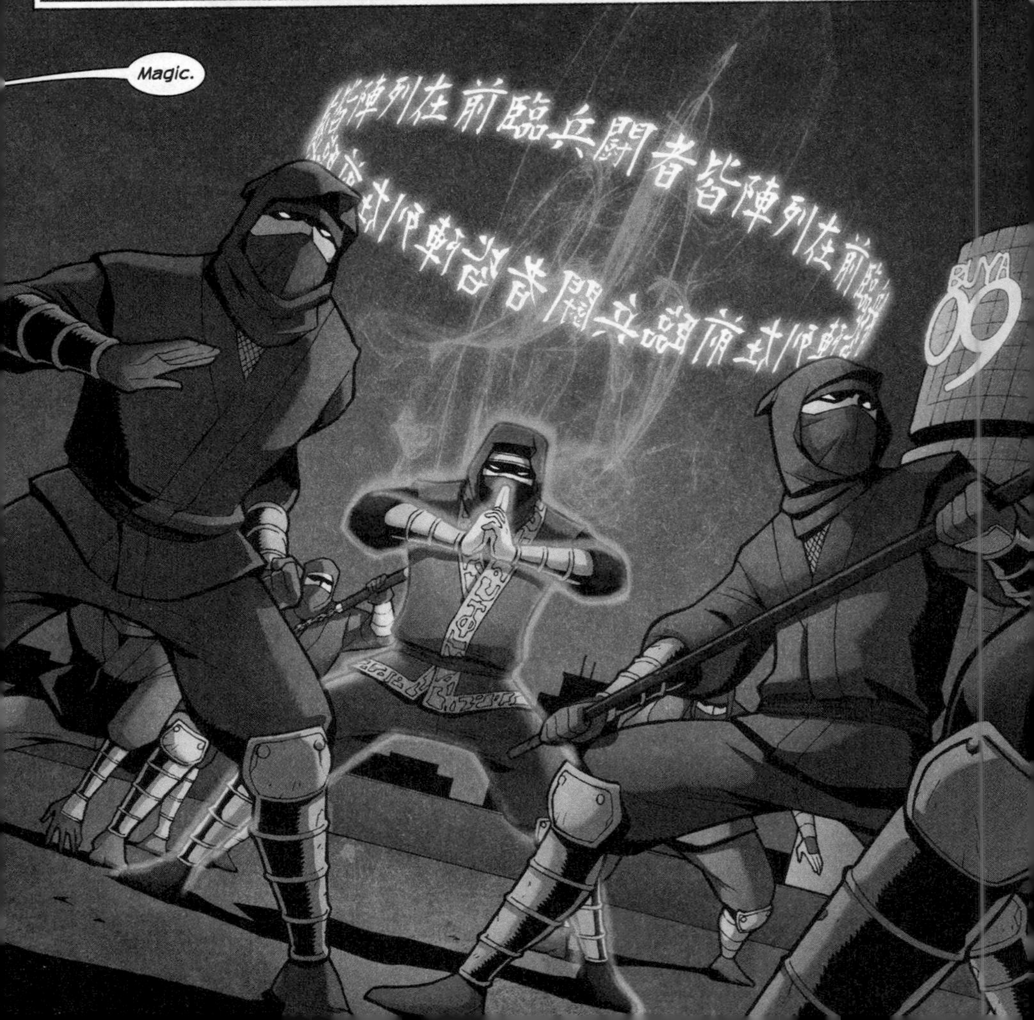
Magic.

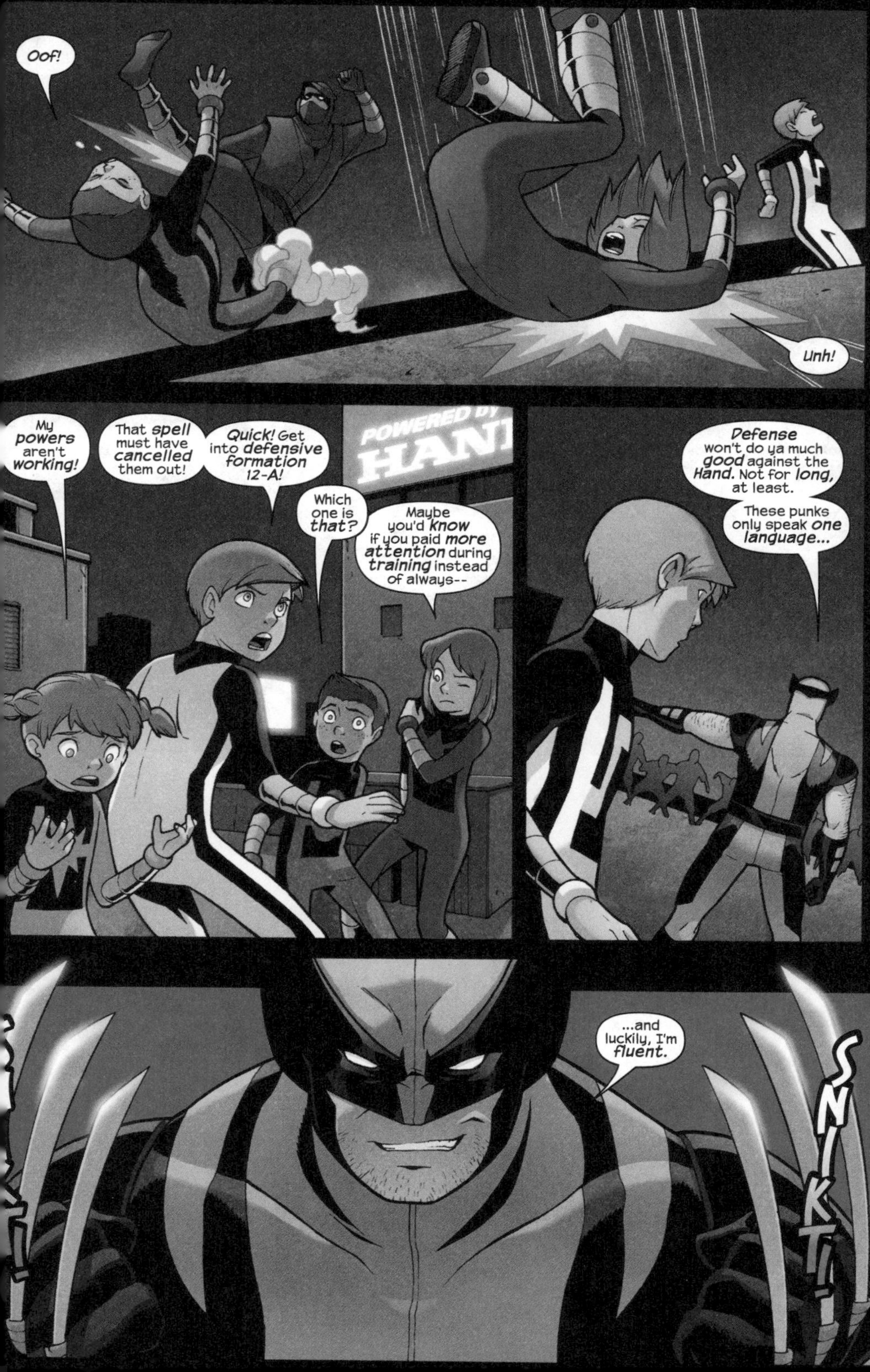

Oof!
Unh!
My powers aren't working!
That spell must have cancelled them out!
Quick! Get into defensive formation 12-A!
POWERED by HAN
Which one is that?
Maybe you'd know if you paid more attention during training instead of always--
Defense won't do ya much good against the Hand. Not for long, at least.
These punks only speak one language...
...and luckily, I'm fluent.
SNIKT!

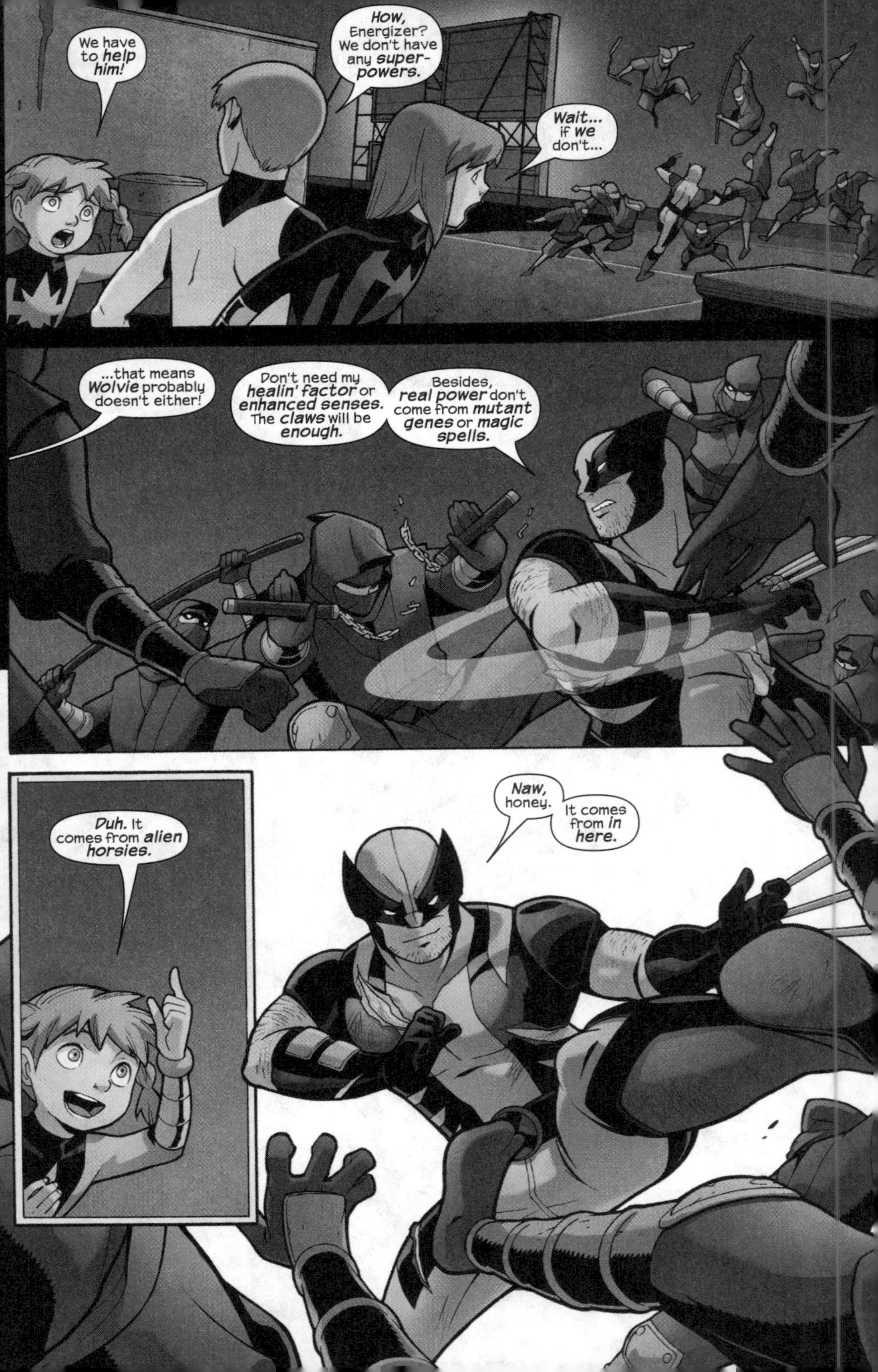
We have to help him!
How, Energizer? We don't have any super-powers.
Wait... if we don't...
...that means Wolvie probably doesn't either!
Don't need my healin' factor or enhanced senses. The claws will be enough.
Besides, real power don't come from mutant genes or magic spells.
Duh. It comes from alien horsies.
Naw, honey.
It comes from in here.

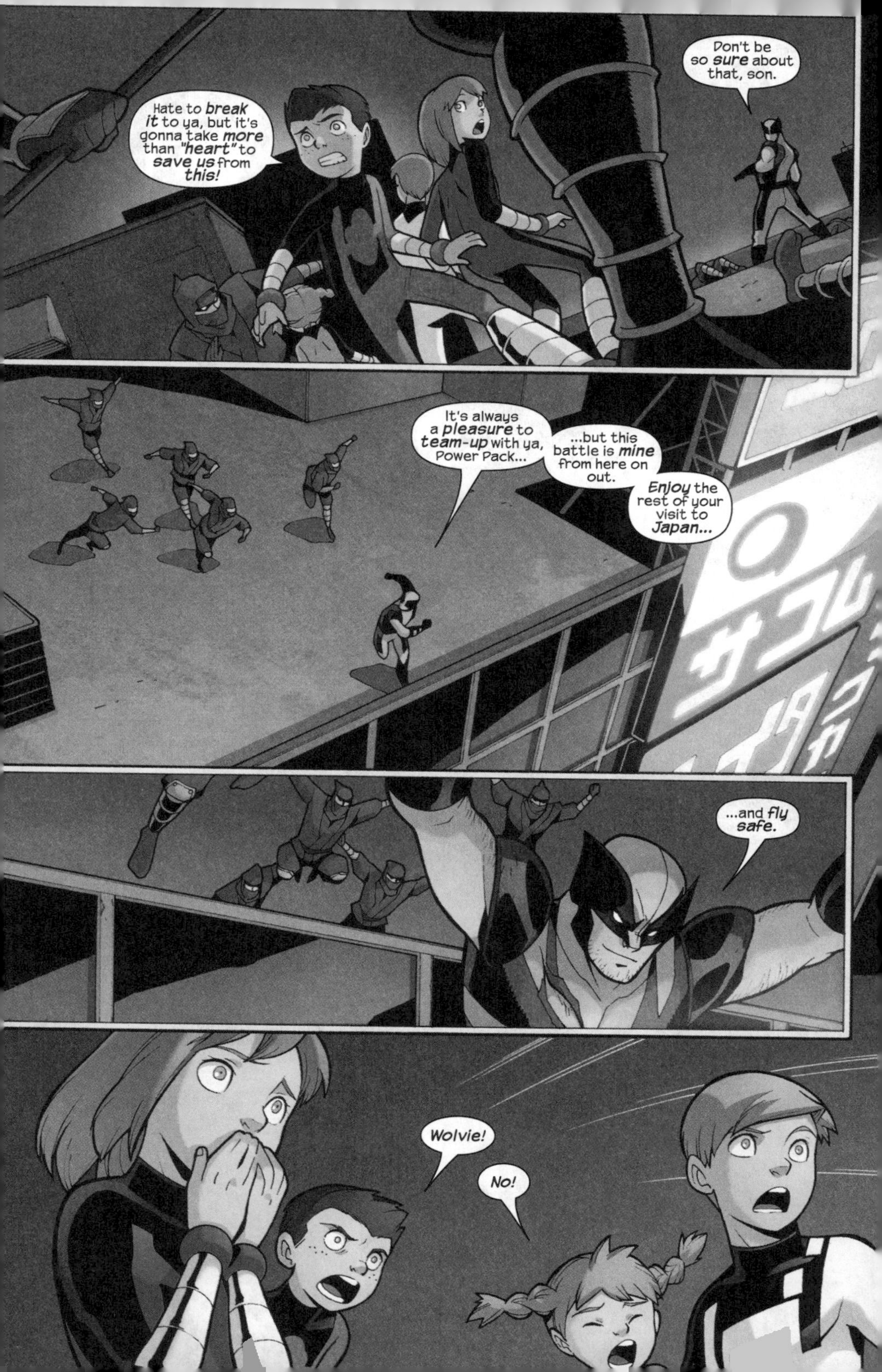
Hate to break it to ya, but it's gonna take more than "heart" to save us from this!
Don't be so sure about that, son.
It's always a pleasure to team-up with ya, Power Pack...
...but this battle is mine from here on out.
Enjoy the rest of your visit to Japan...
...and fly safe.
Wolvie!
No!

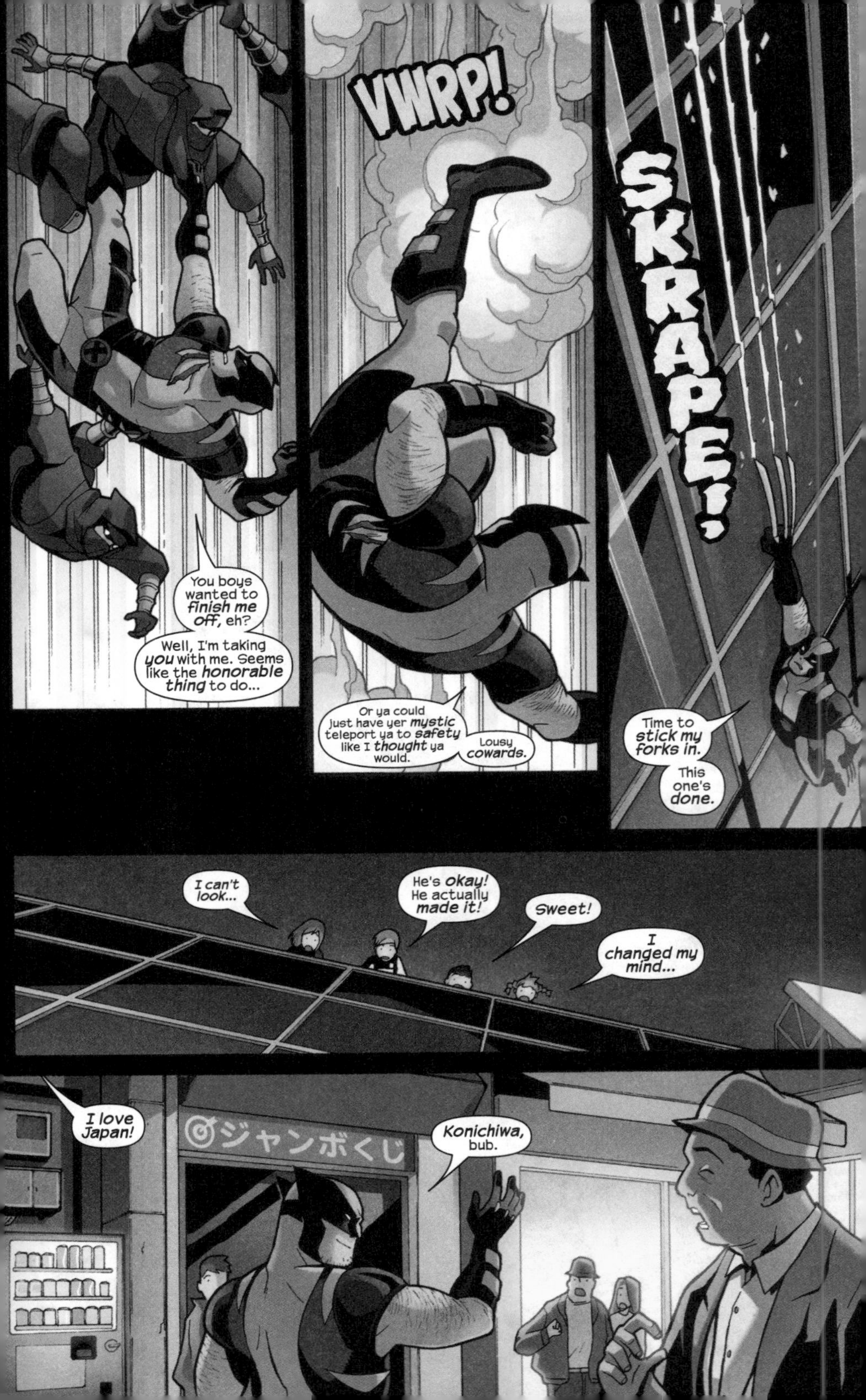

You boys wanted to finish me off, eh?
Well, I'm taking you with me. Seems like the honorable thing to do...
VWRP!
Or ya could just have yer mystic teleport ya to safety like I thought ya would.
Lousy cowards.
SKRAPE!
Time to stick my forks in.
This one's done.
I can't look...
He's okay! He actually made it!
Sweet!
I changed my mind...
I love Japan!
ジャンボくじ
Konichiwa, bub.

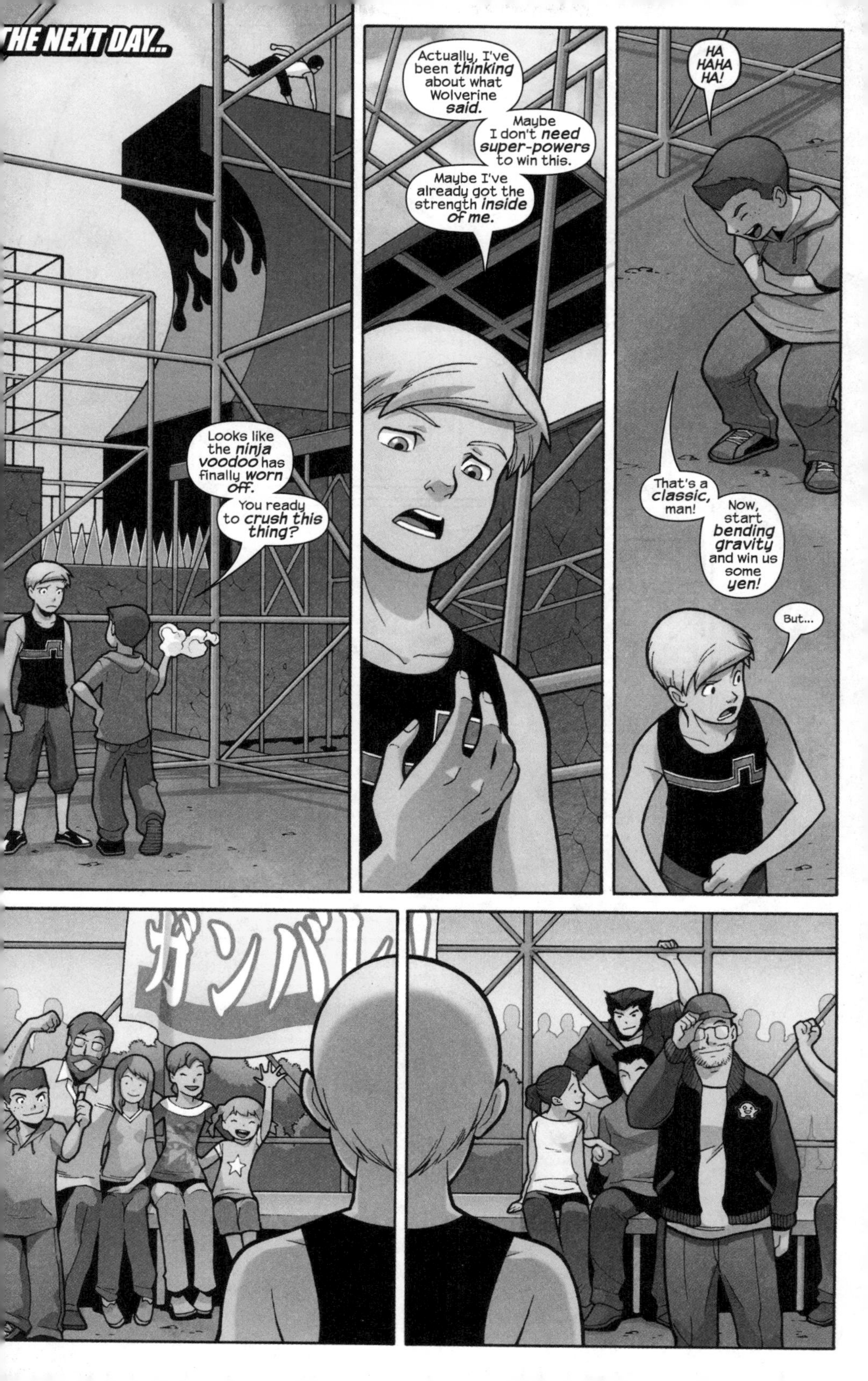
THE NEXT DAY...
Looks like the ninja voodoo has finally worn off.
You ready to crush this thing?
Actually, I've been thinking about what Wolverine said.
Maybe I don't need super-powers to win this.
Maybe I've already got the strength inside of me.
HA HAHA HA!
That's a classic, man!
Now, start bending gravity and win us some yen!
But...
ガンバレ

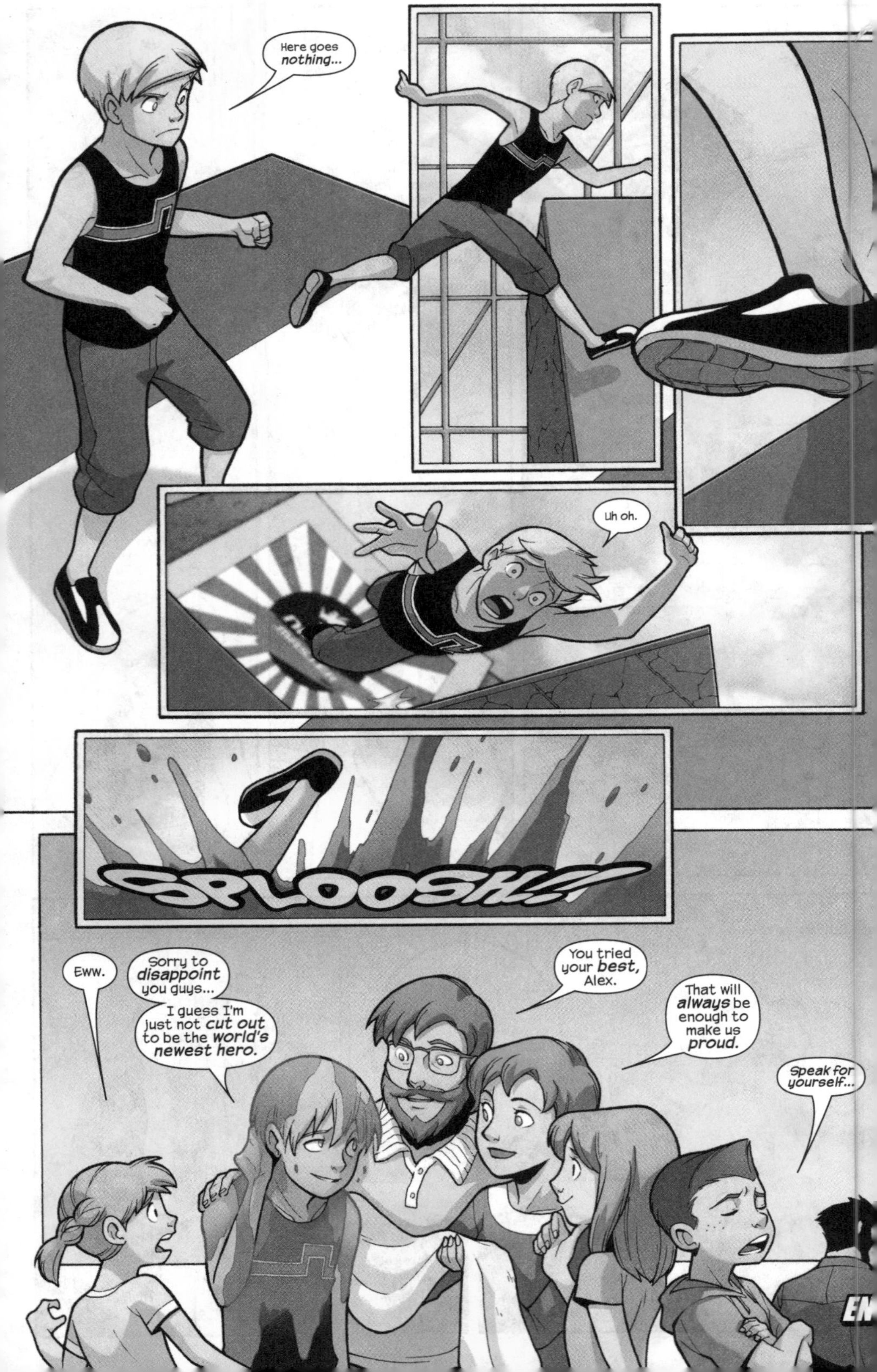
Here goes nothing...
Uh oh.
SPLOOSH!!
Eww.
Sorry to disappoint you guys...
I guess I'm just not cut out to be the world's newest hero.
You tried your best, Alex.
That will always be enough to make us proud.
Speak for yourself...